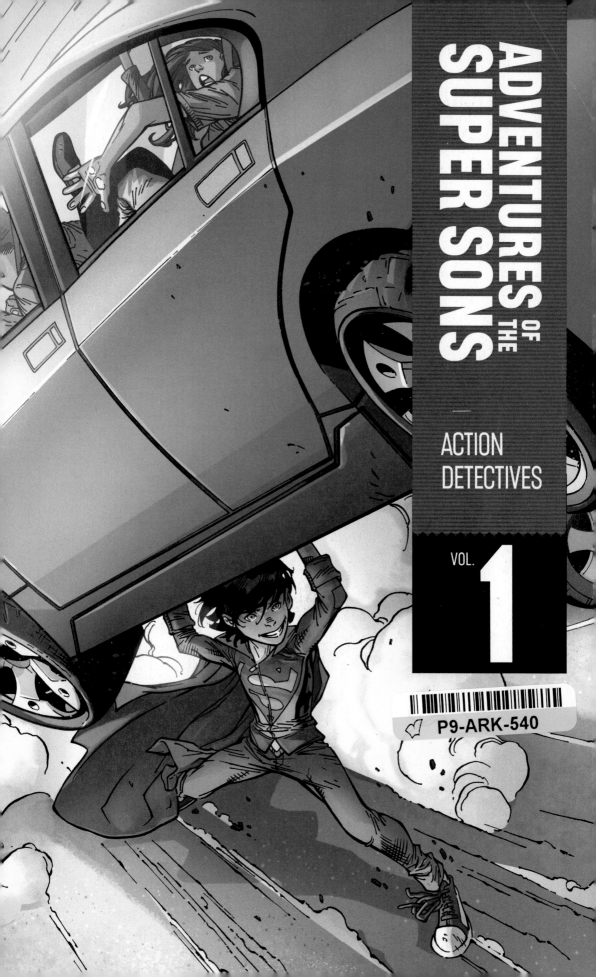

ADVENTURES OF THE SUPER SONS

ACTION DETECTIVES

VOL. 1

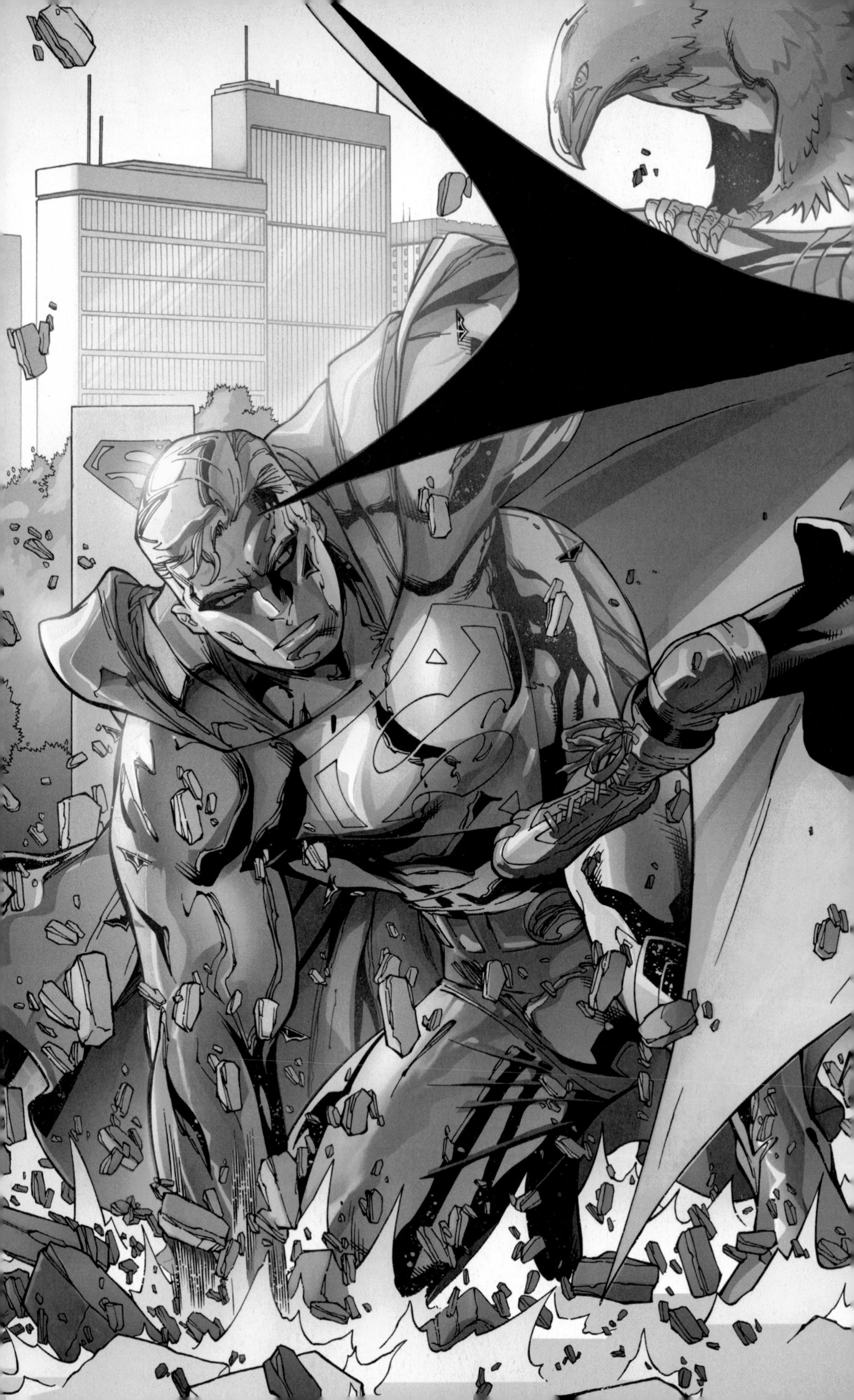

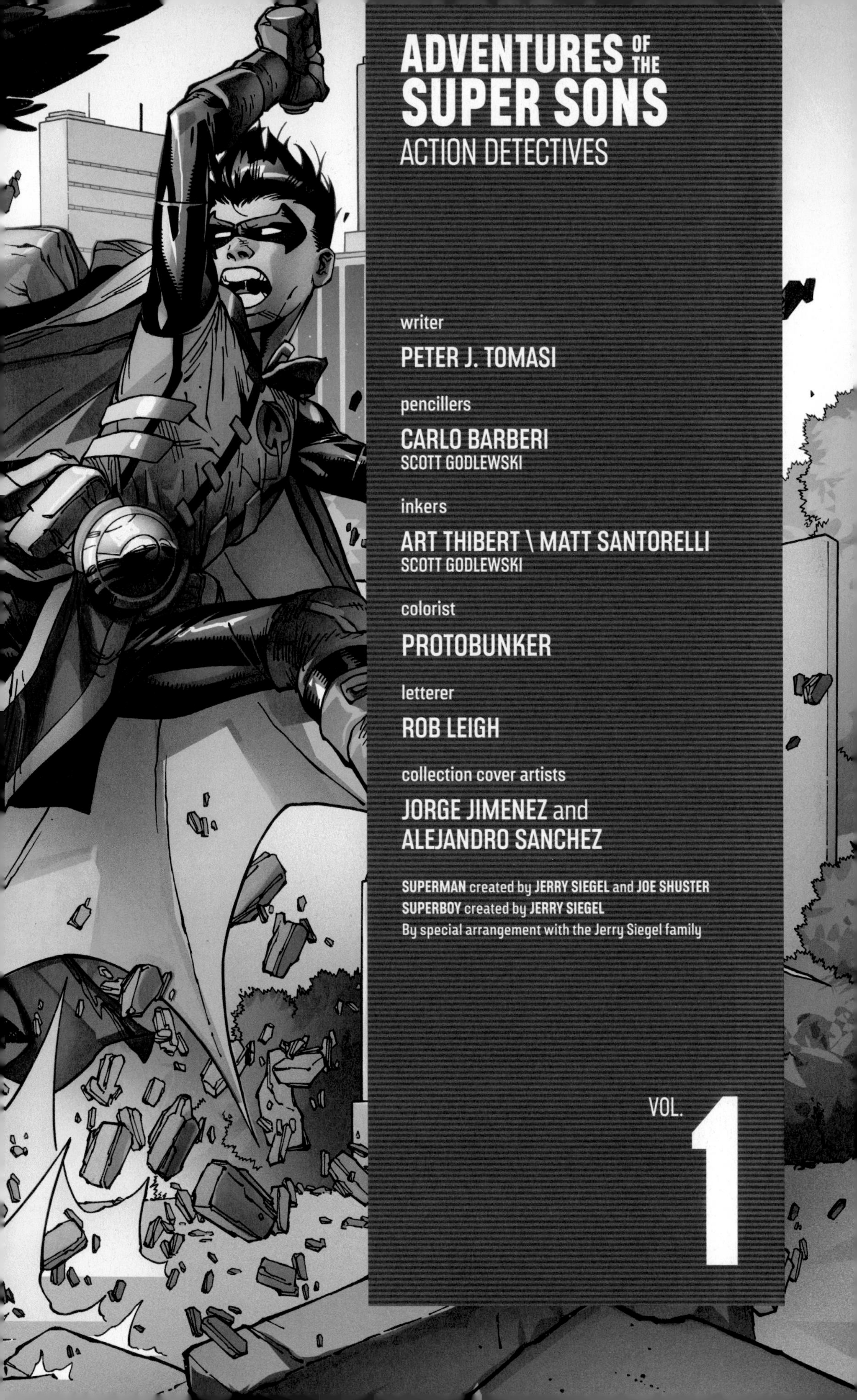

ADVENTURES OF THE SUPER SONS

ACTION DETECTIVES

writer

PETER J. TOMASI

pencillers

CARLO BARBERI
SCOTT GODLEWSKI

inkers

ART THIBERT \ MATT SANTORELLI
SCOTT GODLEWSKI

colorist

PROTOBUNKER

letterer

ROB LEIGH

collection cover artists

JORGE JIMENEZ and
ALEJANDRO SANCHEZ

SUPERMAN created by **JERRY SIEGEL** and **JOE SHUSTER**
SUPERBOY created by **JERRY SIEGEL**
By special arrangement with the Jerry Siegel family

VOL. 1

PAUL KAMINSKI Editor – Original Series
ANDREW MARINO Assistant Editor – Original Series
JEB WOODARD Group Editor – Collected Editions
ERIKA ROTHBERG Editor – Collected Edition
STEVE COOK Design Director – Books
MONIQUE NARBONETA Publication Design

BOB HARRAS Senior VP – Editor-in-Chief, DC Comics
PAT McCALLUM Executive Editor, DC Comics

DAN DiDIO Publisher
JIM LEE Publisher & Chief Creative Officer
AMIT DESAI Executive VP – Business & Marketing Strategy, Direct to
                    Consumer & Global Franchise Management
BOBBIE CHASE VP & Executive Editor, Young Reader & Talent Development
MARK CHIARELLO Senior VP – Art, Design & Collected Editions
JOHN CUNNINGHAM Senior VP – Sales & Trade Marketing
BRIAR DARDEN VP – Business Affairs
ANNE DePIES Senior VP – Business Strategy, Finance & Administration
DON FALLETTI VP – Manufacturing Operations
LAWRENCE GANEM VP – Editorial Administration & Talent Relations
ALISON GILL Senior VP – Manufacturing & Operations
JASON GREENBERG VP – Business Strategy & Finance
HANK KANALZ Senior VP – Editorial Strategy & Administration
JAY KOGAN Senior VP – Legal Affairs
NICK J. NAPOLITANO VP – Manufacturing Administration
LISETTE OSTERLOH VP – Digital Marketing & Events
EDDIE SCANNELL VP – Consumer Marketing
COURTNEY SIMMONS Senior VP – Publicity & Communications
JIM (SKI) SOKOLOWSKI VP – Comic Book Specialty Sales & Trade Marketing
NANCY SPEARS VP – Mass, Book, Digital Sales & Trade Marketing
MICHELE R. WELLS VP – Content Strategy

ADVENTURES OF THE SUPER SONS VOL. 1: ACTION DETECTIVES

Published by DC Comics. Compilation and all new material Copyright © 2019 DC Comics. All Rights Reserved.
Originally published in single magazine form in ADVENTURES OF THE SUPER SONS 1-6. Copyright © 2018, 2019 DC
Comics. All Rights Reserved. All characters, their distinctive likenesses and related elements featured in this
publication are trademarks of DC Comics. The stories, characters and incidents featured in this publication are
entirely fictional. DC Comics does not read or accept unsolicited submissions of ideas, stories or artwork.

DC Comics, 2900 West Alameda Ave., Burbank, CA 91505
Printed by LSC Communications, Owensville, MO, USA. 3/8/19. First Printing.
ISBN: 978-1-4012-9058-0

Library of Congress Cataloging-in-Publication Data is available.

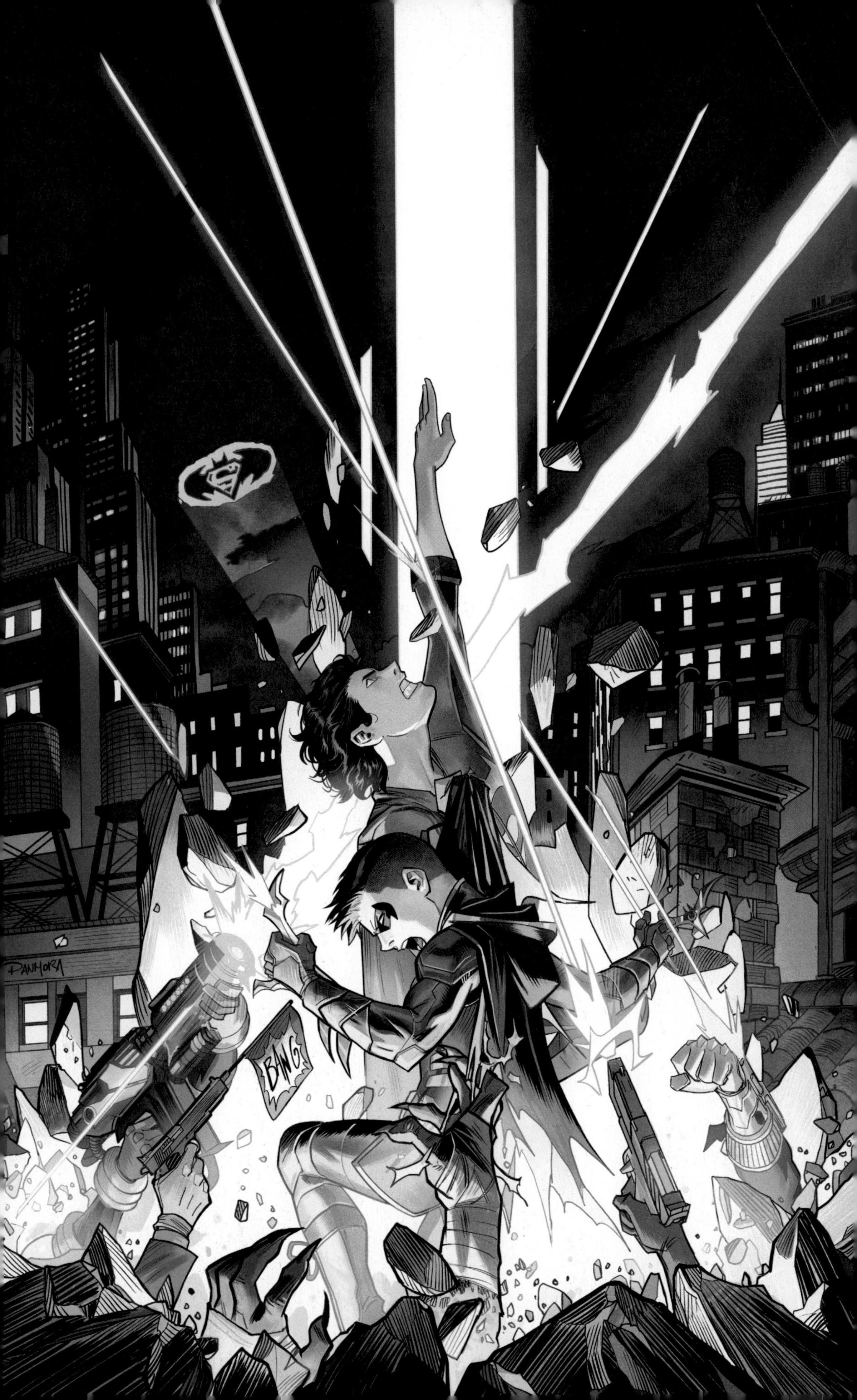
DANMORA
BANG

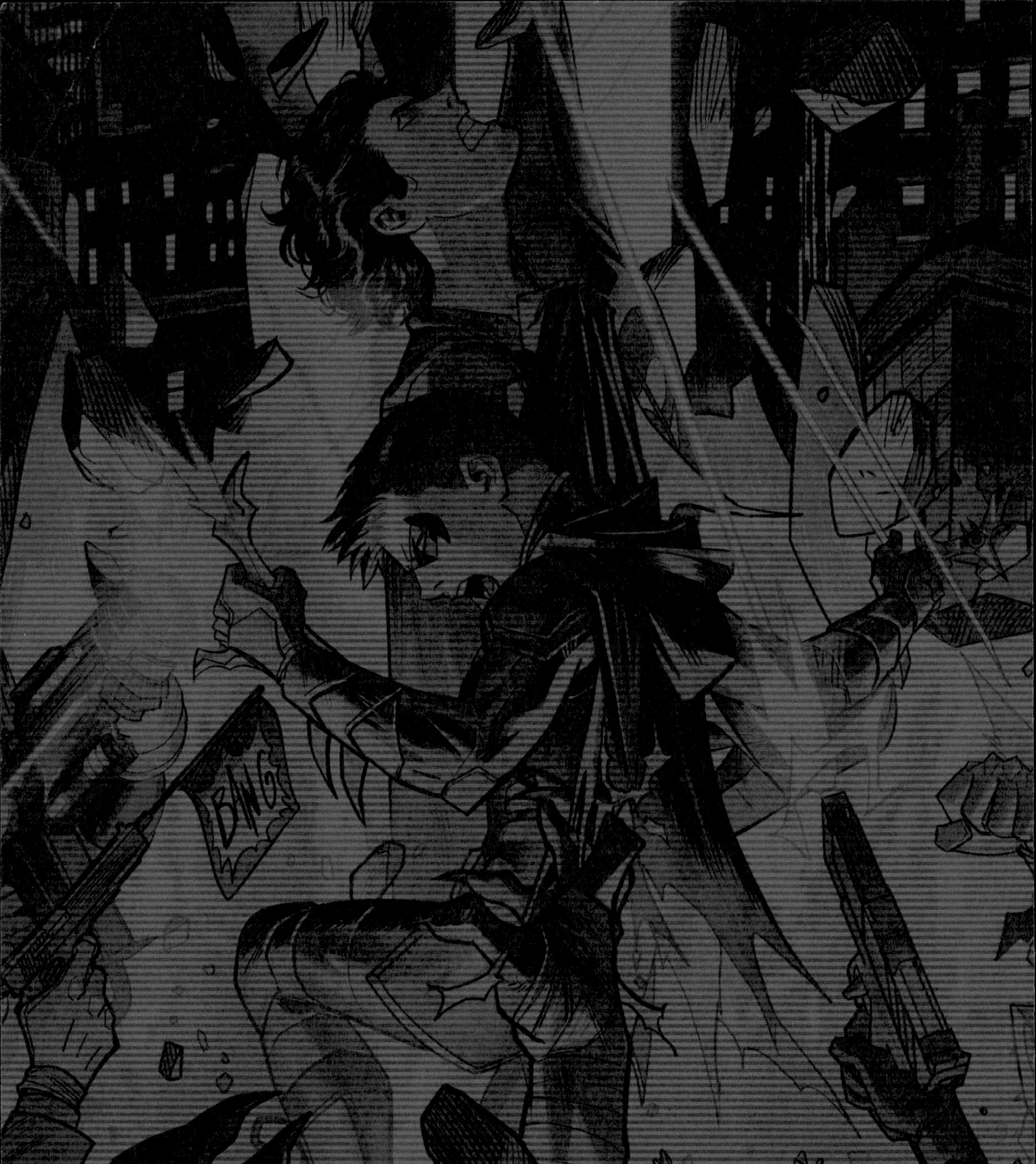
BANG

ADVENTURES OF THE SUPER SONS
#1

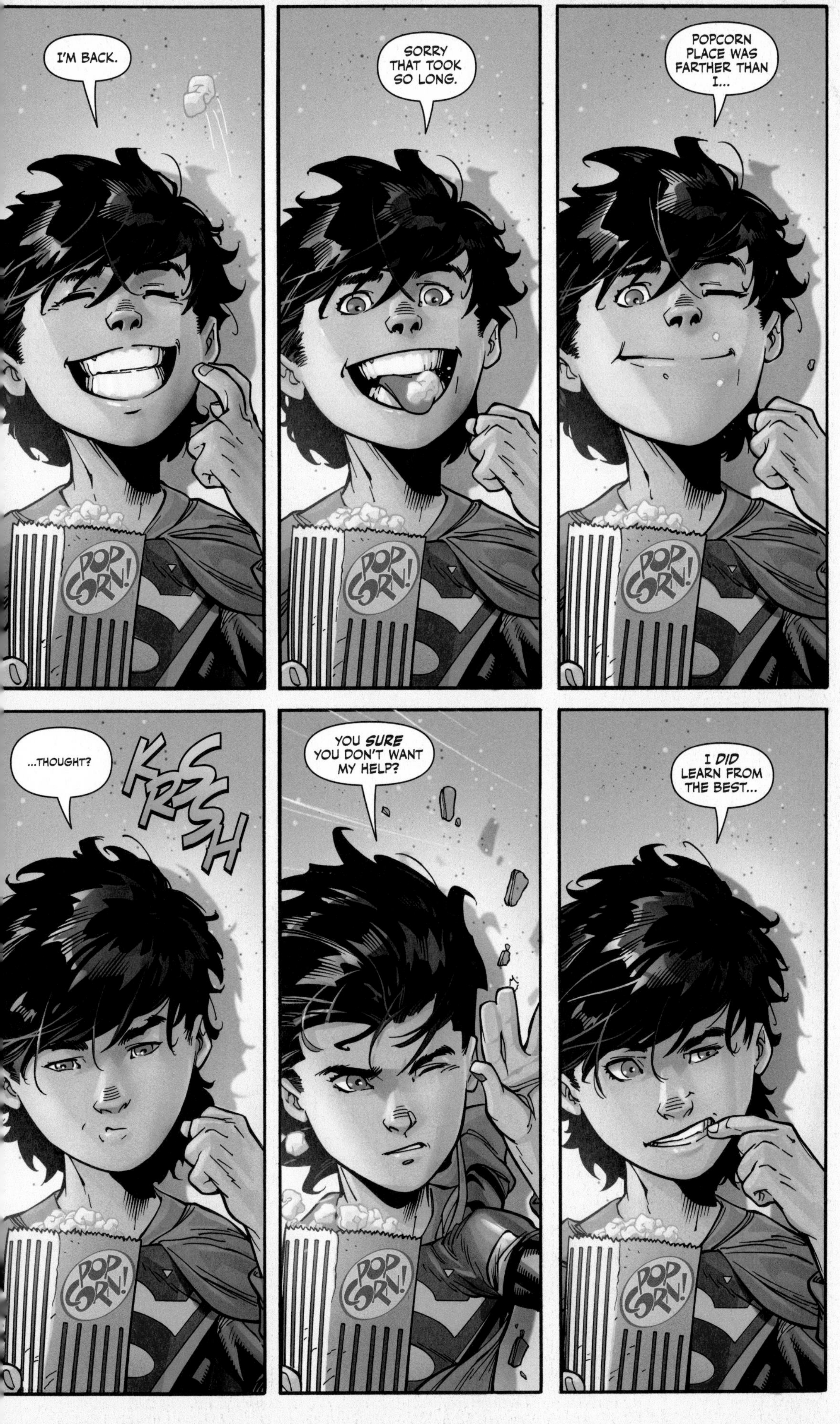
I'M BACK.
SORRY THAT TOOK SO LONG.
POPCORN PLACE WAS FARTHER THAN I...
POP CORN!
...THOUGHT?
KRSSH
YOU SURE YOU DON'T WANT MY HELP?
I DID LEARN FROM THE BEST...

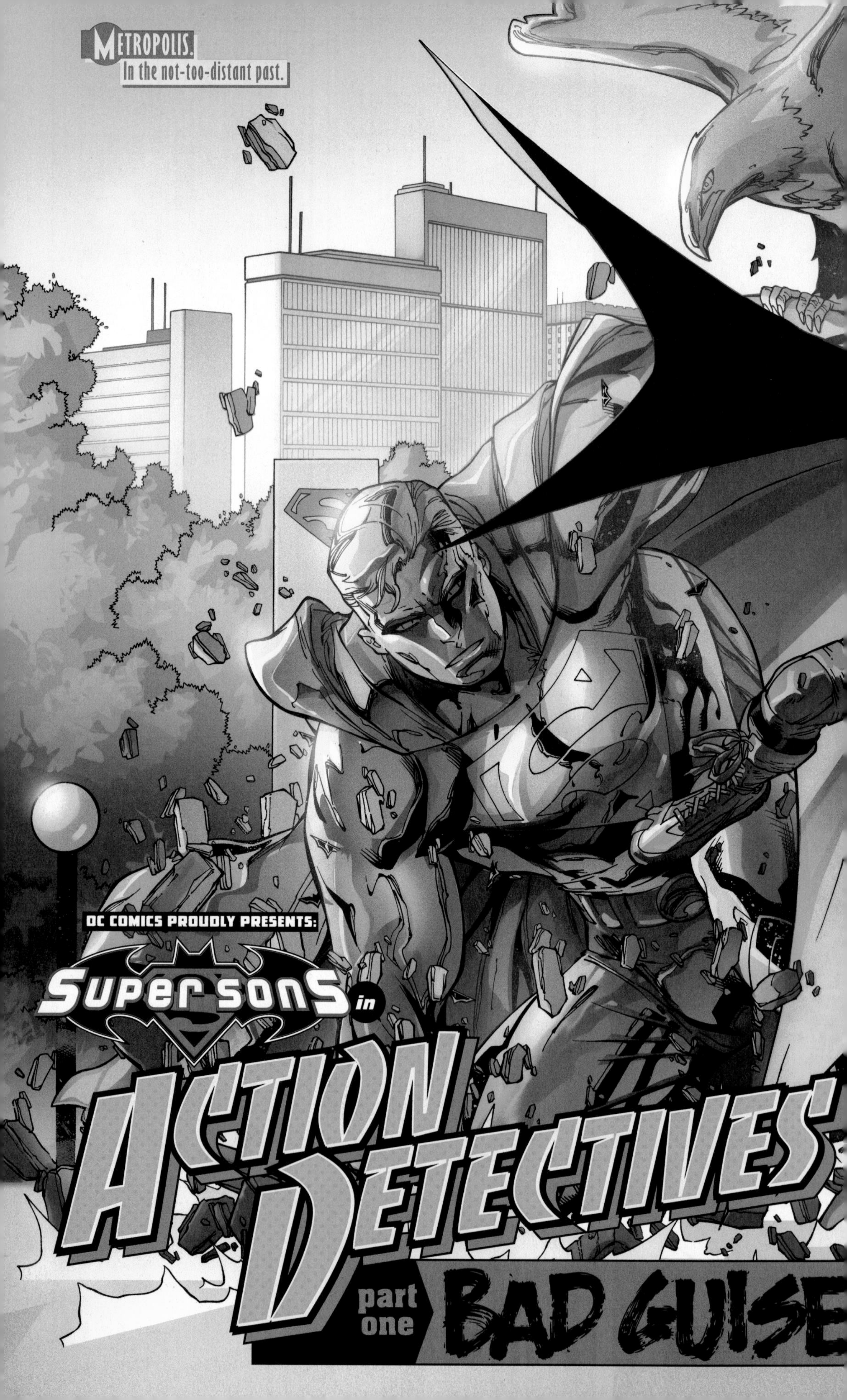
METROPOLIS.
In the not-too-distant past.
DC COMICS PROUDLY PRESENTS:
SUPER SONS in
ACTION DETECTIVES
part one
BAD GUISE

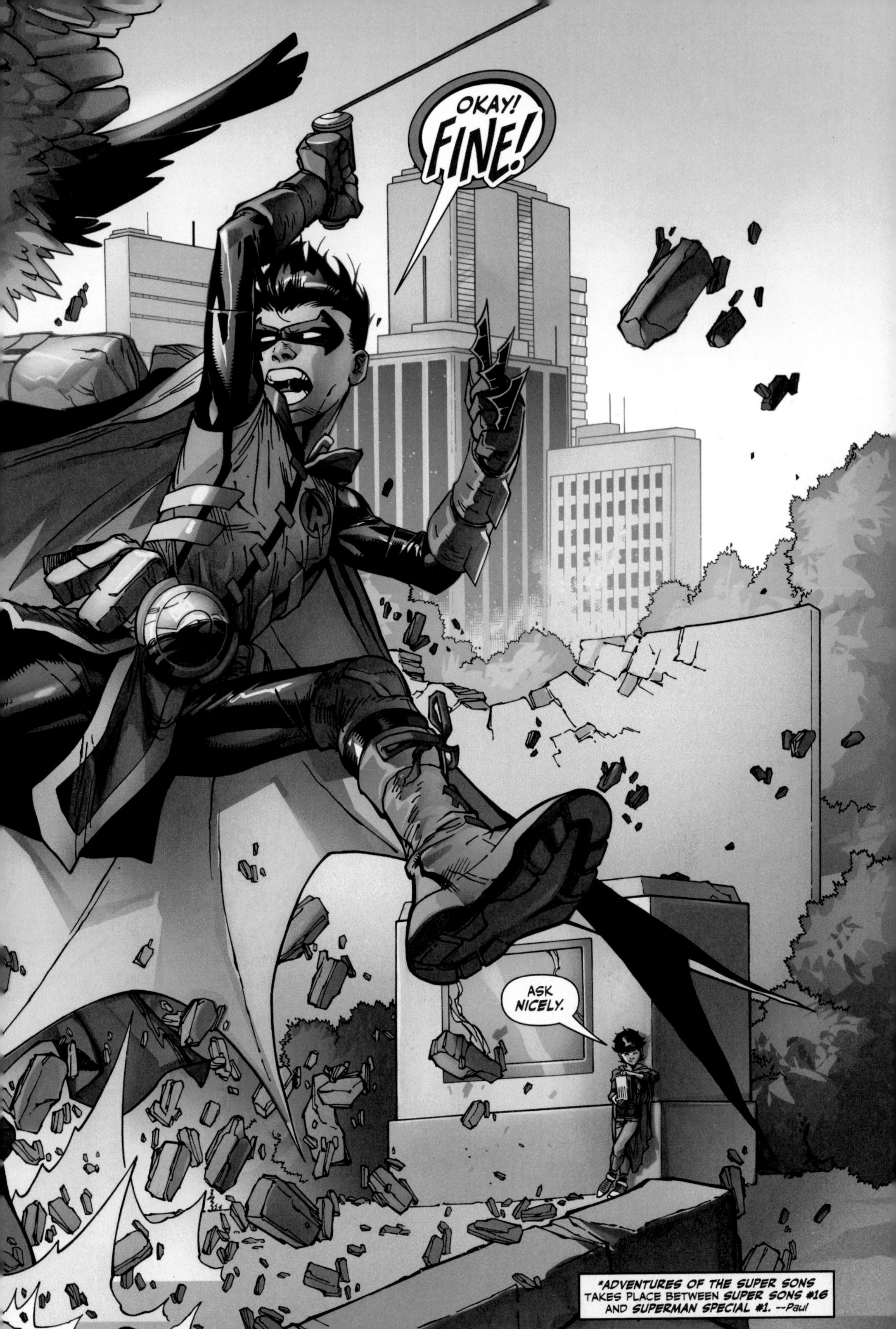
OKAY! FINE!
ASK NICELY.
*ADVENTURES OF THE SUPER SONS TAKES PLACE BETWEEN SUPER SONS #16 AND SUPERMAN SPECIAL #1. --Paul

PETER J. TOMASI story and words • **CARLO BARBERI** pencils
ART THIBERT inks • **PROTOBUNKER** colors • **ROB LEIGH** letters
DAN MORA cover • **ANDREW MARINO** assistant editor • **PAUL KAMINSKI** editor
MARIE JAVINS group editor

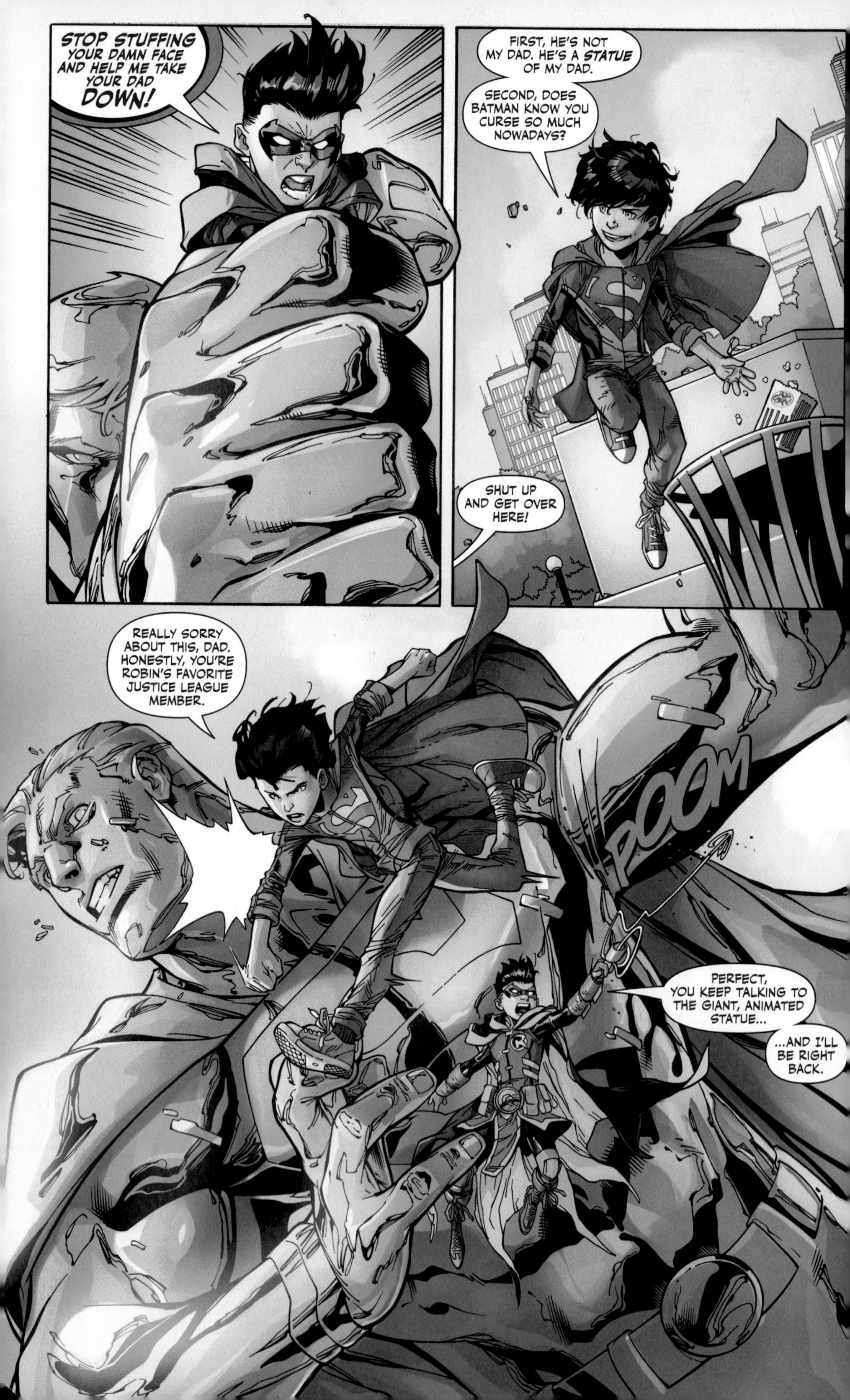
STOP STUFFING YOUR DAMN FACE AND HELP ME TAKE YOUR DAD DOWN!
FIRST, HE'S NOT MY DAD. HE'S A STATUE OF MY DAD.
SECOND, DOES BATMAN KNOW YOU CURSE SO MUCH NOWADAYS?
SHUT UP AND GET OVER HERE!
REALLY SORRY ABOUT THIS, DAD. HONESTLY, YOU'RE ROBIN'S FAVORITE JUSTICE LEAGUE MEMBER.
BOOM
PERFECT, YOU KEEP TALKING TO THE GIANT, ANIMATED STATUE...
...AND I'LL BE RIGHT BACK.

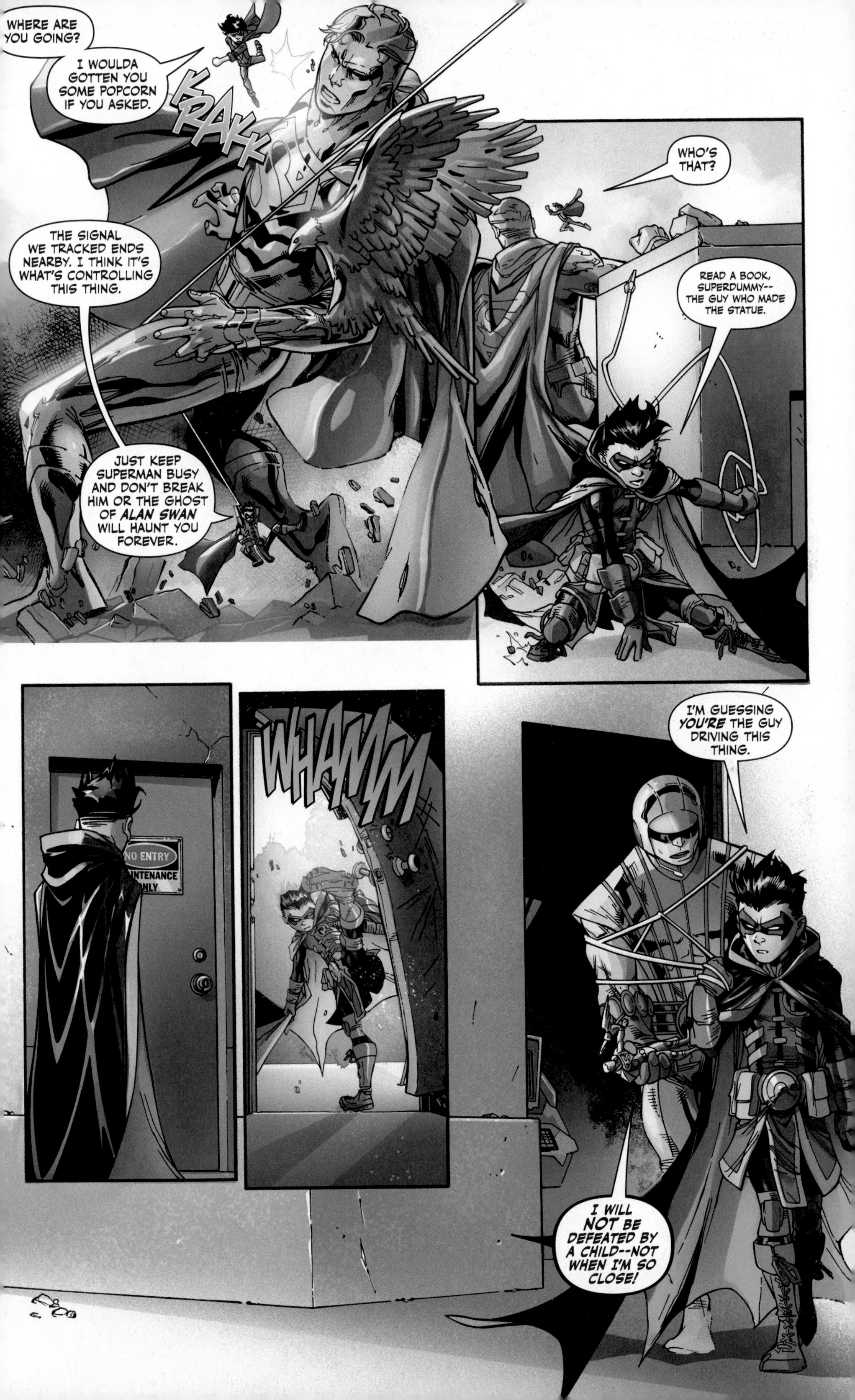

WHERE ARE YOU GOING?
I WOULDA GOTTEN YOU SOME POPCORN IF YOU ASKED.
KRAKK
WHO'S THAT?
THE SIGNAL WE TRACKED ENDS NEARBY. I THINK IT'S WHAT'S CONTROLLING THIS THING.
READ A BOOK, SUPERDUMMY-- THE GUY WHO MADE THE STATUE.
JUST KEEP SUPERMAN BUSY AND DON'T BREAK HIM OR THE GHOST OF ALAN SWAN WILL HAUNT YOU FOREVER.
NO ENTRY
WHAMM
I'M GUESSING YOU'RE THE GUY DRIVING THIS THING.
I WILL NOT BE DEFEATED BY A CHILD--NOT WHEN I'M SO CLOSE!

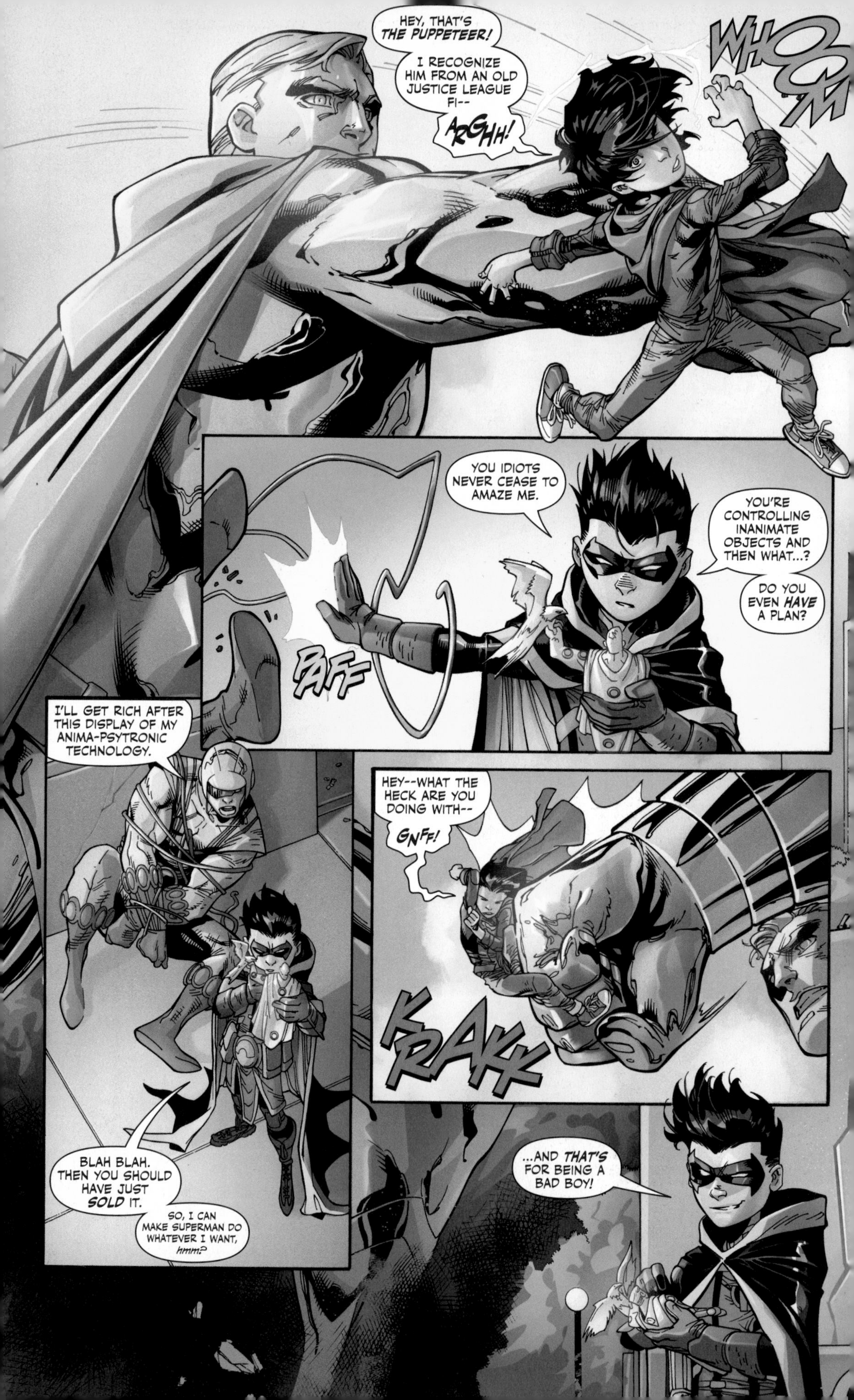
HEY, THAT'S *THE PUPPETEER!*
I RECOGNIZE HIM FROM AN OLD JUSTICE LEAGUE FI--
ARGHH!
WHOOM
YOU IDIOTS NEVER CEASE TO AMAZE ME.
YOU'RE CONTROLLING INANIMATE OBJECTS AND THEN WHAT...?
DO YOU EVEN *HAVE* A PLAN?
PAFF
I'LL GET RICH AFTER THIS DISPLAY OF MY ANIMA-PSYTRONIC TECHNOLOGY.
BLAH BLAH. THEN YOU SHOULD HAVE JUST *SOLD* IT.
SO, I CAN MAKE SUPERMAN DO WHATEVER I WANT, *hmm?*
HEY--WHAT THE HECK ARE YOU DOING WITH--
GNFF!
KRAKK
...AND *THAT'S* FOR BEING A BAD BOY!

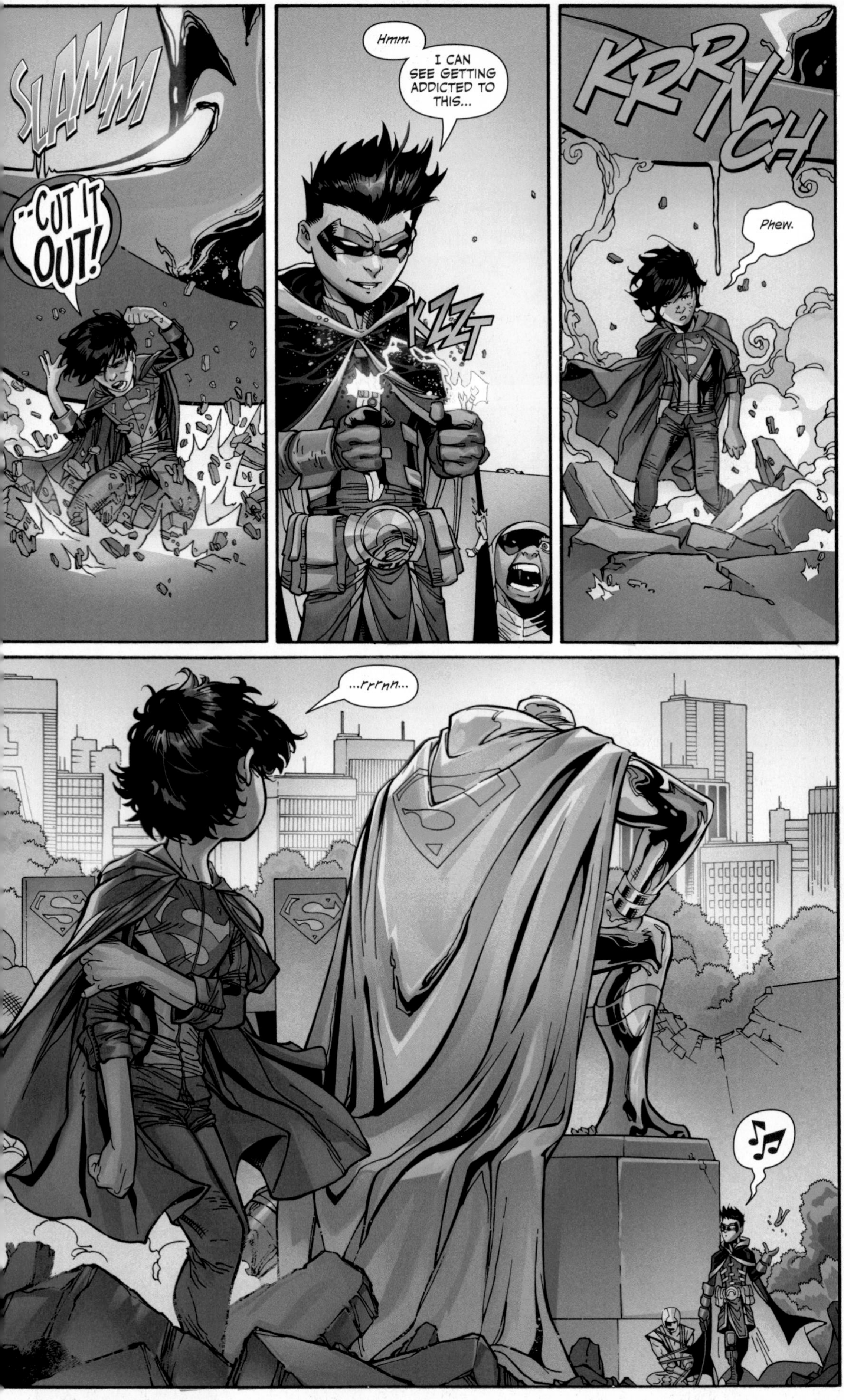
SLAMM
--CUT IT OUT!
Hmm.
I CAN SEE GETTING ADDICTED TO THIS...
KZZT
KRRNCH
Phew.
...rrrnn...

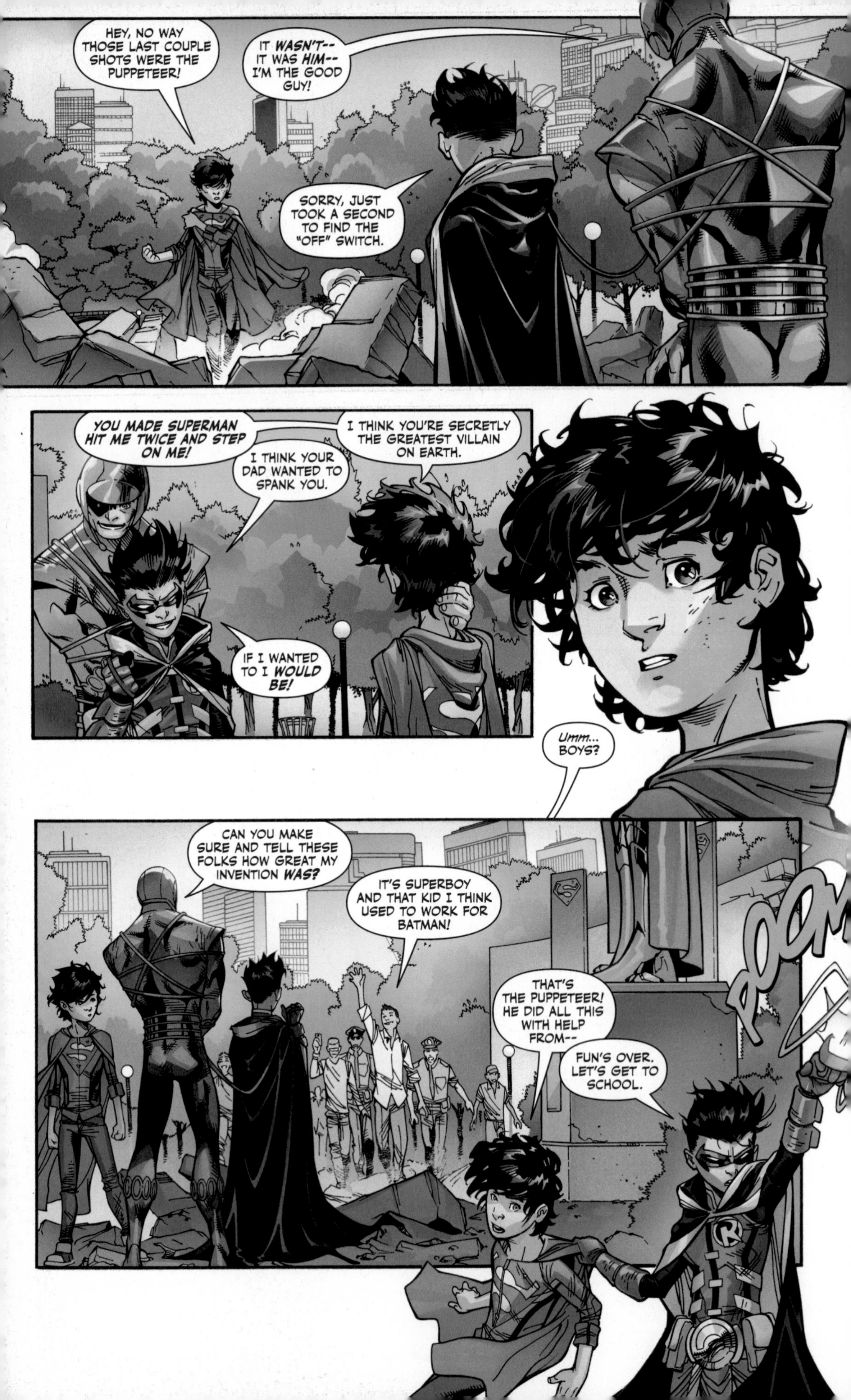
HEY, NO WAY THOSE LAST COUPLE SHOTS WERE THE PUPPETEER!
IT *WASN'T*-- IT WAS *HIM*-- I'M THE GOOD GUY!
SORRY, JUST TOOK A SECOND TO FIND THE "OFF" SWITCH.
YOU MADE SUPERMAN HIT ME TWICE AND STEP ON ME!
I THINK YOU'RE SECRETLY THE GREATEST VILLAIN ON EARTH.
I THINK YOUR DAD WANTED TO SPANK YOU.
IF I WANTED TO I *WOULD BE!*
Umm... BOYS?
CAN YOU MAKE SURE AND TELL THESE FOLKS HOW GREAT MY INVENTION *WAS?*
IT'S SUPERBOY AND THAT KID I THINK USED TO WORK FOR BATMAN!
THAT'S THE PUPPETEER! HE DID ALL THIS WITH HELP FROM--
FUN'S OVER. LET'S GET TO SCHOOL.

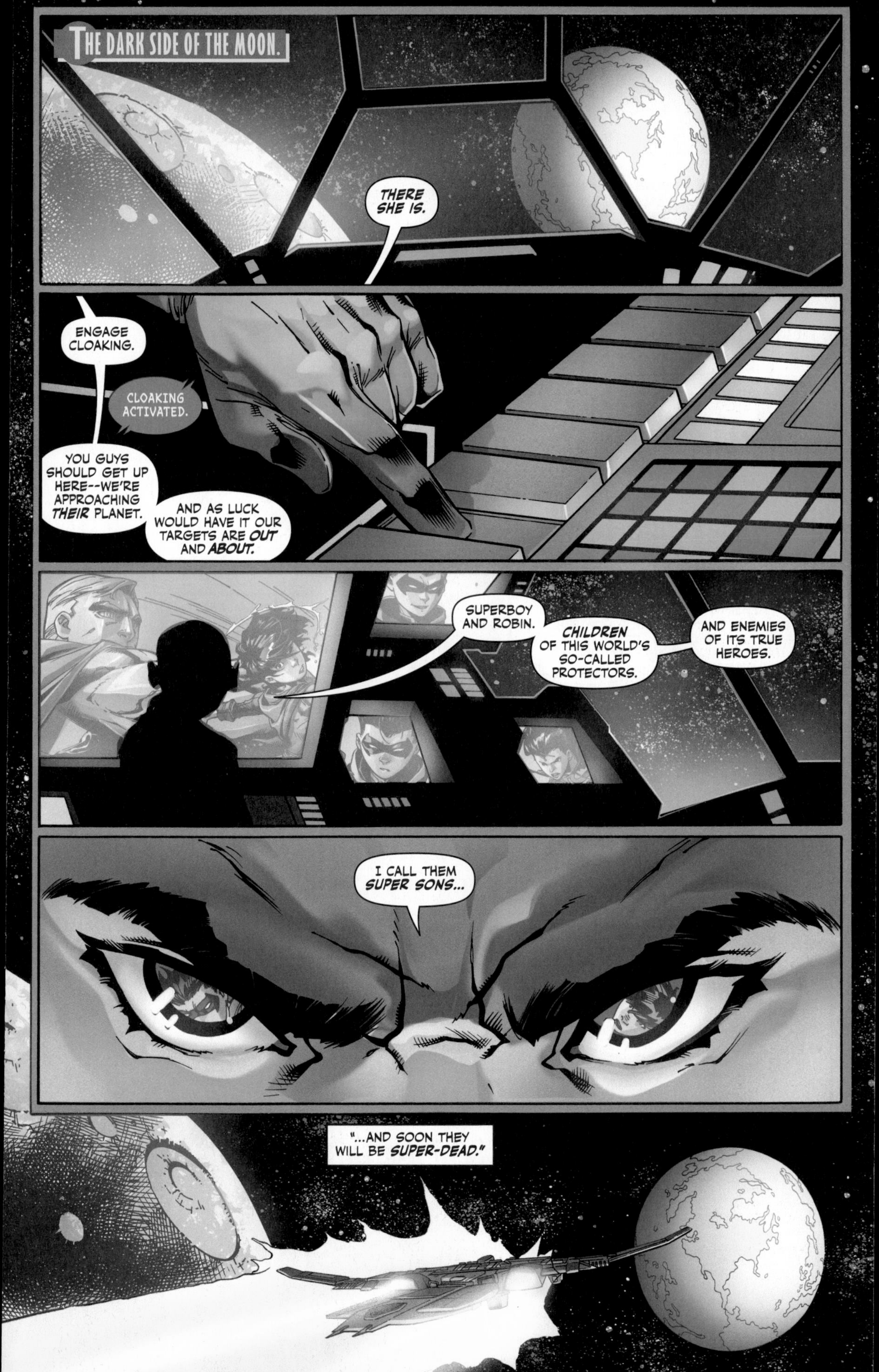
THE DARK SIDE OF THE MOON.
THERE SHE IS.
ENGAGE CLOAKING.
CLOAKING ACTIVATED.
YOU GUYS SHOULD GET UP HERE--WE'RE APPROACHING THEIR PLANET.
AND AS LUCK WOULD HAVE IT OUR TARGETS ARE OUT AND ABOUT.
SUPERBOY AND ROBIN.
CHILDREN OF THIS WORLD'S SO-CALLED PROTECTORS.
AND ENEMIES OF ITS TRUE HEROES.
I CALL THEM SUPER SONS...
"...AND SOON THEY WILL BE SUPER-DEAD."

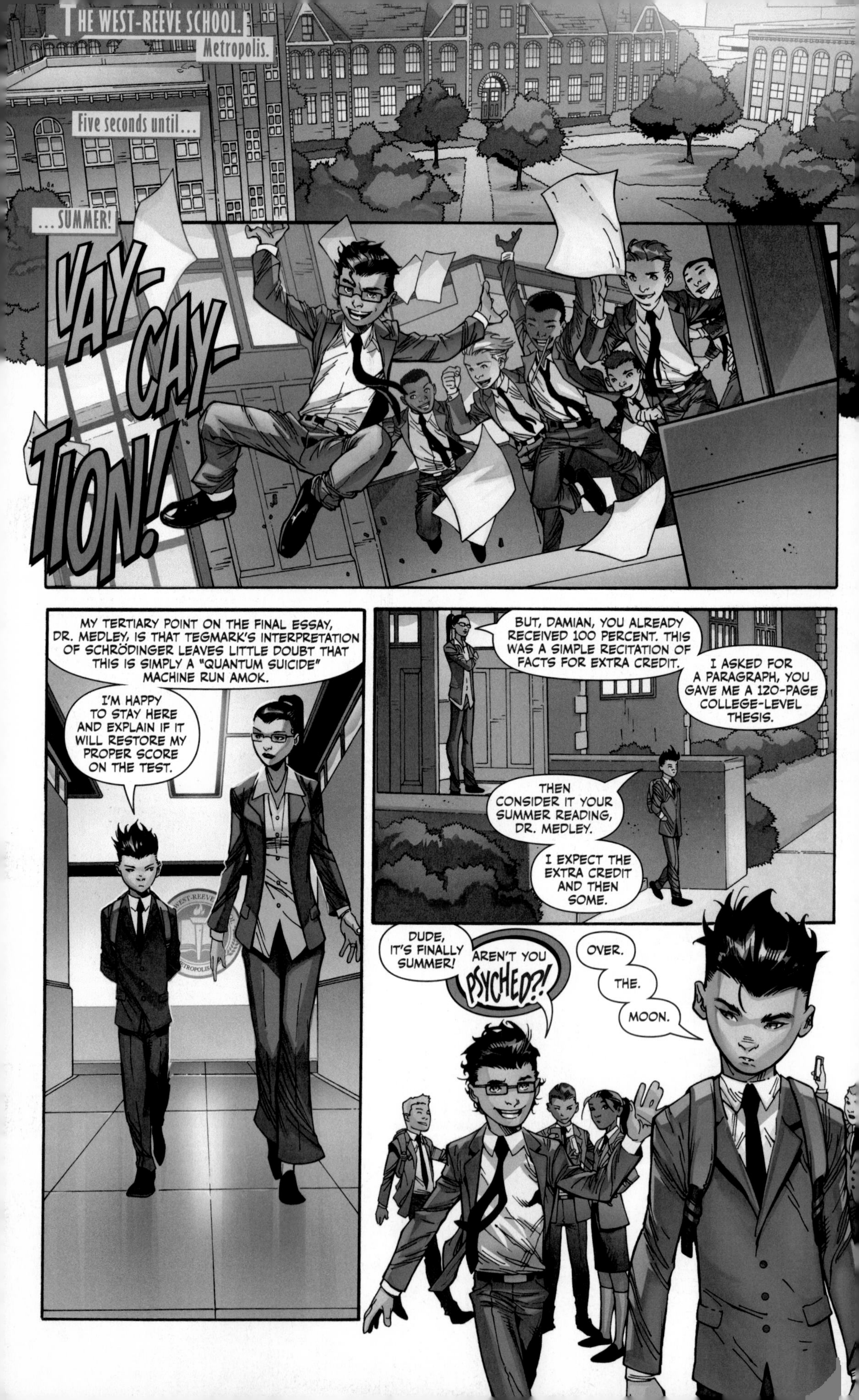
THE WEST-REEVE SCHOOL.
Metropolis.
Five seconds until...
...SUMMER!
VAY-CAY-TION!
MY TERTIARY POINT ON THE FINAL ESSAY, DR. MEDLEY, IS THAT TEGMARK'S INTERPRETATION OF SCHRÖDINGER LEAVES LITTLE DOUBT THAT THIS IS SIMPLY A "QUANTUM SUICIDE" MACHINE RUN AMOK.
I'M HAPPY TO STAY HERE AND EXPLAIN IF IT WILL RESTORE MY PROPER SCORE ON THE TEST.
WEST-REEVE
METROPOLIS
BUT, DAMIAN, YOU ALREADY RECEIVED 100 PERCENT. THIS WAS A SIMPLE RECITATION OF FACTS FOR EXTRA CREDIT.
I ASKED FOR A PARAGRAPH, YOU GAVE ME A 120-PAGE COLLEGE-LEVEL THESIS.
THEN CONSIDER IT YOUR SUMMER READING, DR. MEDLEY.
I EXPECT THE EXTRA CREDIT AND THEN SOME.
DUDE, IT'S FINALLY SUMMER!
AREN'T YOU PSYCHED?!
OVER.
THE.
MOON.

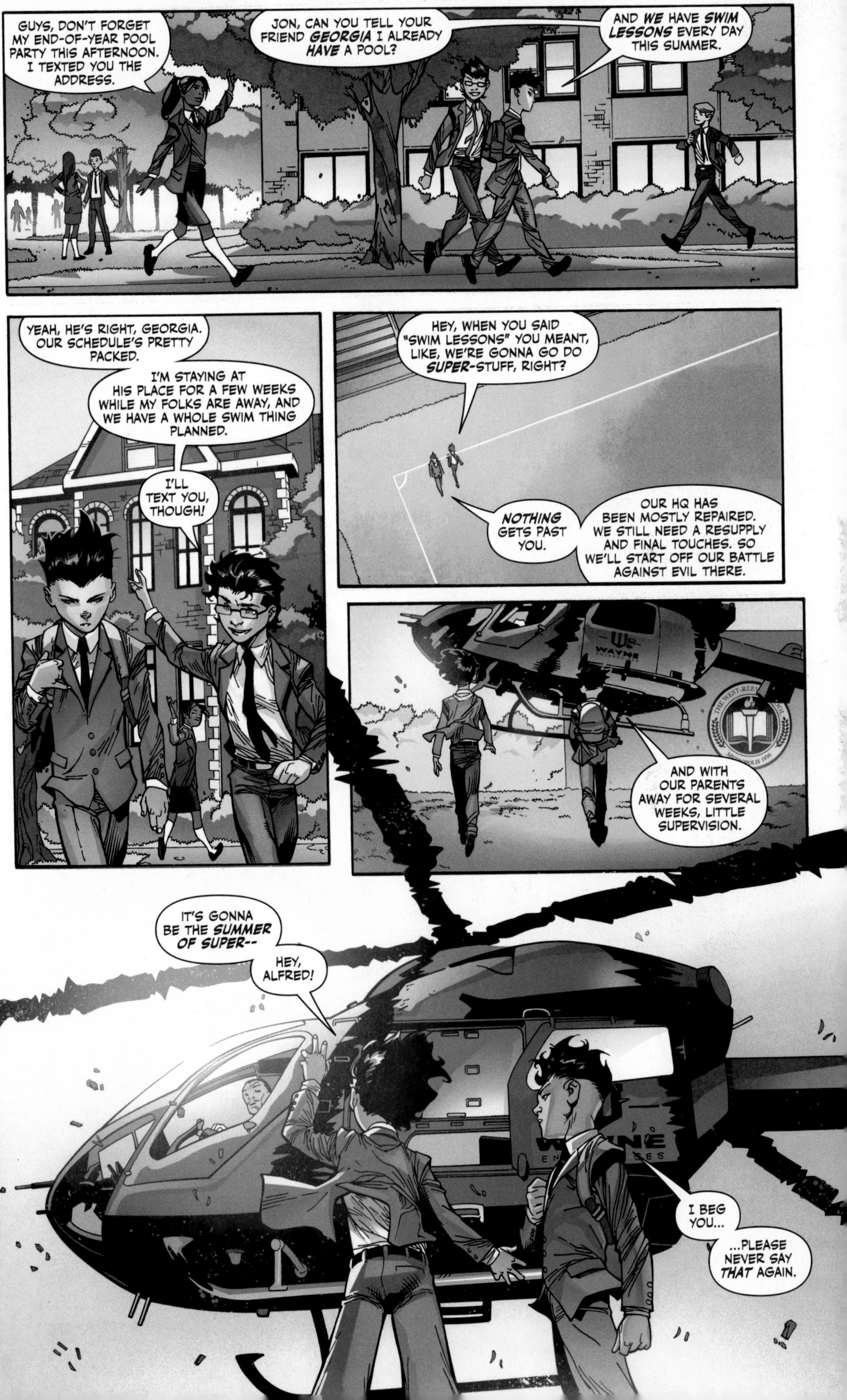

GUYS, DON'T FORGET MY END-OF-YEAR POOL PARTY THIS AFTERNOON. I TEXTED YOU THE ADDRESS.
JON, CAN YOU TELL YOUR FRIEND GEORGIA I ALREADY HAVE A POOL?
AND WE HAVE SWIM LESSONS EVERY DAY THIS SUMMER.
YEAH, HE'S RIGHT, GEORGIA. OUR SCHEDULE'S PRETTY PACKED.
I'M STAYING AT HIS PLACE FOR A FEW WEEKS WHILE MY FOLKS ARE AWAY, AND WE HAVE A WHOLE SWIM THING PLANNED.
I'LL TEXT YOU, THOUGH!
HEY, WHEN YOU SAID "SWIM LESSONS" YOU MEANT, LIKE, WE'RE GONNA GO DO SUPER-STUFF, RIGHT?
NOTHING GETS PAST YOU.
OUR HQ HAS BEEN MOSTLY REPAIRED. WE STILL NEED A RESUPPLY AND FINAL TOUCHES. SO WE'LL START OFF OUR BATTLE AGAINST EVIL THERE.
WAYNE
AND WITH OUR PARENTS AWAY FOR SEVERAL WEEKS, LITTLE SUPERVISION.
IT'S GONNA BE THE SUMMER OF SUPER--
HEY, ALFRED!
I BEG YOU...
...PLEASE NEVER SAY THAT AGAIN.

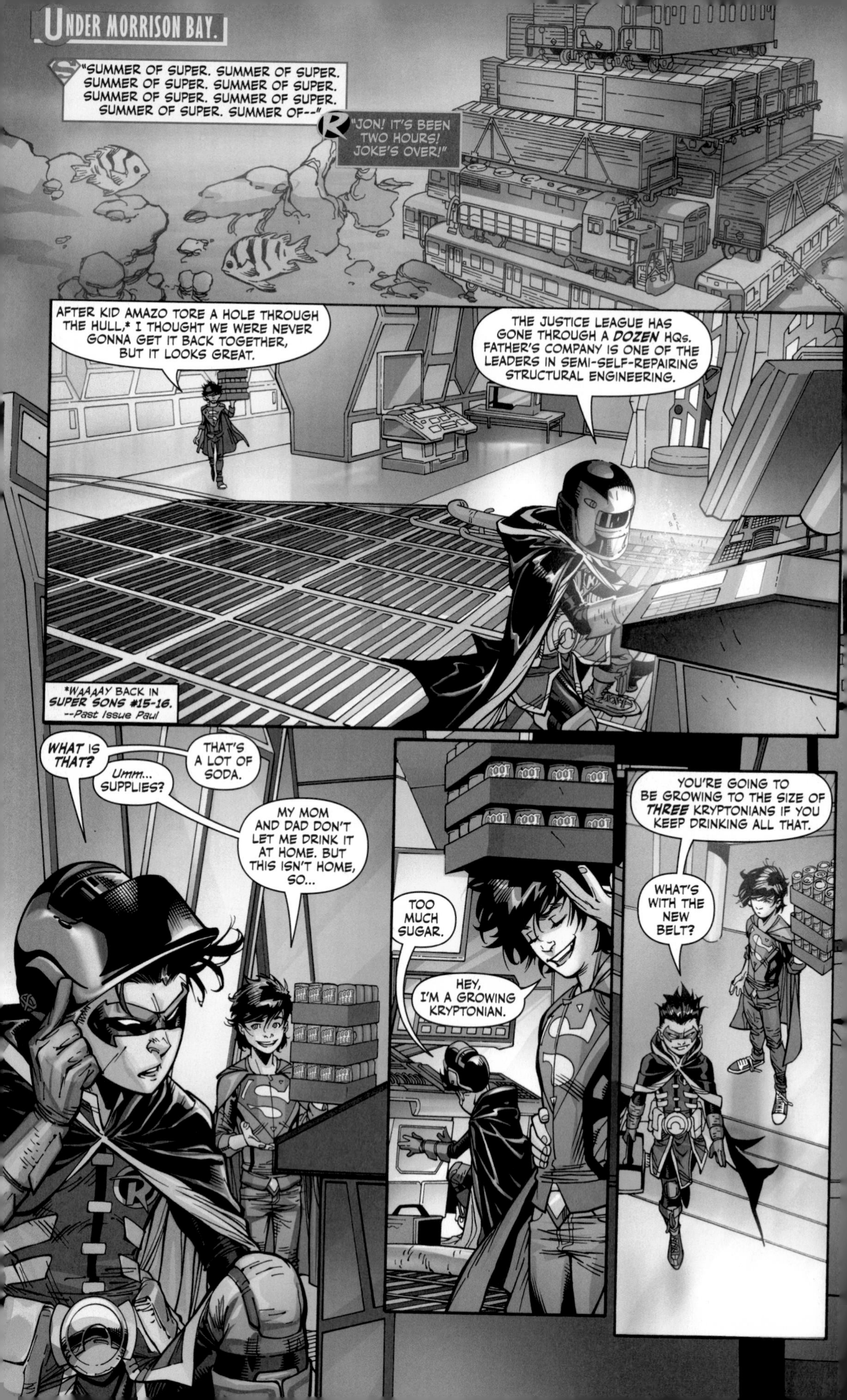
UNDER MORRISON BAY.
"SUMMER OF SUPER. SUMMER OF SUPER. SUMMER OF SUPER. SUMMER OF SUPER. SUMMER OF SUPER. SUMMER OF SUPER. SUMMER OF SUPER. SUMMER OF--"
"JON! IT'S BEEN TWO HOURS! JOKE'S OVER!"
AFTER KID AMAZO TORE A HOLE THROUGH THE HULL,* I THOUGHT WE WERE NEVER GONNA GET IT BACK TOGETHER, BUT IT LOOKS GREAT.
THE JUSTICE LEAGUE HAS GONE THROUGH A DOZEN HQs. FATHER'S COMPANY IS ONE OF THE LEADERS IN SEMI-SELF-REPAIRING STRUCTURAL ENGINEERING.
*WAAAAY BACK IN SUPER SONS #15-16. --Past Issue Paul
WHAT IS THAT?
Umm... SUPPLIES?
THAT'S A LOT OF SODA.
MY MOM AND DAD DON'T LET ME DRINK IT AT HOME. BUT THIS ISN'T HOME, SO...
TOO MUCH SUGAR.
HEY, I'M A GROWING KRYPTONIAN.
YOU'RE GOING TO BE GROWING TO THE SIZE OF THREE KRYPTONIANS IF YOU KEEP DRINKING ALL THAT.
WHAT'S WITH THE NEW BELT?

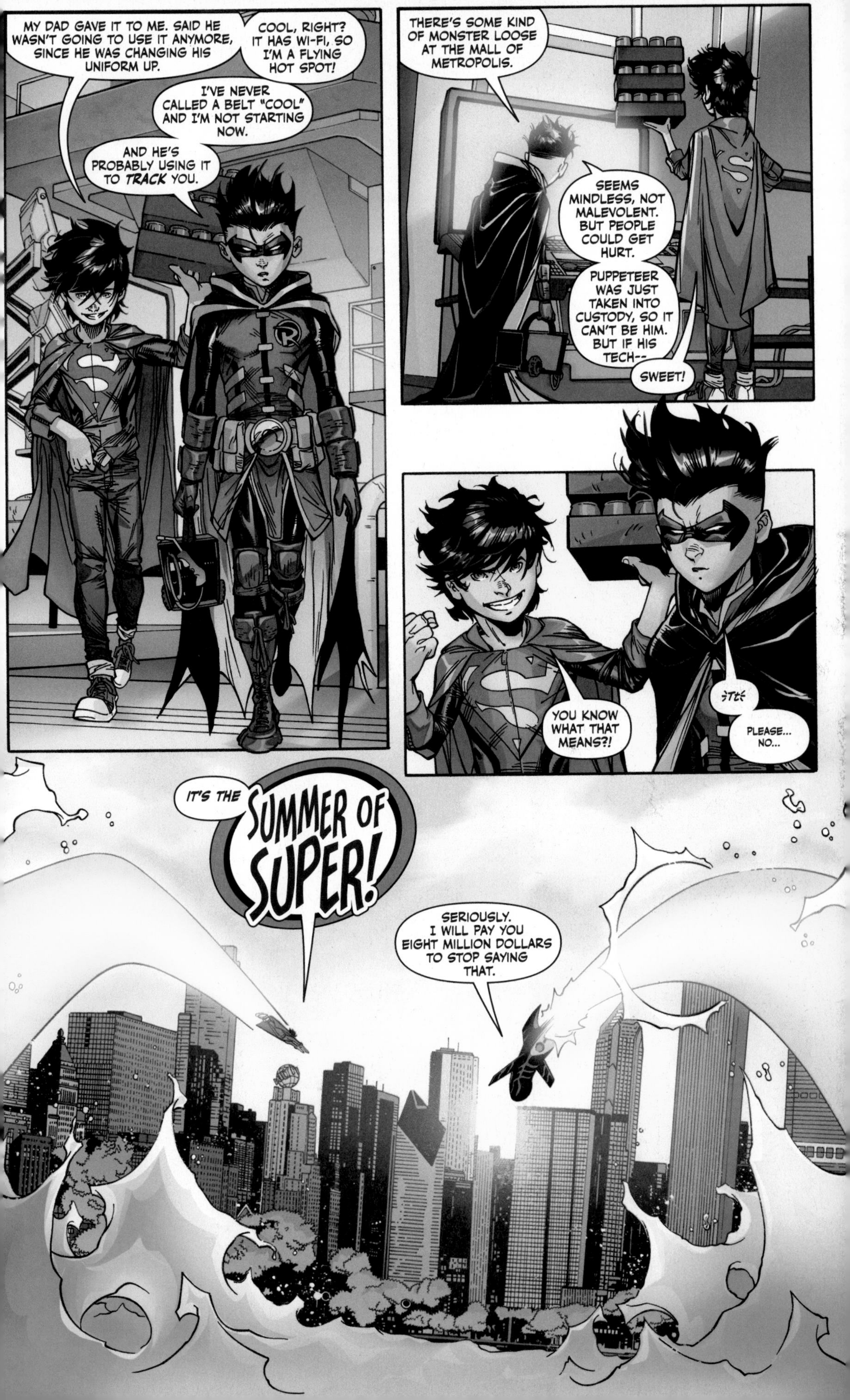
MY DAD GAVE IT TO ME. SAID HE WASN'T GOING TO USE IT ANYMORE, SINCE HE WAS CHANGING HIS UNIFORM UP.
COOL, RIGHT? IT HAS WI-FI, SO I'M A FLYING HOT SPOT!
I'VE NEVER CALLED A BELT "COOL" AND I'M NOT STARTING NOW.
AND HE'S PROBABLY USING IT TO TRACK YOU.
THERE'S SOME KIND OF MONSTER LOOSE AT THE MALL OF METROPOLIS.
SEEMS MINDLESS, NOT MALEVOLENT. BUT PEOPLE COULD GET HURT.
PUPPETEER WAS JUST TAKEN INTO CUSTODY, SO IT CAN'T BE HIM. BUT IF HIS TECH--
SWEET!
YOU KNOW WHAT THAT MEANS?!
TT.
PLEASE... NO...
IT'S THE SUMMER OF SUPER!
SERIOUSLY. I WILL PAY YOU EIGHT MILLION DOLLARS TO STOP SAYING THAT.

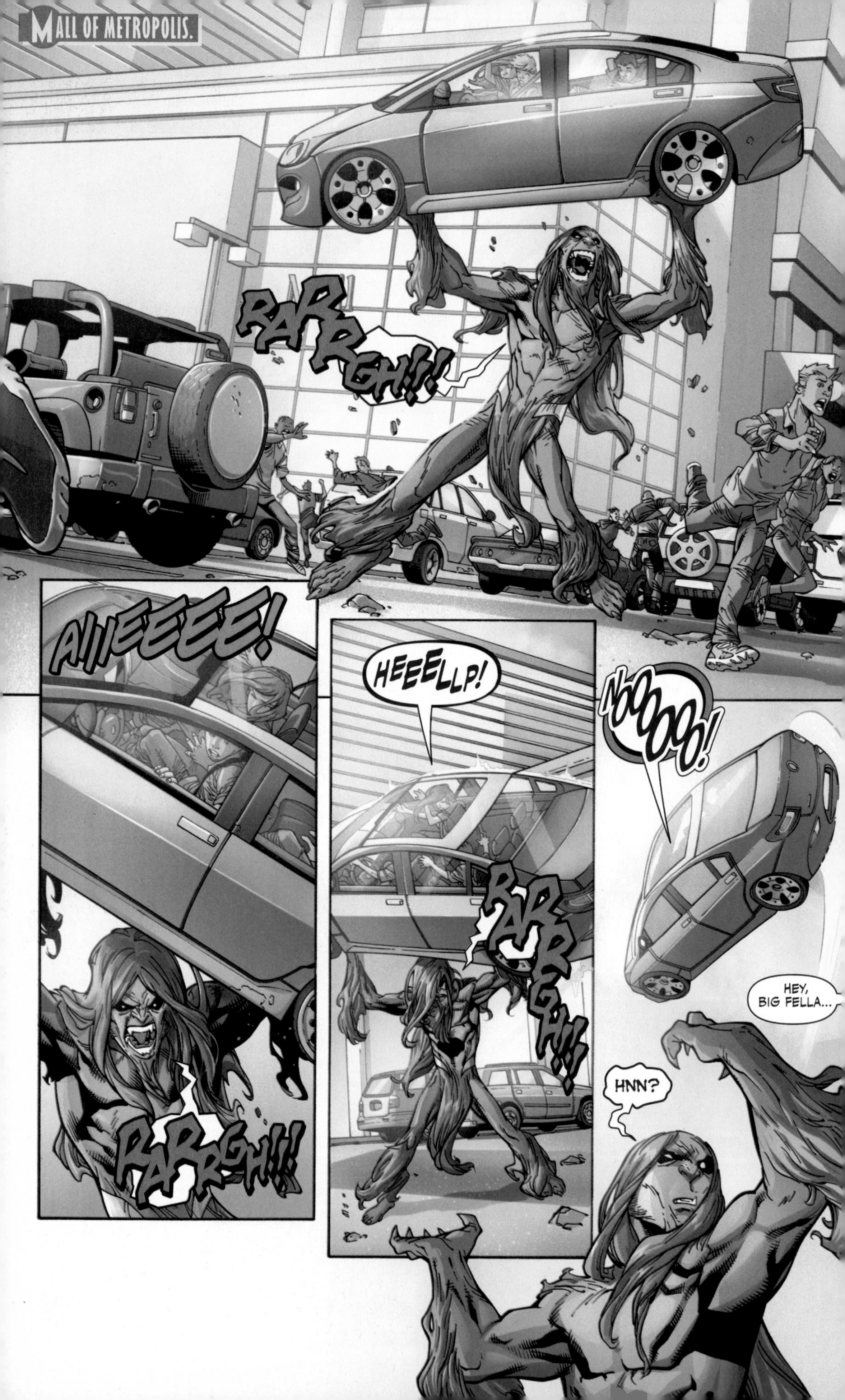
MALL OF METROPOLIS.
RARRGH!!
AIIIEEEEE!
RARRGH!!
HEEELLP!
RARRGH!!
NOOOOOO!
HEY, BIG FELLA...
HNN?

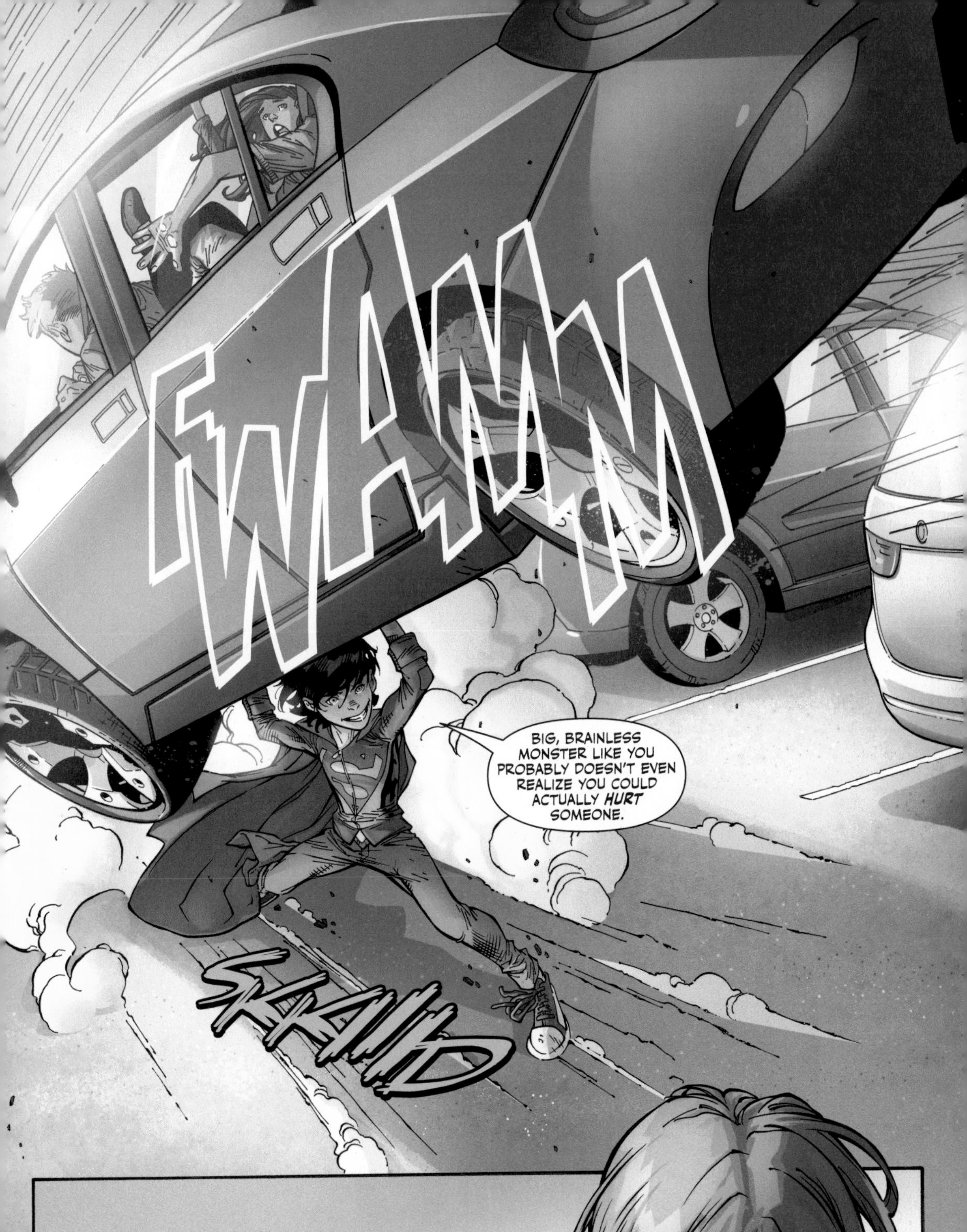
FWAMM
BIG, BRAINLESS MONSTER LIKE YOU PROBABLY DOESN'T EVEN REALIZE YOU COULD ACTUALLY *HURT* SOMEONE.
SKRAIID

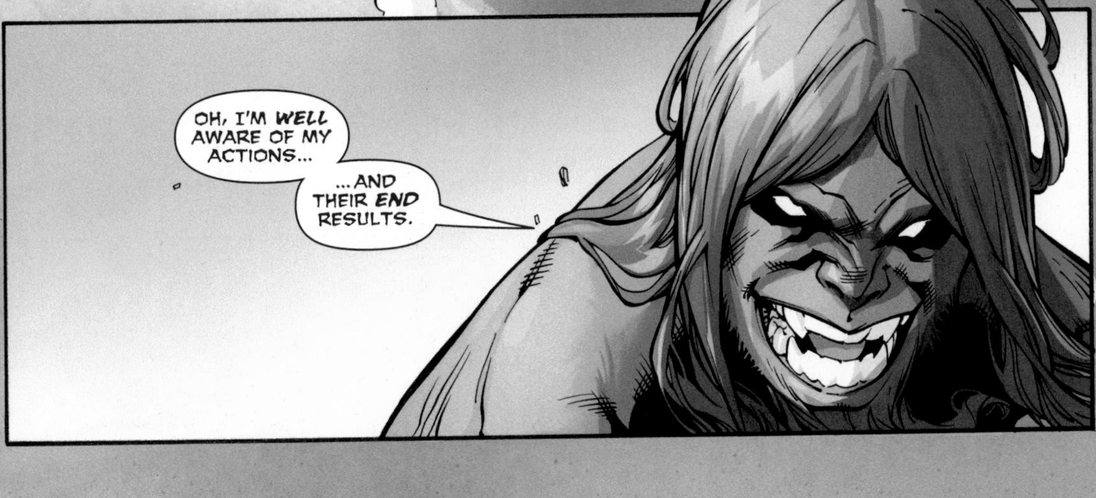
OH, I'M *WELL* AWARE OF MY ACTIONS...
...AND THEIR *END* RESULTS.

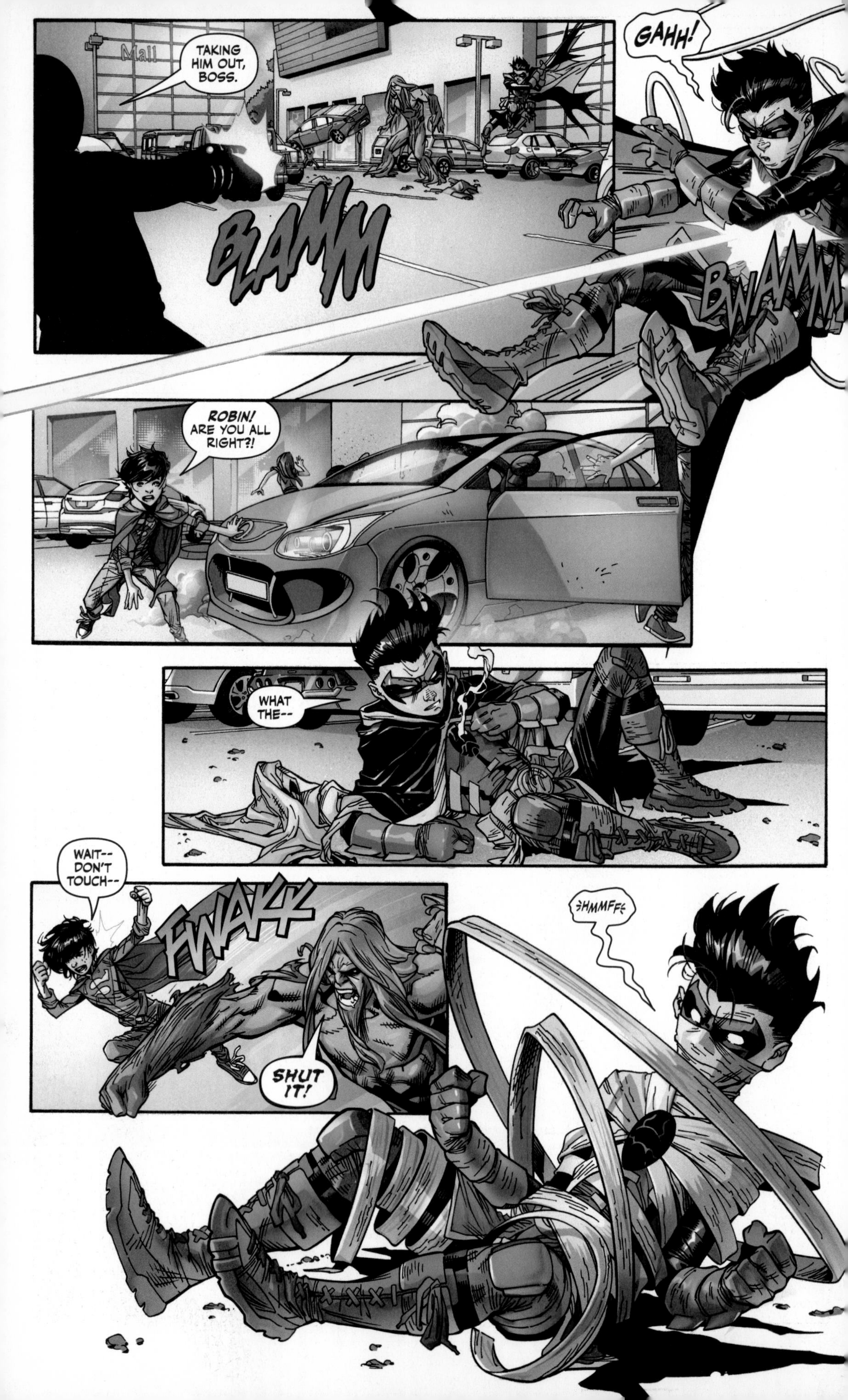

Mall
TAKING HIM OUT, BOSS.
BLAMM
GAHH!
BWAMM
ROBIN! ARE YOU ALL RIGHT?!
WHAT THE--
WAIT-- DON'T TOUCH--
FWAKK
SHUT IT!
HMMFF

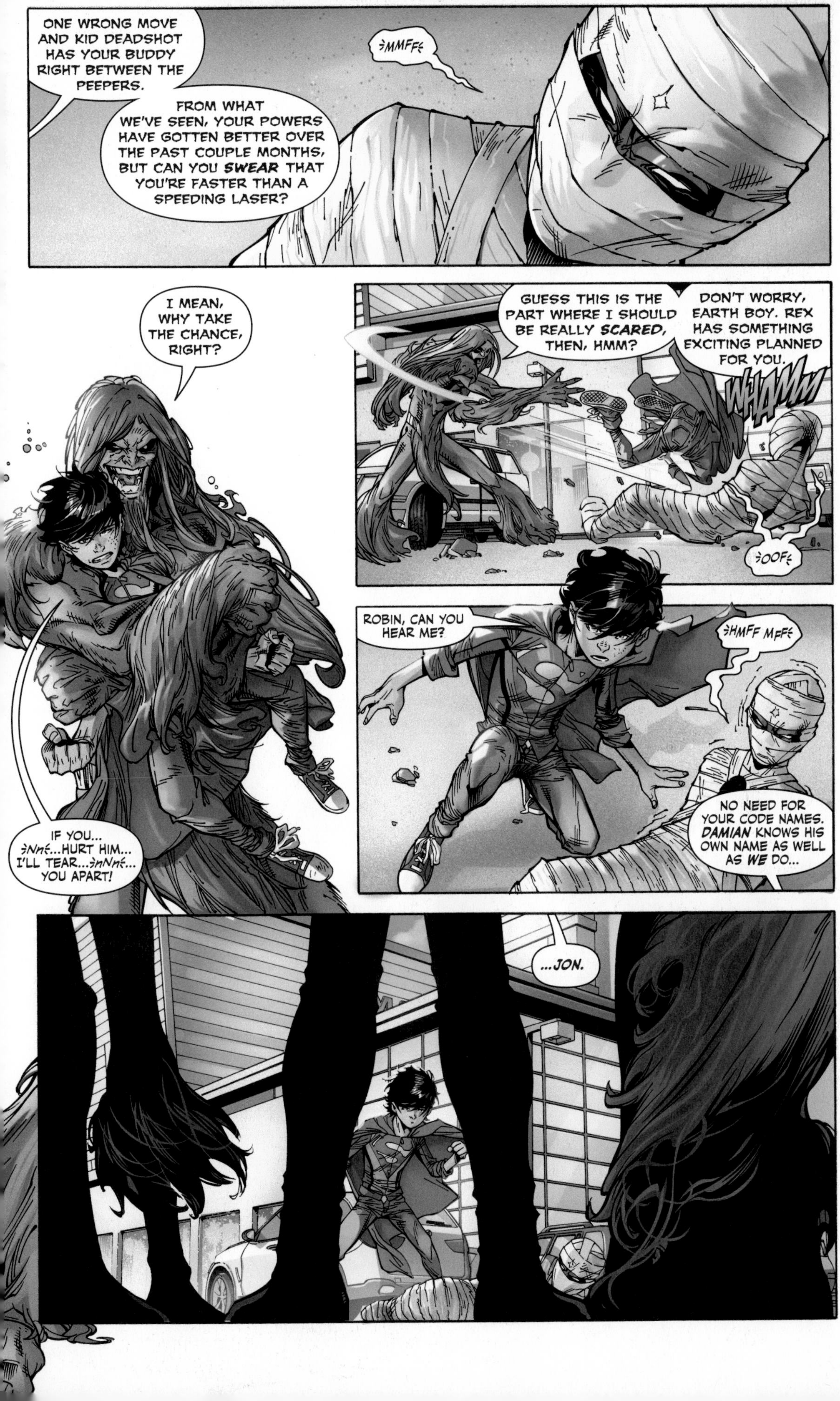
ONE WRONG MOVE AND KID DEADSHOT HAS YOUR BUDDY RIGHT BETWEEN THE PEEPERS.
FROM WHAT WE'VE SEEN, YOUR POWERS HAVE GOTTEN BETTER OVER THE PAST COUPLE MONTHS, BUT CAN YOU **SWEAR** THAT YOU'RE FASTER THAN A SPEEDING LASER?
MMFF
I MEAN, WHY TAKE THE CHANCE, RIGHT?
IF YOU... NNN...HURT HIM... I'LL TEAR...NNN... YOU APART!
GUESS THIS IS THE PART WHERE I SHOULD BE REALLY **SCARED**, THEN, HMM?
DON'T WORRY, EARTH BOY. REX HAS SOMETHING EXCITING PLANNED FOR YOU.
WHAMM
OOF
ROBIN, CAN YOU HEAR ME?
HMFF MFF
NO NEED FOR YOUR CODE NAMES. **DAMIAN** KNOWS HIS OWN NAME AS WELL AS **WE** DO...
...JON.

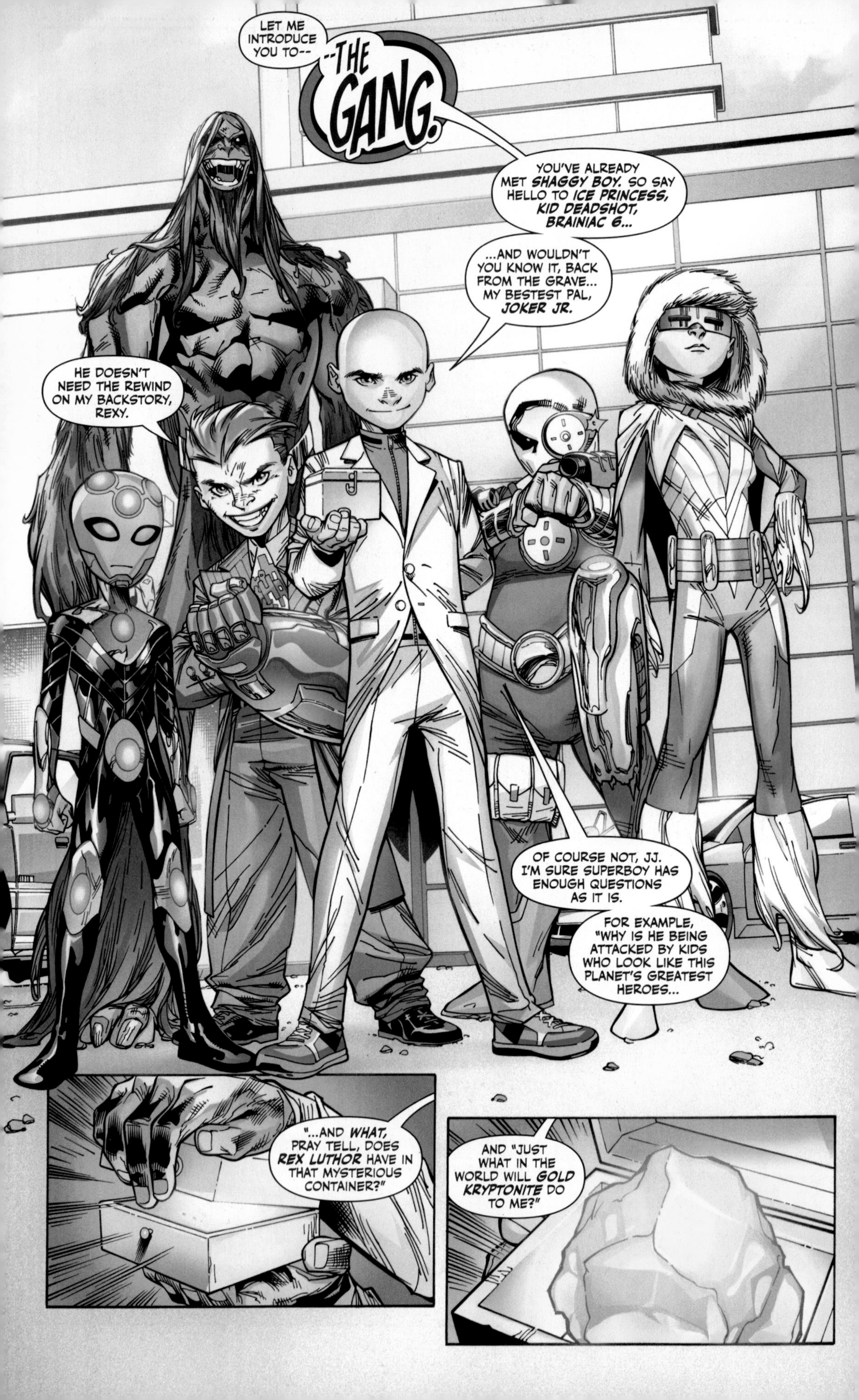

LET ME INTRODUCE YOU TO--
--THE GANG.
YOU'VE ALREADY MET SHAGGY BOY. SO SAY HELLO TO ICE PRINCESS, KID DEADSHOT, BRAINIAC 6...
...AND WOULDN'T YOU KNOW IT, BACK FROM THE GRAVE... MY BESTEST PAL, JOKER JR.
HE DOESN'T NEED THE REWIND ON MY BACKSTORY, REXY.
OF COURSE NOT, JJ. I'M SURE SUPERBOY HAS ENOUGH QUESTIONS AS IT IS.
FOR EXAMPLE, "WHY IS HE BEING ATTACKED BY KIDS WHO LOOK LIKE THIS PLANET'S GREATEST HEROES...
"...AND WHAT, PRAY TELL, DOES REX LUTHOR HAVE IN THAT MYSTERIOUS CONTAINER?"
AND "JUST WHAT IN THE WORLD WILL GOLD KRYPTONITE DO TO ME?"

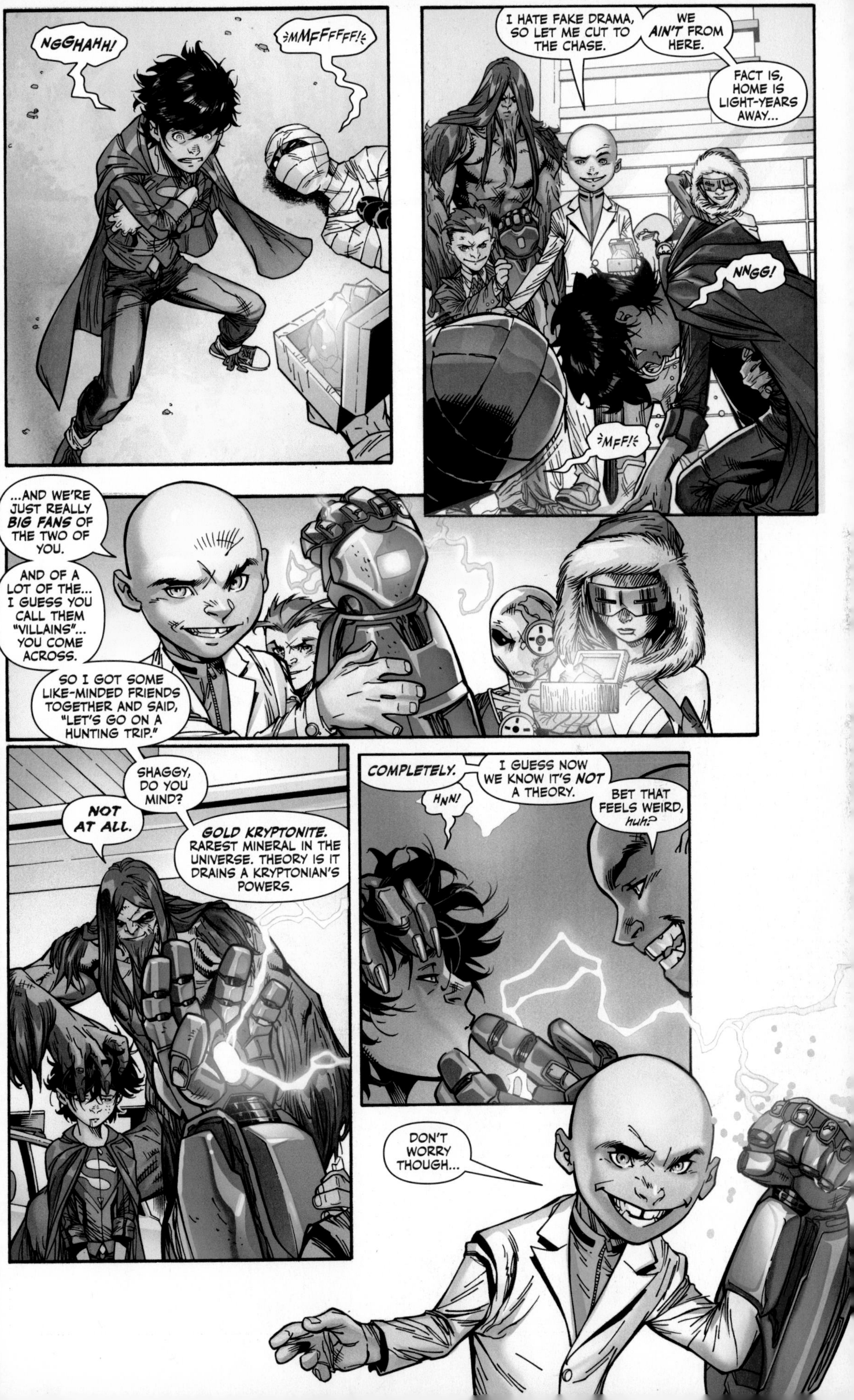
NGGHAHH!
MMFFFFFF!
I HATE FAKE DRAMA, SO LET ME CUT TO THE CHASE.
WE AIN'T FROM HERE.
FACT IS, HOME IS LIGHT-YEARS AWAY...
NNGG!
MFF!
...AND WE'RE JUST REALLY BIG FANS OF THE TWO OF YOU.
AND OF A LOT OF THE... I GUESS YOU CALL THEM "VILLAINS"... YOU COME ACROSS.
SO I GOT SOME LIKE-MINDED FRIENDS TOGETHER AND SAID, "LET'S GO ON A HUNTING TRIP."
SHAGGY, DO YOU MIND?
NOT AT ALL.
GOLD KRYPTONITE. RAREST MINERAL IN THE UNIVERSE. THEORY IS IT DRAINS A KRYPTONIAN'S POWERS.
COMPLETELY.
HNN!
I GUESS NOW WE KNOW IT'S NOT A THEORY.
BET THAT FEELS WEIRD, huh?
DON'T WORRY THOUGH...

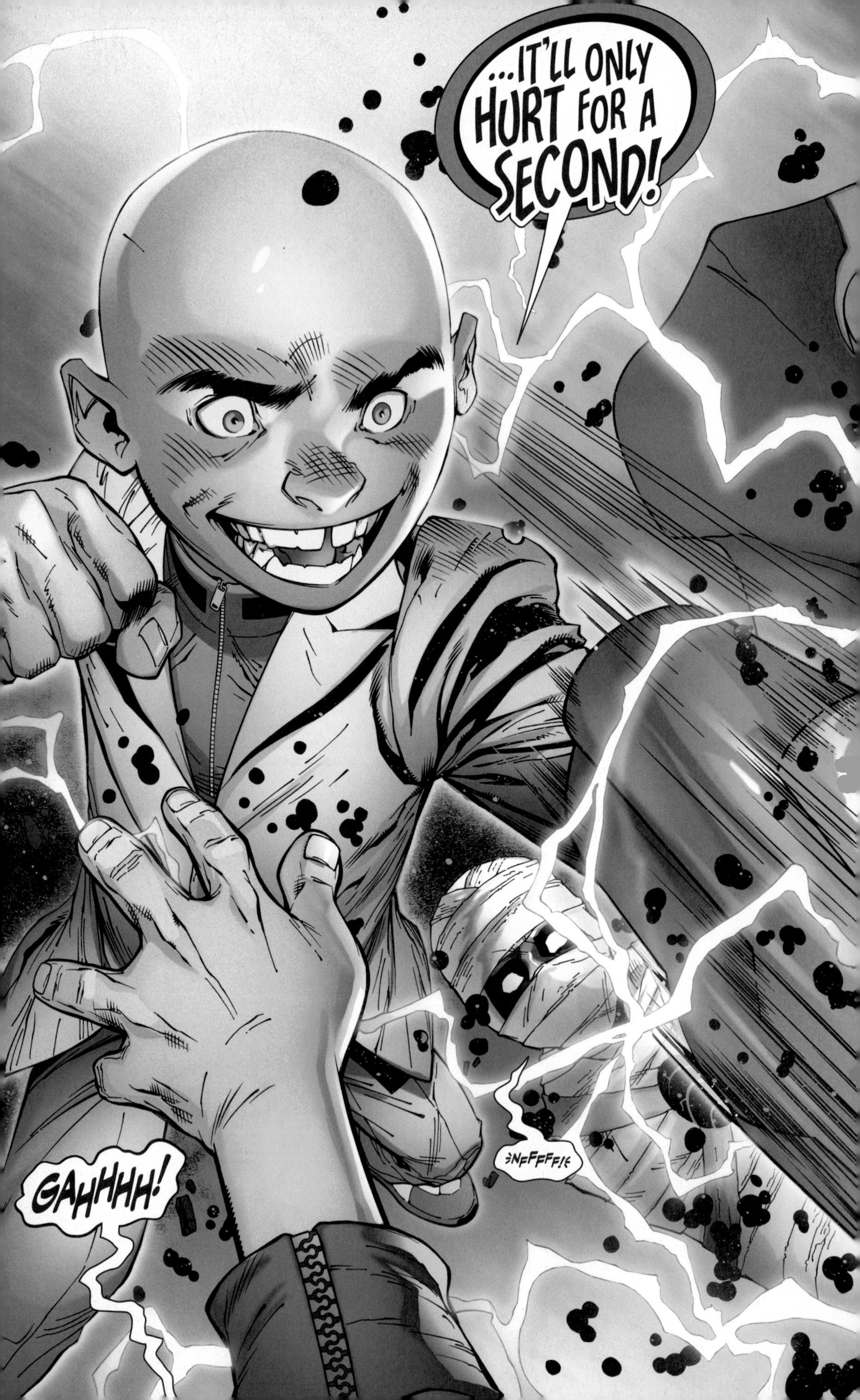
...IT'LL ONLY HURT FOR A SECOND!
GAHHHH!
NFFFF!

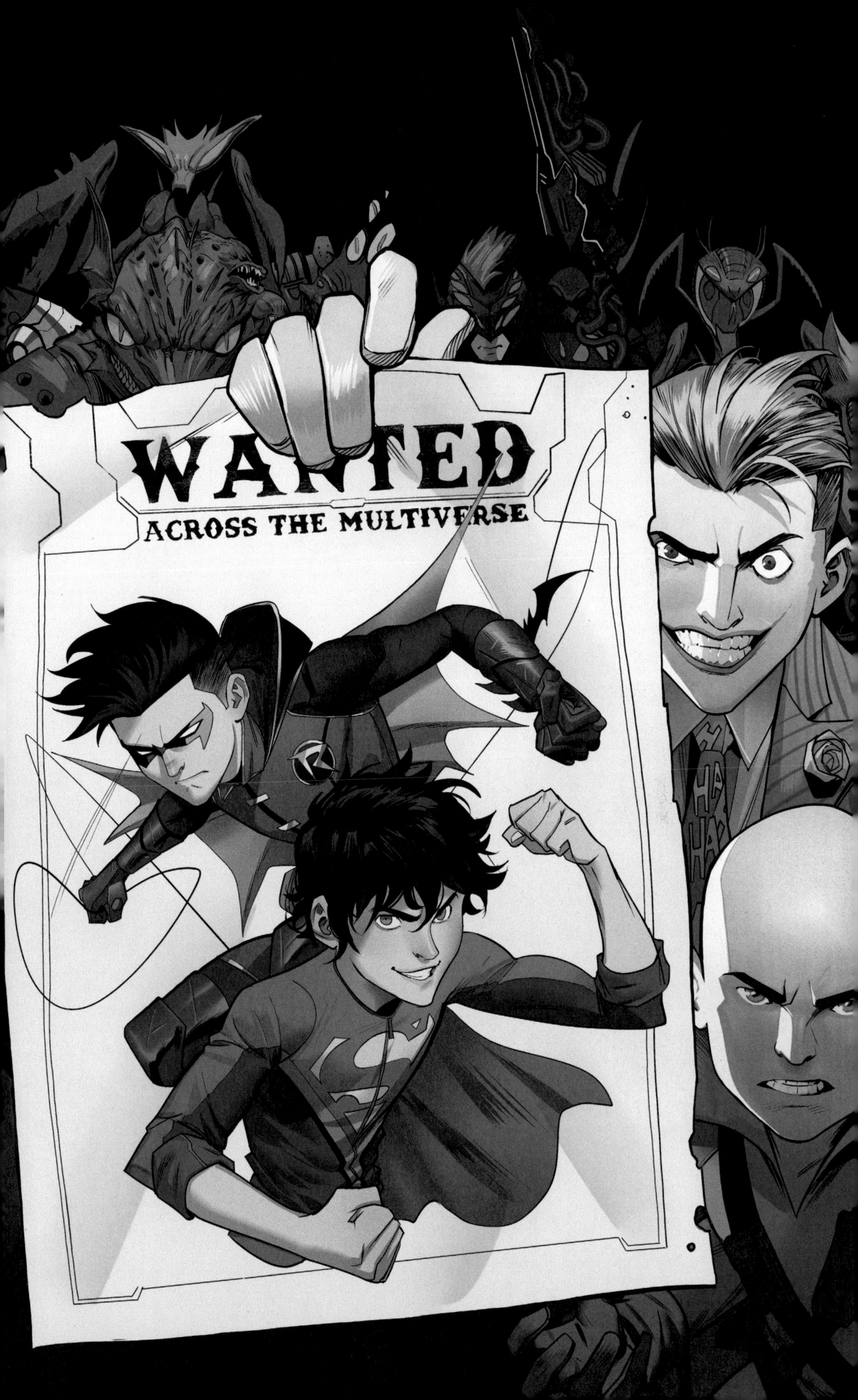
WANTED
ACROSS THE MULTIVERSE
HA
HA
HA

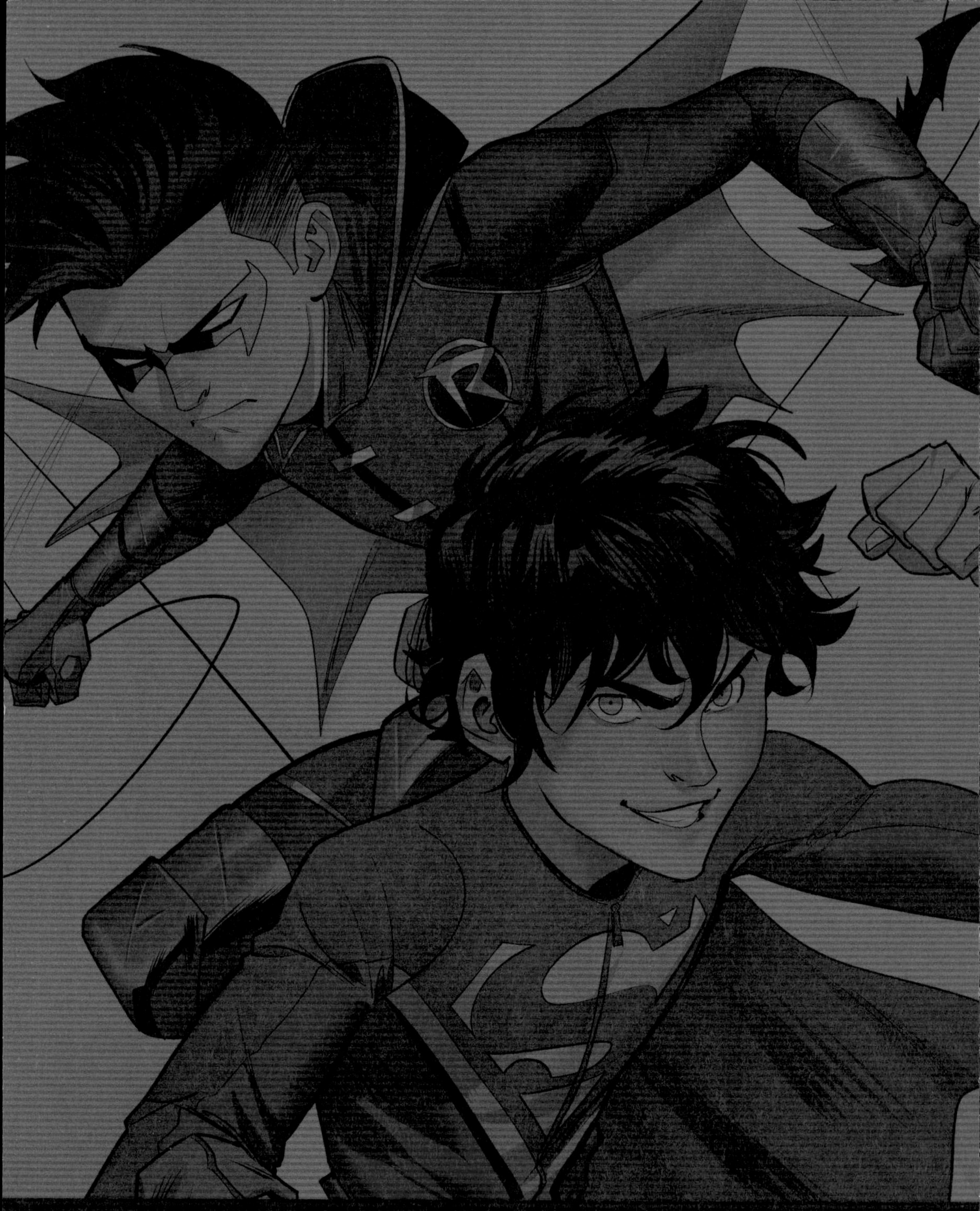

ADVENTURES OF THE SUPER SONS
#2

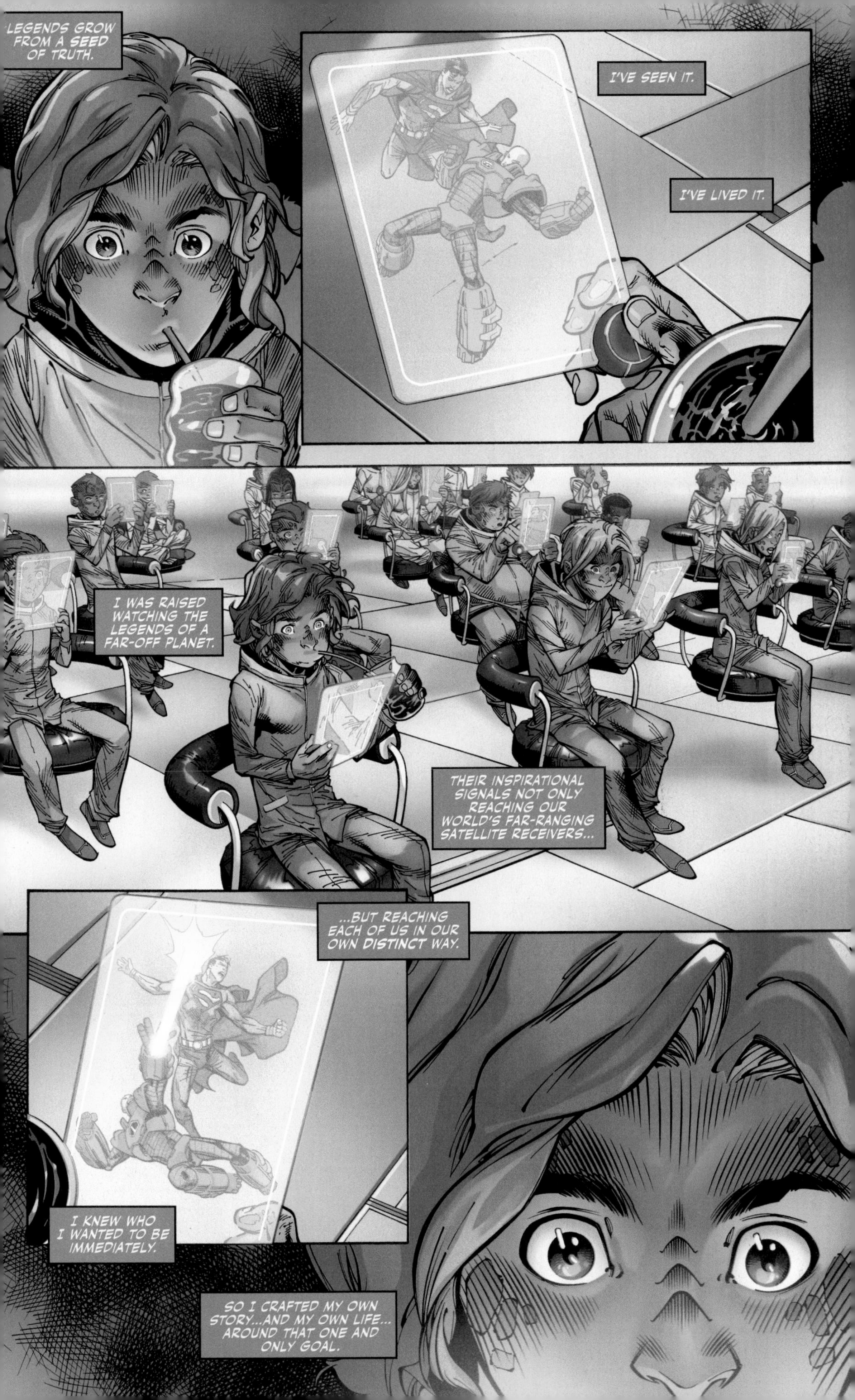
LEGENDS GROW FROM A SEED OF TRUTH.
I'VE SEEN IT.
I'VE LIVED IT.
I WAS RAISED WATCHING THE LEGENDS OF A FAR-OFF PLANET.
THEIR INSPIRATIONAL SIGNALS NOT ONLY REACHING OUR WORLD'S FAR-RANGING SATELLITE RECEIVERS...
...BUT REACHING EACH OF US IN OUR OWN DISTINCT WAY.
I KNEW WHO I WANTED TO BE IMMEDIATELY.
SO I CRAFTED MY OWN STORY...AND MY OWN LIFE... AROUND THAT ONE AND ONLY GOAL.

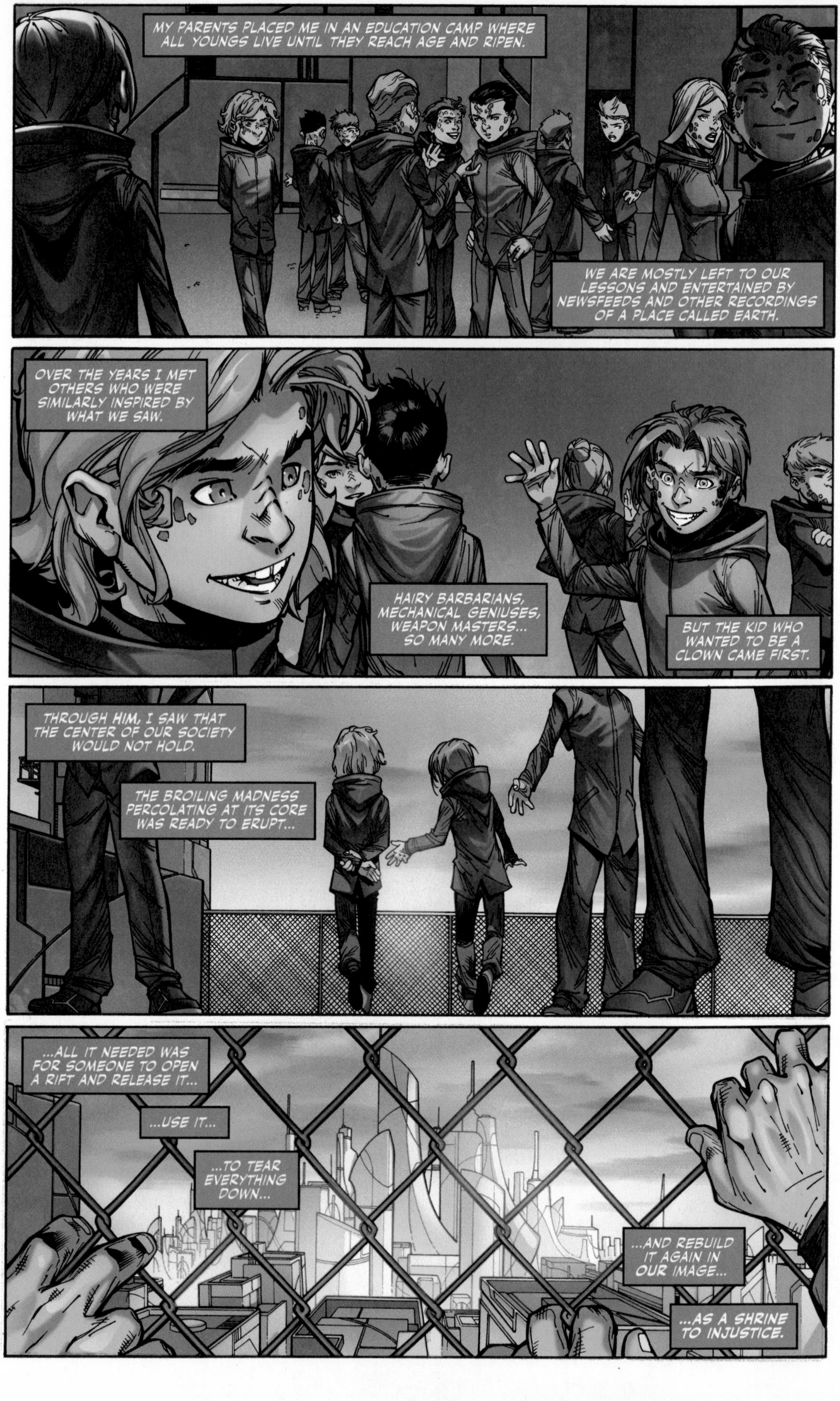
MY PARENTS PLACED ME IN AN EDUCATION CAMP WHERE ALL YOUNGS LIVE UNTIL THEY REACH AGE AND RIPEN.
WE ARE MOSTLY LEFT TO OUR LESSONS AND ENTERTAINED BY NEWSFEEDS AND OTHER RECORDINGS OF A PLACE CALLED EARTH.
OVER THE YEARS I MET OTHERS WHO WERE SIMILARLY INSPIRED BY WHAT WE SAW.
HAIRY BARBARIANS, MECHANICAL GENIUSES, WEAPON MASTERS... SO MANY MORE.
BUT THE KID WHO WANTED TO BE A CLOWN CAME FIRST.
THROUGH HIM, I SAW THAT THE CENTER OF OUR SOCIETY WOULD NOT HOLD.
THE BROILING MADNESS PERCOLATING AT ITS CORE WAS READY TO ERUPT...
...ALL IT NEEDED WAS FOR SOMEONE TO OPEN A RIFT AND RELEASE IT...
...USE IT...
...TO TEAR EVERYTHING DOWN...
...AND REBUILD IT AGAIN IN OUR IMAGE...
...AS A SHRINE TO INJUSTICE.

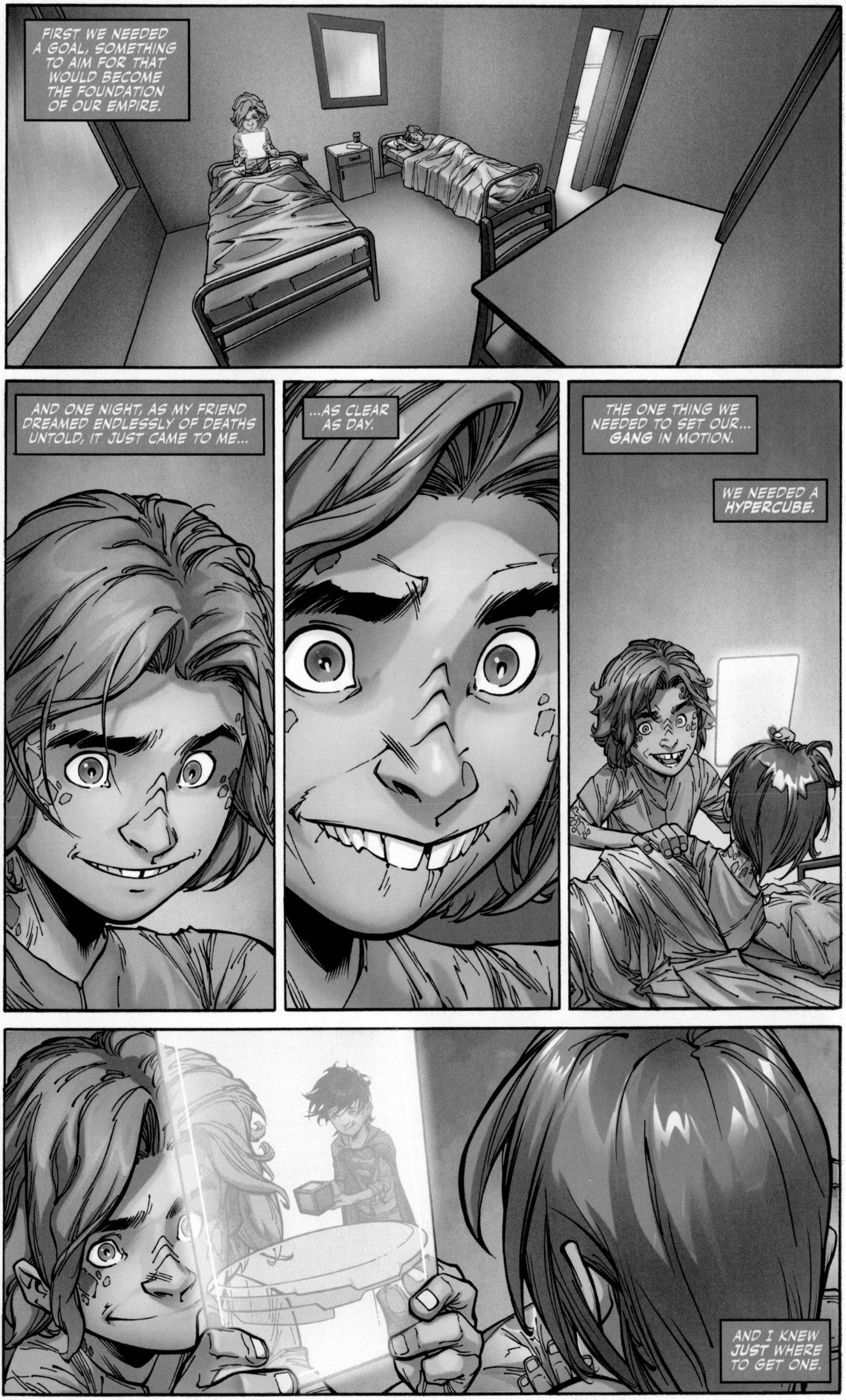
FIRST WE NEEDED A GOAL, SOMETHING TO AIM FOR THAT WOULD BECOME THE FOUNDATION OF OUR EMPIRE.
AND ONE NIGHT, AS MY FRIEND DREAMED ENDLESSLY OF DEATHS UNTOLD, IT JUST CAME TO ME...
...AS CLEAR AS DAY.
THE ONE THING WE NEEDED TO SET OUR... GANG IN MOTION.
WE NEEDED A HYPERCUBE.
AND I KNEW JUST WHERE TO GET ONE.

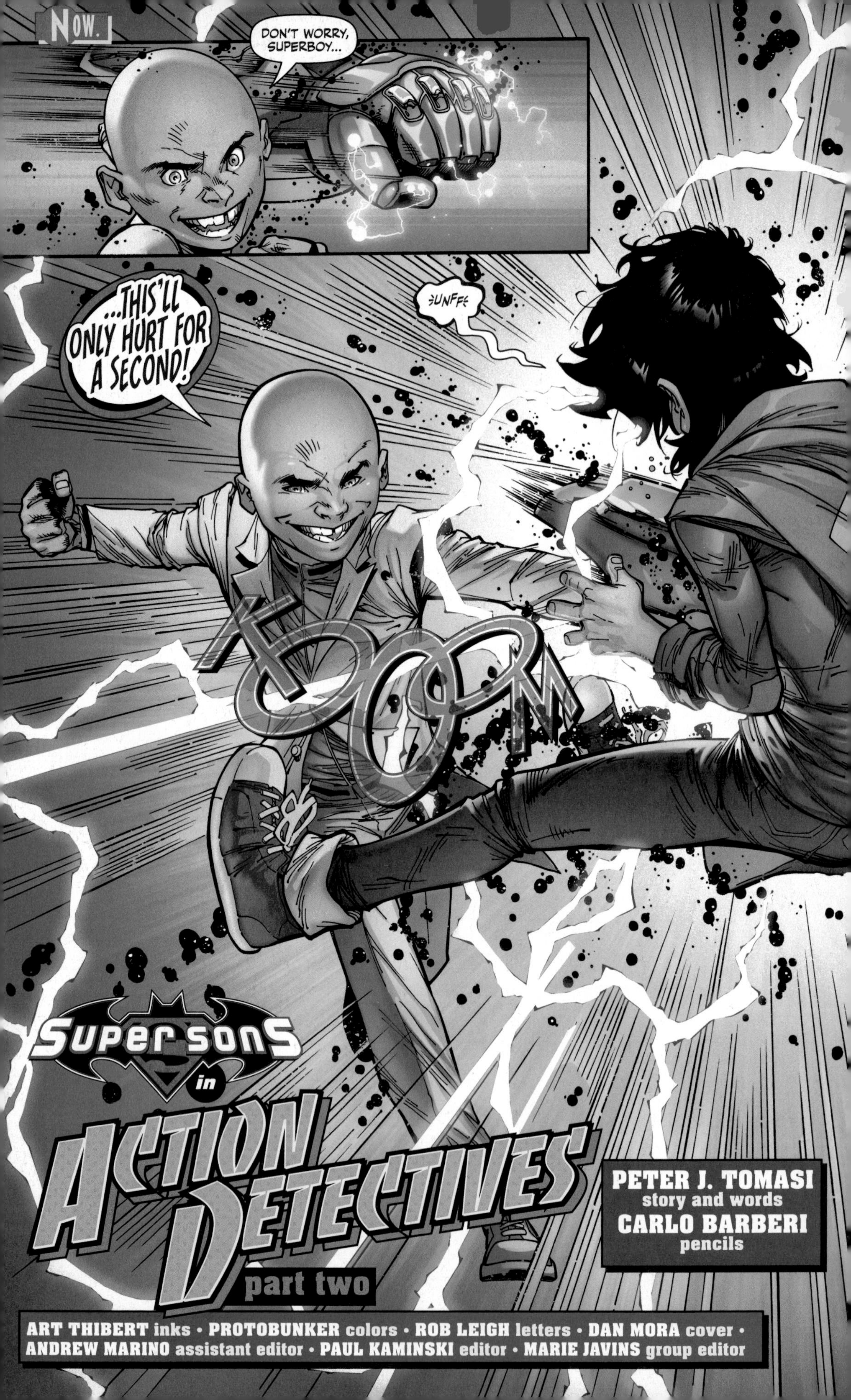
NOW.
DON'T WORRY, SUPERBOY...
...THIS'LL ONLY HURT FOR A SECOND!
UNFF
KOOOM
SUPER SONS
in
ACTION DETECTIVES
part two
PETER J. TOMASI story and words
CARLO BARBERI pencils
ART THIBERT inks • PROTOBUNKER colors • ROB LEIGH letters • DAN MORA cover •
ANDREW MARINO assistant editor • PAUL KAMINSKI editor • MARIE JAVINS group editor

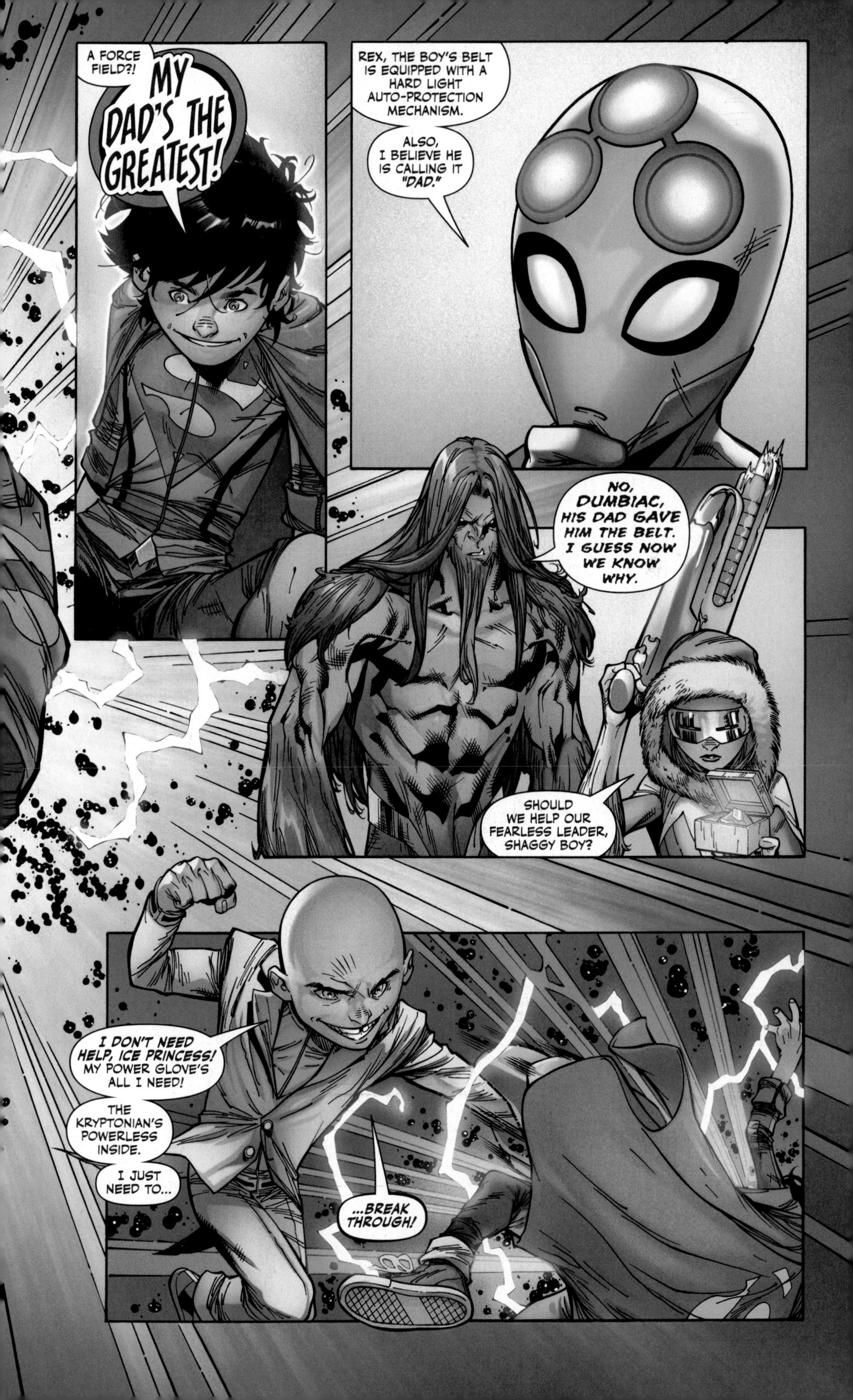
A FORCE FIELD?!
MY DAD'S THE GREATEST!
REX, THE BOY'S BELT IS EQUIPPED WITH A HARD LIGHT AUTO-PROTECTION MECHANISM.
ALSO, I BELIEVE HE IS CALLING IT "DAD."
NO, DUMBIAC, HIS DAD GAVE HIM THE BELT. I GUESS NOW WE KNOW WHY.
SHOULD WE HELP OUR FEARLESS LEADER, SHAGGY BOY?
I DON'T NEED HELP, ICE PRINCESS! MY POWER GLOVE'S ALL I NEED!
THE KRYPTONIAN'S POWERLESS INSIDE.
I JUST NEED TO...
...BREAK THROUGH!

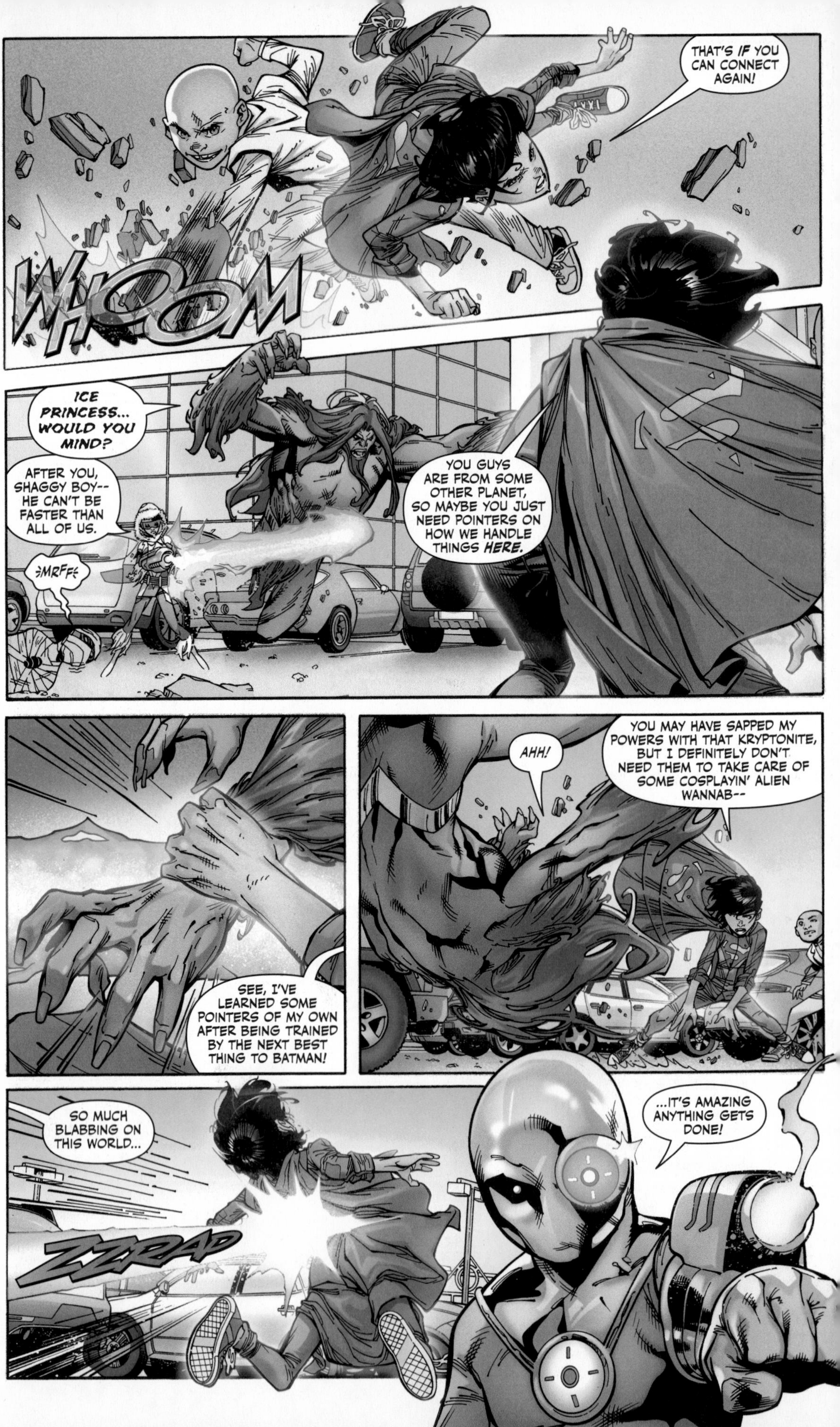
THAT'S *IF* YOU CAN CONNECT AGAIN!
WHOOM
ICE PRINCESS... WOULD YOU MIND?
AFTER YOU, SHAGGY BOY-- HE CAN'T BE FASTER THAN ALL OF US.
MRFF
YOU GUYS ARE FROM SOME OTHER PLANET, SO MAYBE YOU JUST NEED POINTERS ON HOW WE HANDLE THINGS *HERE.*
SEE, I'VE LEARNED SOME POINTERS OF MY OWN AFTER BEING TRAINED BY THE NEXT BEST THING TO BATMAN!
AHH!
YOU MAY HAVE SAPPED MY POWERS WITH THAT KRYPTONITE, BUT I DEFINITELY DON'T NEED THEM TO TAKE CARE OF SOME COSPLAYIN' ALIEN WANNAB--
SO MUCH BLABBING ON THIS WORLD...
ZZRAP
...IT'S AMAZING ANYTHING GETS DONE!

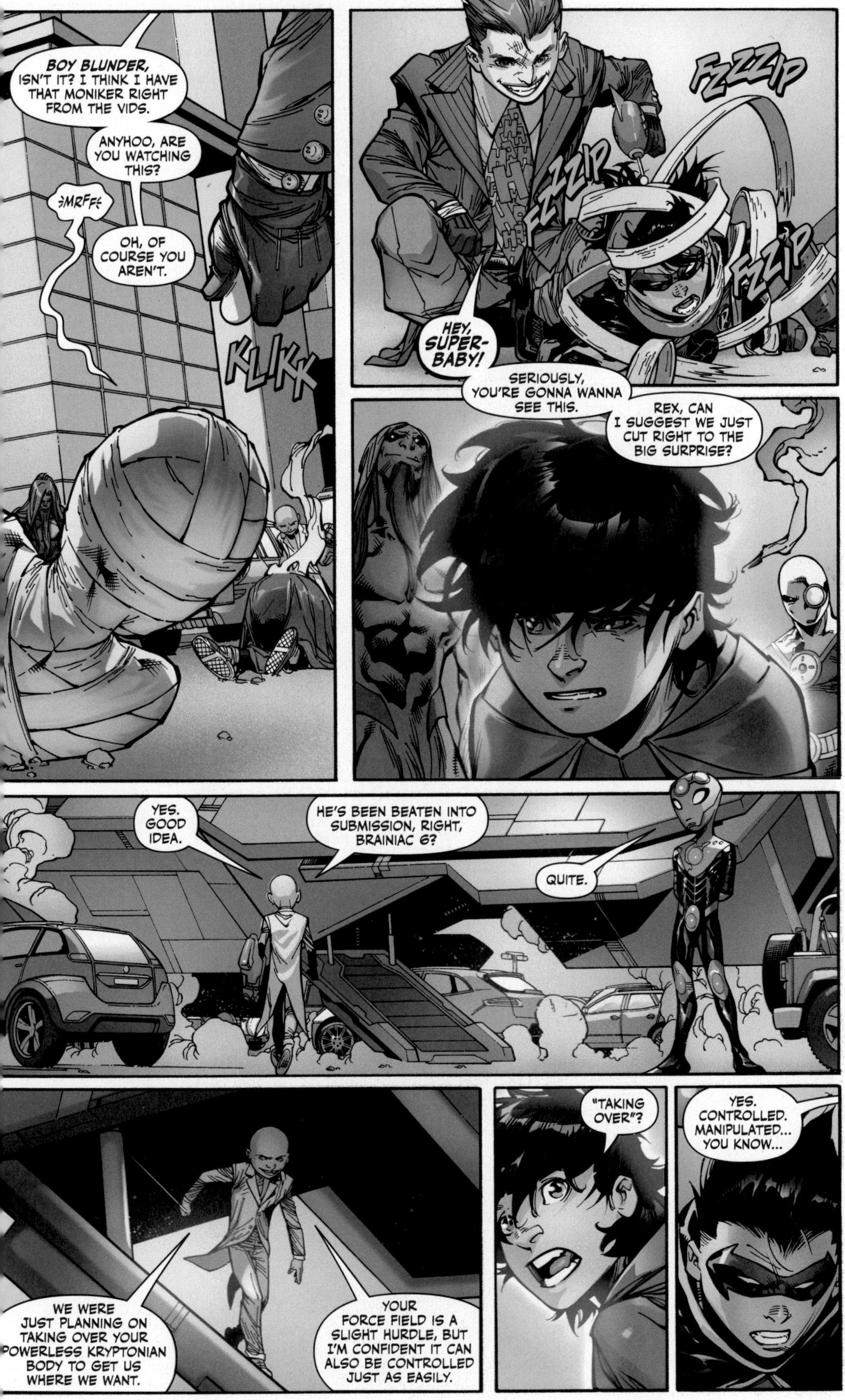

BOY BLUNDER, ISN'T IT? I THINK I HAVE THAT MONIKER RIGHT FROM THE VIDS.
ANYHOO, ARE YOU WATCHING THIS?
MRFF
OH, OF COURSE YOU AREN'T.
KLIKK
FZZZIP
FZZZIP
FZZIP
HEY, SUPER-BABY!
SERIOUSLY, YOU'RE GONNA WANNA SEE THIS.
REX, CAN I SUGGEST WE JUST CUT RIGHT TO THE BIG SURPRISE?
YES. GOOD IDEA.
HE'S BEEN BEATEN INTO SUBMISSION, RIGHT, BRAINIAC 6?
QUITE.
WE WERE JUST PLANNING ON TAKING OVER YOUR POWERLESS KRYPTONIAN BODY TO GET US WHERE WE WANT.
YOUR FORCE FIELD IS A SLIGHT HURDLE, BUT I'M CONFIDENT IT CAN ALSO BE CONTROLLED JUST AS EASILY.
"TAKING OVER"?
YES. CONTROLLED. MANIPULATED... YOU KNOW...

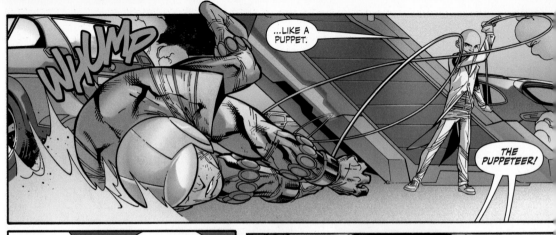

WHUMP

...LIKE A PUPPET.

THE PUPPETEER!

CORRECT. YOU'VE MET.

IN FACT, WATCHING YOUR BATTLE IS HOW I GOT THE IDEA.

YOU KNOW WHAT WE NEED, JORDAN WEIR.

AND HERE'S YOUR TECHNOLOGY WE RETRIEVED.

IF YOU THINK I'M GONNA LET THIS THIRD-RATE BAD GUY USE ME IN SOME PLAN OF--

OH, YOU WILL, OTHERWISE *BLAMMO*, YOUR FRIEND'S BIRD BRAIN WILL TURN INTO A...

...Uh... uh...

...A JACKSON POLLOCK PAINTING!

Heh. SORRY. SORTA DRIFTED OFF THERE.

ANYWAY, YOU STAND STILL OR *BLAMMO*!

THE FORCE FIELD BEING INORGANIC ACTUALLY MAKES THIS EASIER. HUMAN PUPPETS ARE ALWAYS A LITTLE MORE COMPLI--

ENOUGH! JUST DO WHATEVER A PUPPETEER DOES. WE *ARE* ON A TIMELINE!

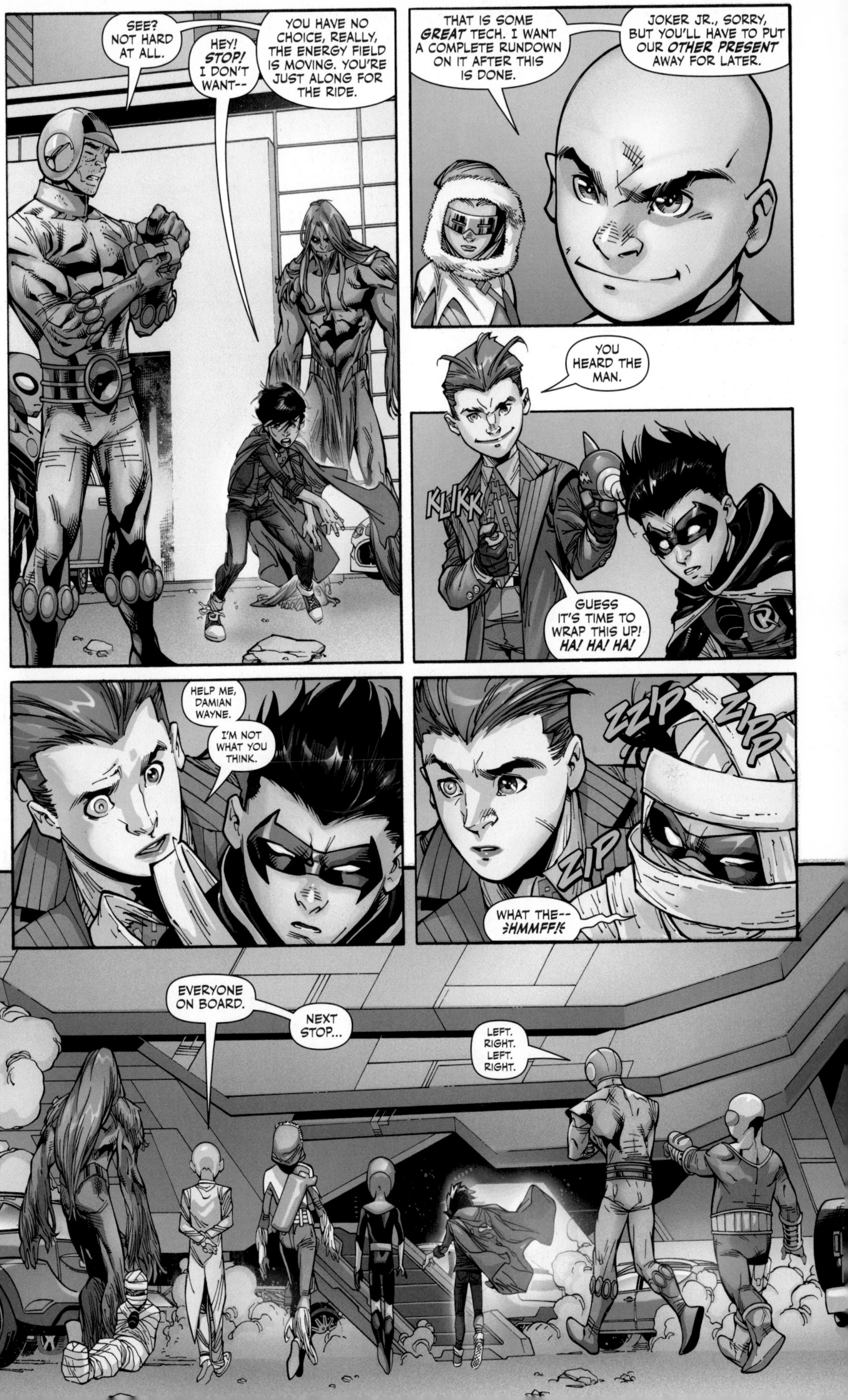
SEE? NOT HARD AT ALL.
HEY! STOP! I DON'T WANT--
YOU HAVE NO CHOICE, REALLY, THE ENERGY FIELD IS MOVING. YOU'RE JUST ALONG FOR THE RIDE.
THAT IS SOME GREAT TECH. I WANT A COMPLETE RUNDOWN ON IT AFTER THIS IS DONE.
JOKER JR., SORRY, BUT YOU'LL HAVE TO PUT OUR OTHER PRESENT AWAY FOR LATER.
YOU HEARD THE MAN.
KLIKK
GUESS IT'S TIME TO WRAP THIS UP! HA! HA! HA!
HELP ME, DAMIAN WAYNE.
I'M NOT WHAT YOU THINK.
ZZIP
ZIPP
ZIP
WHAT THE-- HMMFF!
EVERYONE ON BOARD.
NEXT STOP...
LEFT. RIGHT. LEFT. RIGHT.

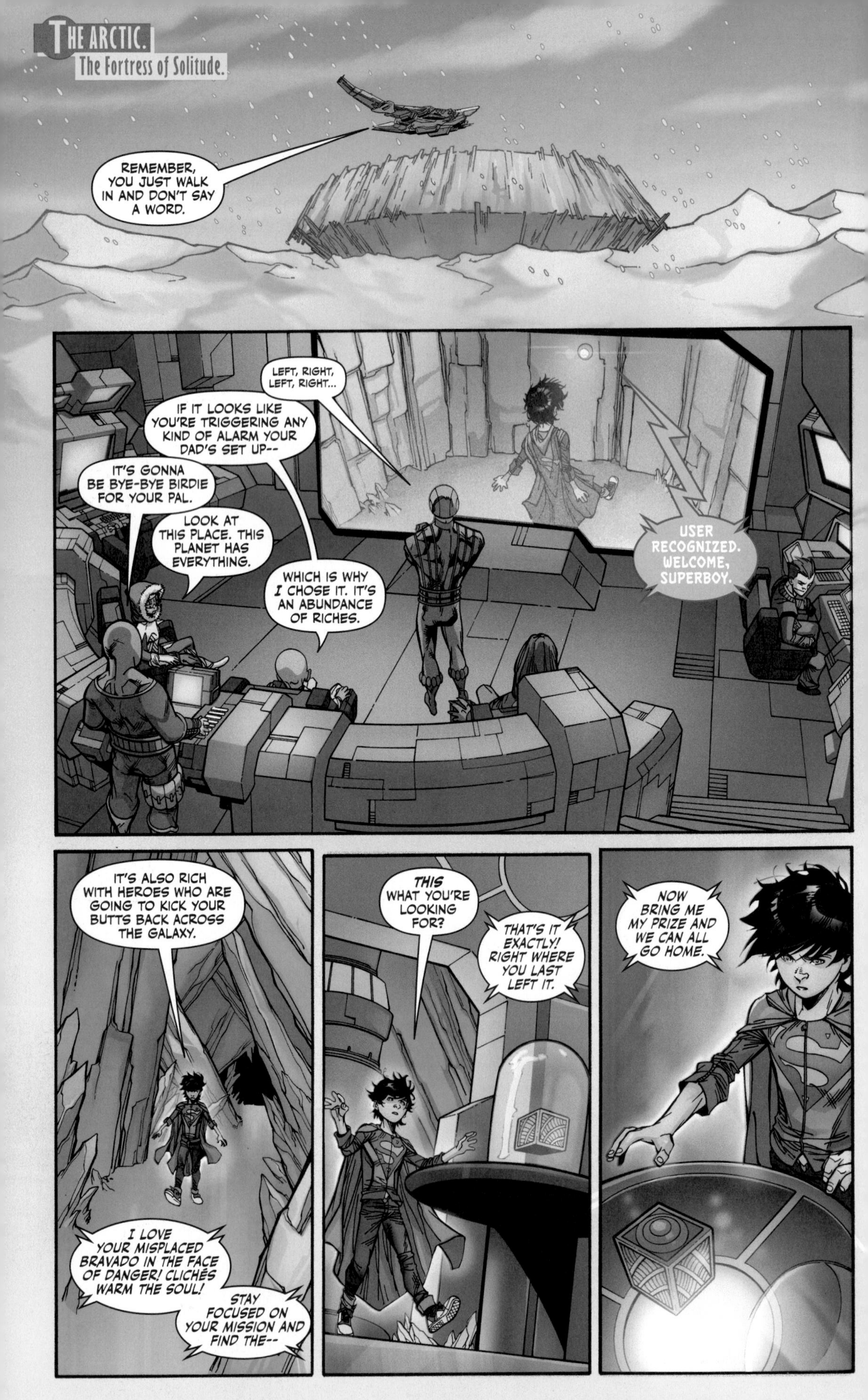
THE ARCTIC.
The Fortress of Solitude.
REMEMBER, YOU JUST WALK IN AND DON'T SAY A WORD.
LEFT, RIGHT, LEFT, RIGHT...
IF IT LOOKS LIKE YOU'RE TRIGGERING ANY KIND OF ALARM YOUR DAD'S SET UP--
IT'S GONNA BE BYE-BYE BIRDIE FOR YOUR PAL.
LOOK AT THIS PLACE. THIS PLANET HAS EVERYTHING.
WHICH IS WHY I CHOSE IT. IT'S AN ABUNDANCE OF RICHES.
USER RECOGNIZED. WELCOME, SUPERBOY.
IT'S ALSO RICH WITH HEROES WHO ARE GOING TO KICK YOUR BUTTS BACK ACROSS THE GALAXY.
I LOVE YOUR MISPLACED BRAVADO IN THE FACE OF DANGER! CLICHÉS WARM THE SOUL!
STAY FOCUSED ON YOUR MISSION AND FIND THE--
THIS WHAT YOU'RE LOOKING FOR?
THAT'S IT EXACTLY! RIGHT WHERE YOU LAST LEFT IT.
NOW BRING ME MY PRIZE AND WE CAN ALL GO HOME.

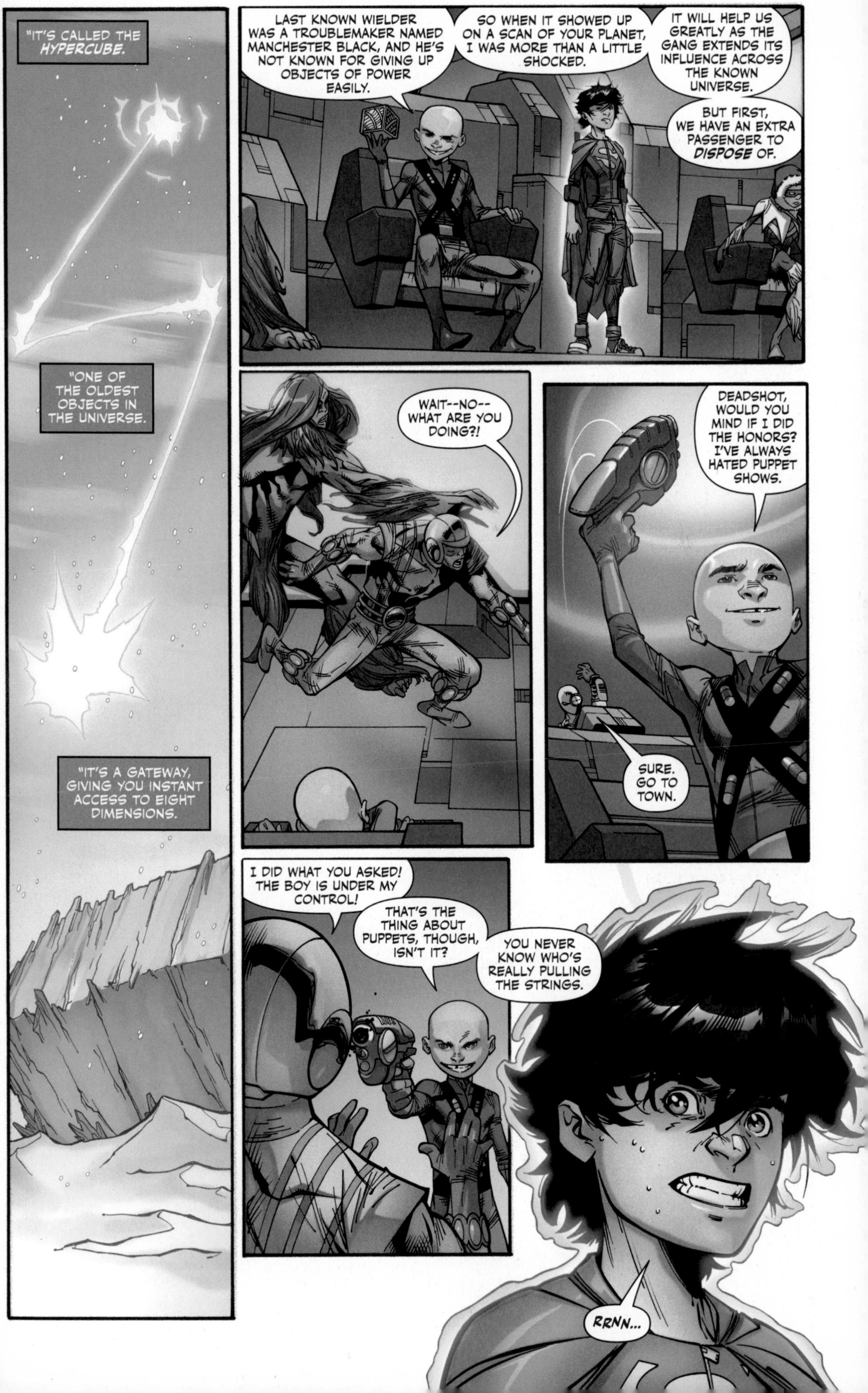
"IT'S CALLED THE HYPERCUBE.
LAST KNOWN WIELDER WAS A TROUBLEMAKER NAMED MANCHESTER BLACK, AND HE'S NOT KNOWN FOR GIVING UP OBJECTS OF POWER EASILY.
SO WHEN IT SHOWED UP ON A SCAN OF YOUR PLANET, I WAS MORE THAN A LITTLE SHOCKED.
IT WILL HELP US GREATLY AS THE GANG EXTENDS ITS INFLUENCE ACROSS THE KNOWN UNIVERSE.
BUT FIRST, WE HAVE AN EXTRA PASSENGER TO DISPOSE OF.
"ONE OF THE OLDEST OBJECTS IN THE UNIVERSE.
WAIT--NO-- WHAT ARE YOU DOING?!
DEADSHOT, WOULD YOU MIND IF I DID THE HONORS? I'VE ALWAYS HATED PUPPET SHOWS.
SURE. GO TO TOWN.
"IT'S A GATEWAY, GIVING YOU INSTANT ACCESS TO EIGHT DIMENSIONS.
I DID WHAT YOU ASKED! THE BOY IS UNDER MY CONTROL!
THAT'S THE THING ABOUT PUPPETS, THOUGH, ISN'T IT?
YOU NEVER KNOW WHO'S REALLY PULLING THE STRINGS.
RRNN...

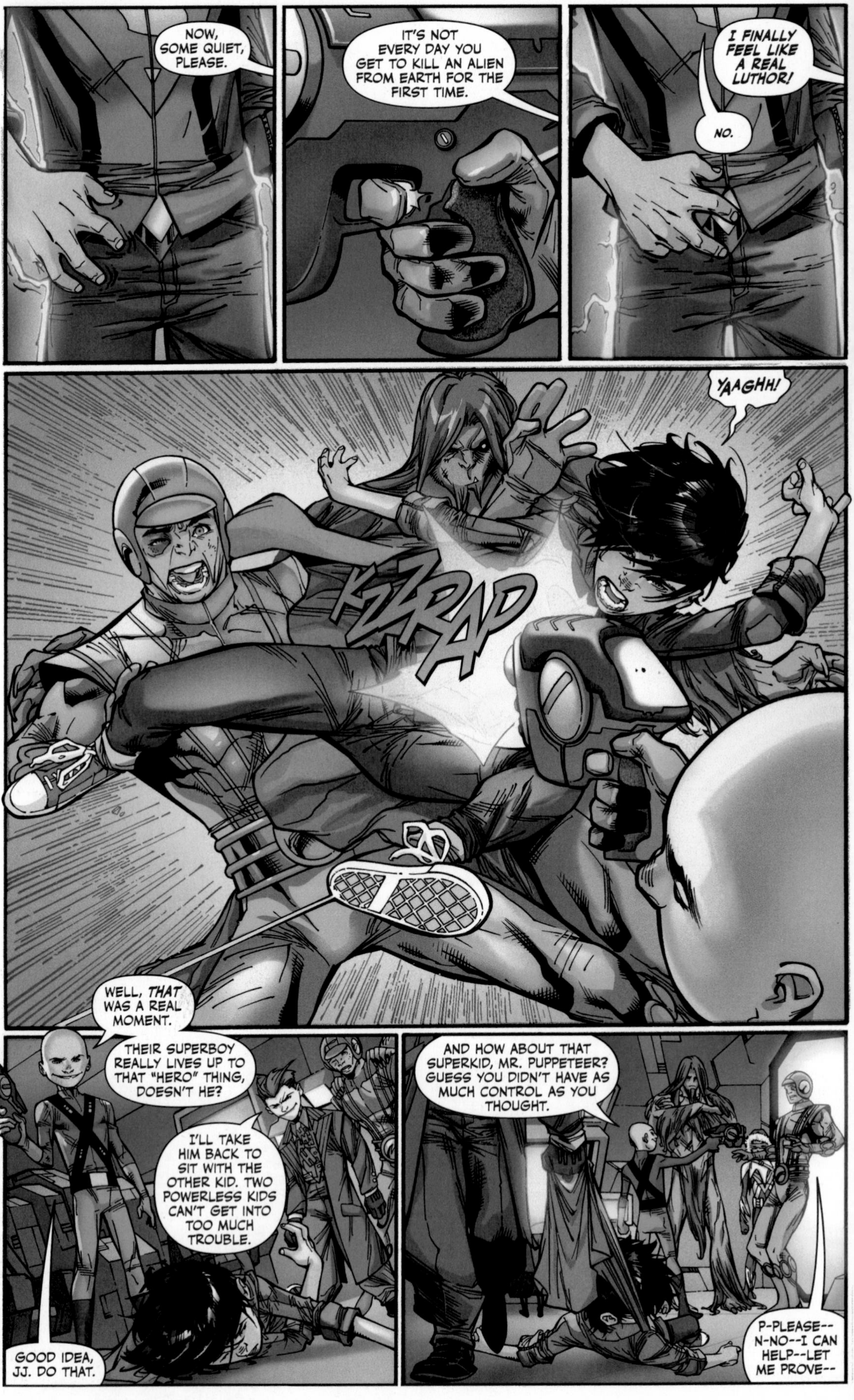
NOW, SOME QUIET, PLEASE.
IT'S NOT EVERY DAY YOU GET TO KILL AN ALIEN FROM EARTH FOR THE FIRST TIME.
I FINALLY FEEL LIKE A REAL LUTHOR!
NO.
YAAGHH!
KZZRAP
WELL, THAT WAS A REAL MOMENT.
THEIR SUPERBOY REALLY LIVES UP TO THAT "HERO" THING, DOESN'T HE?
I'LL TAKE HIM BACK TO SIT WITH THE OTHER KID. TWO POWERLESS KIDS CAN'T GET INTO TOO MUCH TROUBLE.
GOOD IDEA, JJ. DO THAT.
AND HOW ABOUT THAT SUPERKID, MR. PUPPETEER? GUESS YOU DIDN'T HAVE AS MUCH CONTROL AS YOU THOUGHT.
P-PLEASE-- N-NO--I CAN HELP--LET ME PROVE--

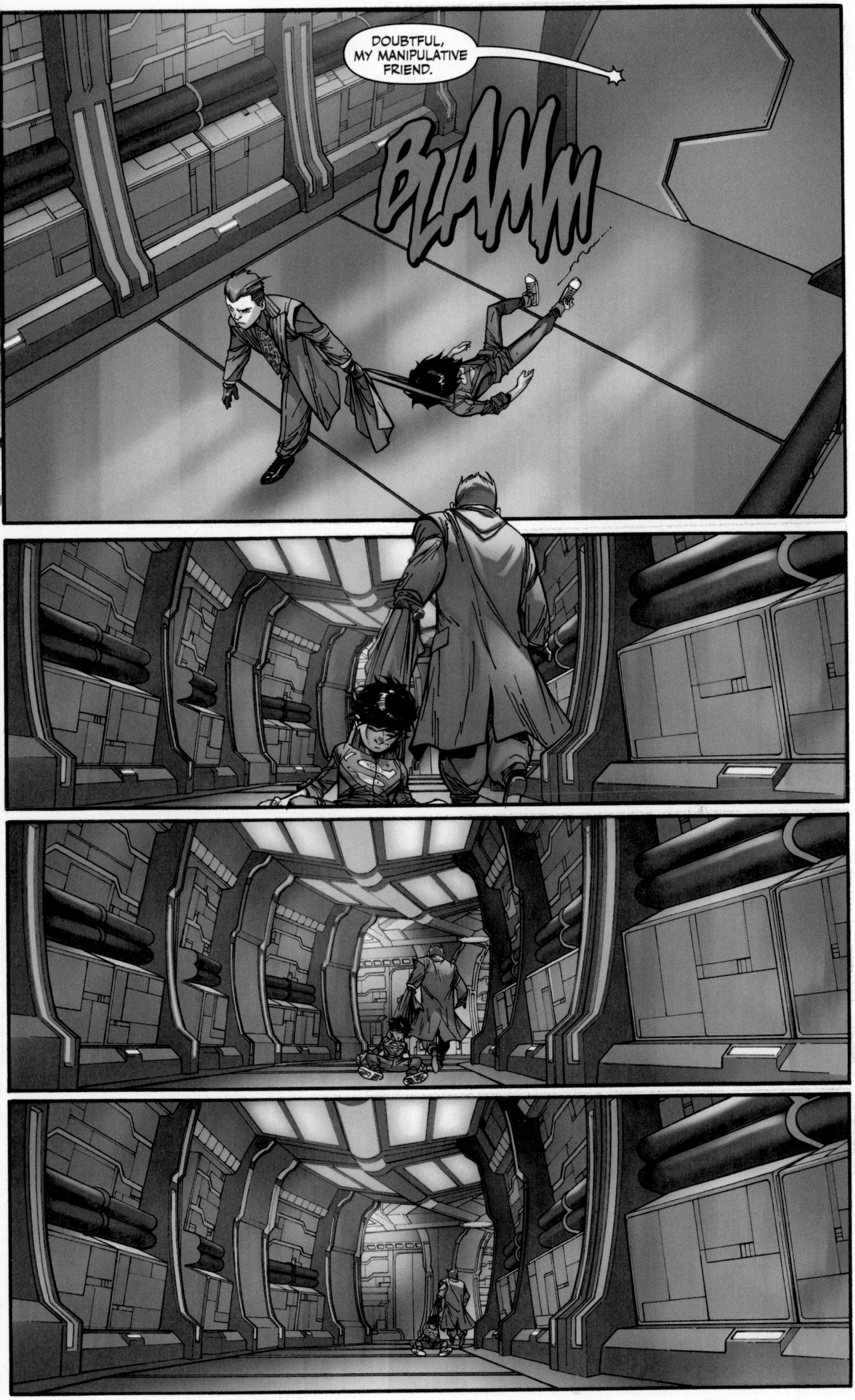
DOUBTFUL, MY MANIPULATIVE FRIEND.
BLAMM

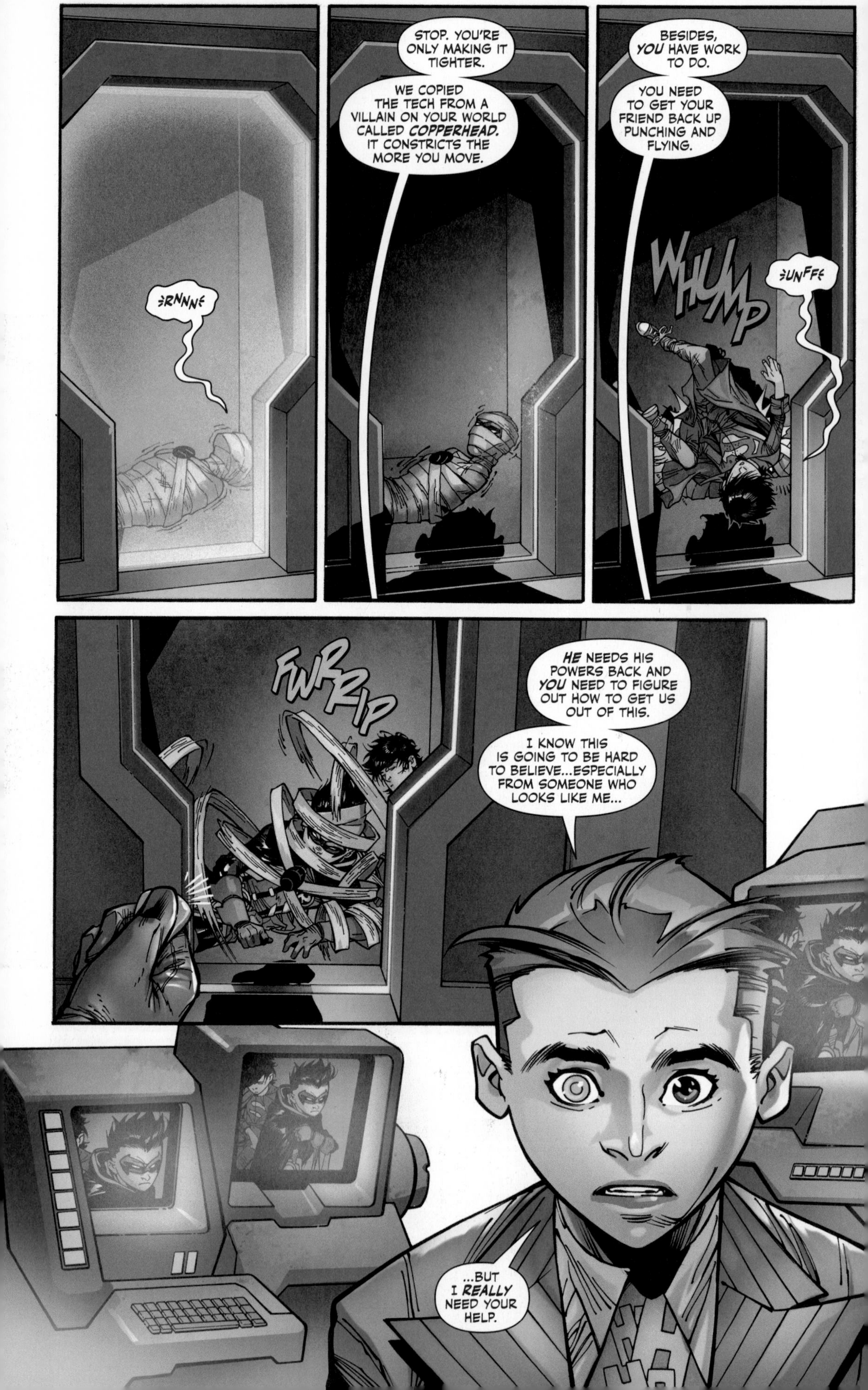

RNNN
STOP. YOU'RE ONLY MAKING IT TIGHTER.
WE COPIED THE TECH FROM A VILLAIN ON YOUR WORLD CALLED COPPERHEAD. IT CONSTRICTS THE MORE YOU MOVE.
BESIDES, YOU HAVE WORK TO DO.
YOU NEED TO GET YOUR FRIEND BACK UP PUNCHING AND FLYING.
WHUMP
UNFF
FWRRIP
HE NEEDS HIS POWERS BACK AND YOU NEED TO FIGURE OUT HOW TO GET US OUT OF THIS.
I KNOW THIS IS GOING TO BE HARD TO BELIEVE...ESPECIALLY FROM SOMEONE WHO LOOKS LIKE ME...
...BUT I REALLY NEED YOUR HELP.

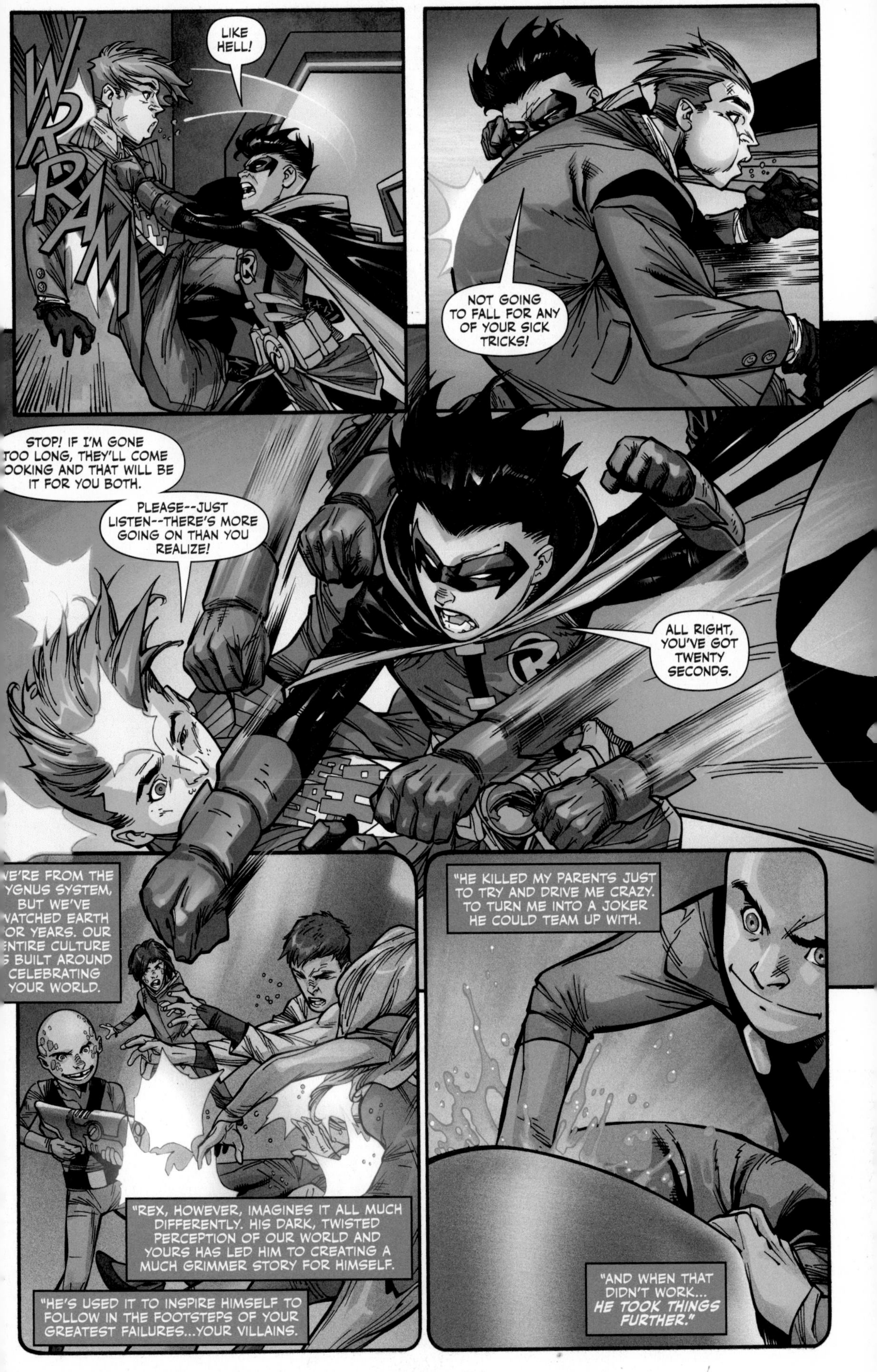
WRAM
LIKE HELL!
NOT GOING TO FALL FOR ANY OF YOUR SICK TRICKS!
STOP! IF I'M GONE TOO LONG, THEY'LL COME LOOKING AND THAT WILL BE IT FOR YOU BOTH.
PLEASE--JUST LISTEN--THERE'S MORE GOING ON THAN YOU REALIZE!
ALL RIGHT, YOU'VE GOT TWENTY SECONDS.
WE'RE FROM THE CYGNUS SYSTEM, BUT WE'VE WATCHED EARTH FOR YEARS. OUR ENTIRE CULTURE IS BUILT AROUND CELEBRATING YOUR WORLD.
"REX, HOWEVER, IMAGINES IT ALL MUCH DIFFERENTLY. HIS DARK, TWISTED PERCEPTION OF OUR WORLD AND YOURS HAS LED HIM TO CREATING A MUCH GRIMMER STORY FOR HIMSELF.
"HE'S USED IT TO INSPIRE HIMSELF TO FOLLOW IN THE FOOTSTEPS OF YOUR GREATEST FAILURES...YOUR VILLAINS.
"HE KILLED MY PARENTS JUST TO TRY AND DRIVE ME CRAZY. TO TURN ME INTO A JOKER HE COULD TEAM UP WITH.
"AND WHEN THAT DIDN'T WORK... *HE TOOK THINGS FURTHER.*"

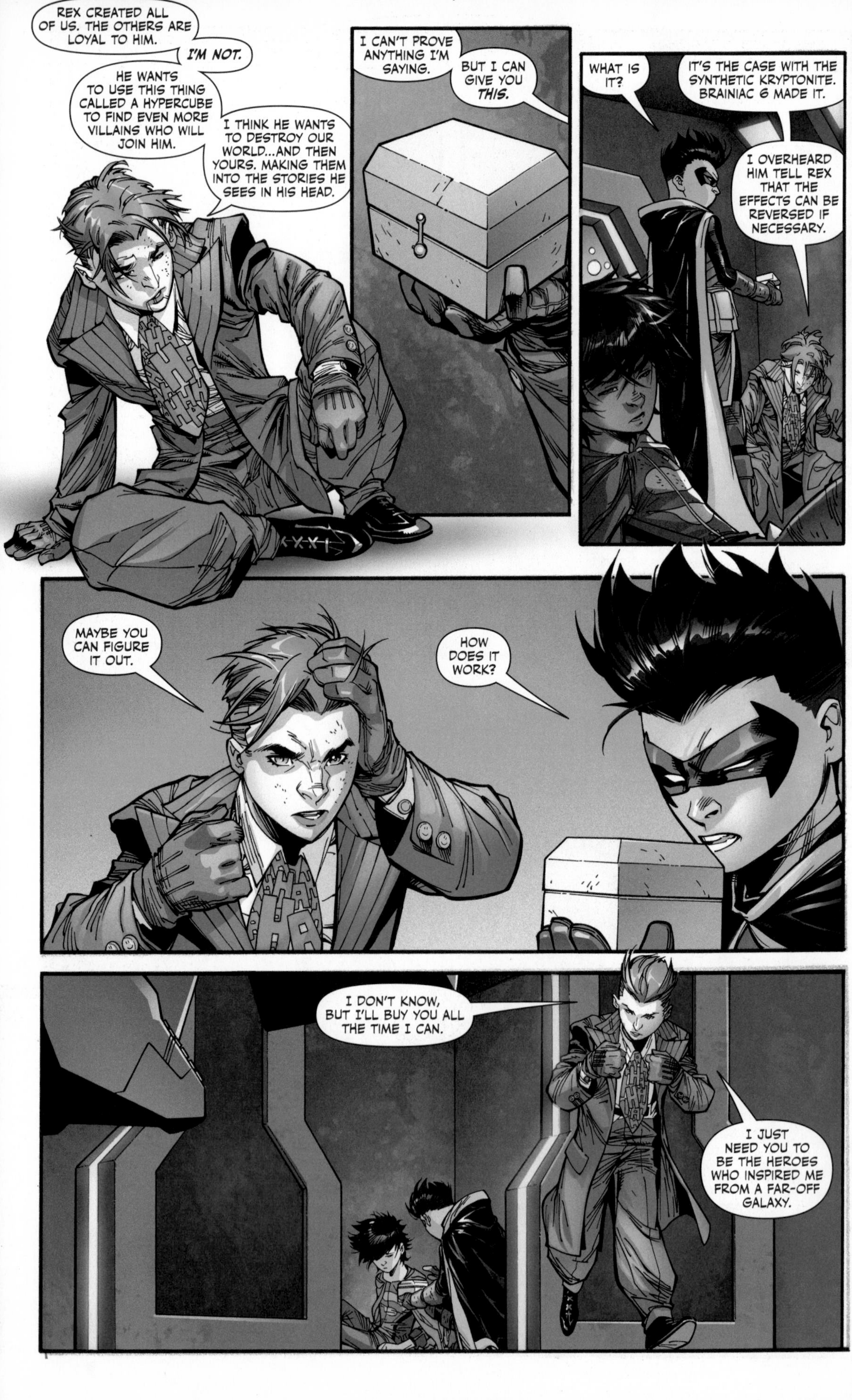
REX CREATED ALL OF US. THE OTHERS ARE LOYAL TO HIM.
I'M NOT.
HE WANTS TO USE THIS THING CALLED A HYPERCUBE TO FIND EVEN MORE VILLAINS WHO WILL JOIN HIM.
I THINK HE WANTS TO DESTROY OUR WORLD...AND THEN YOURS. MAKING THEM INTO THE STORIES HE SEES IN HIS HEAD.
I CAN'T PROVE ANYTHING I'M SAYING.
BUT I CAN GIVE YOU *THIS.*
WHAT IS IT?
IT'S THE CASE WITH THE SYNTHETIC KRYPTONITE. BRAINIAC 6 MADE IT.
I OVERHEARD HIM TELL REX THAT THE EFFECTS CAN BE REVERSED IF NECESSARY.
MAYBE YOU CAN FIGURE IT OUT.
HOW DOES IT WORK?
I DON'T KNOW, BUT I'LL BUY YOU ALL THE TIME I CAN.
I JUST NEED YOU TO BE THE HEROES WHO INSPIRED ME FROM A FAR-OFF GALAXY.

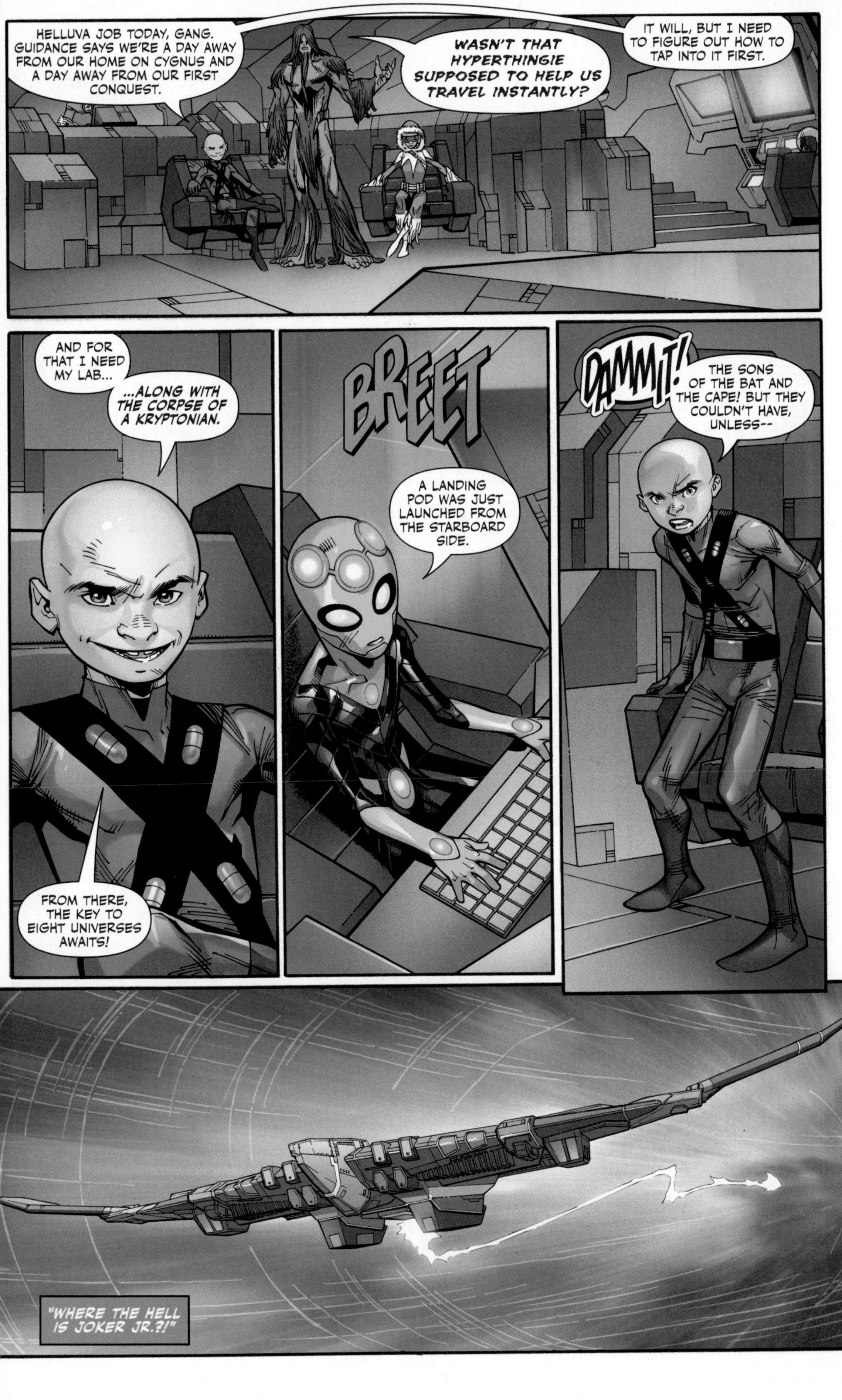
HELLUVA JOB TODAY, GANG. GUIDANCE SAYS WE'RE A DAY AWAY FROM OUR HOME ON CYGNUS AND A DAY AWAY FROM OUR FIRST CONQUEST.
WASN'T THAT HYPERTHINGIE SUPPOSED TO HELP US TRAVEL INSTANTLY?
IT WILL, BUT I NEED TO FIGURE OUT HOW TO TAP INTO IT FIRST.
AND FOR THAT I NEED MY LAB...
...ALONG WITH THE CORPSE OF A KRYPTONIAN.
FROM THERE, THE KEY TO EIGHT UNIVERSES AWAITS!
BREET
A LANDING POD WAS JUST LAUNCHED FROM THE STARBOARD SIDE.
DAMMIT!
THE SONS OF THE BAT AND THE CAPE! BUT THEY COULDN'T HAVE, UNLESS--
"WHERE THE HELL IS JOKER JR.?!"

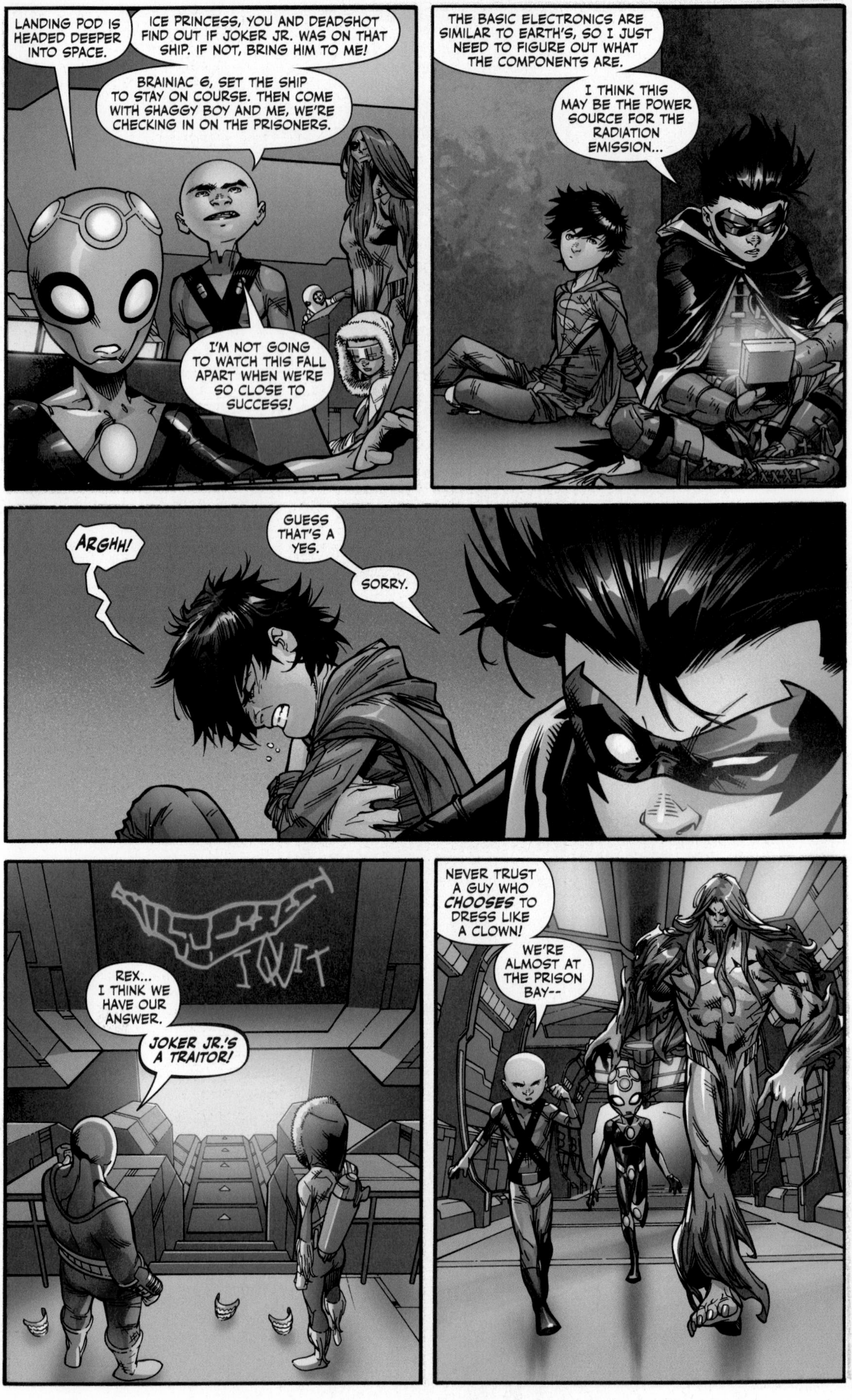
LANDING POD IS HEADED DEEPER INTO SPACE.
ICE PRINCESS, YOU AND DEADSHOT FIND OUT IF JOKER JR. WAS ON THAT SHIP. IF NOT, BRING HIM TO ME!
BRAINIAC 6, SET THE SHIP TO STAY ON COURSE. THEN COME WITH SHAGGY BOY AND ME, WE'RE CHECKING IN ON THE PRISONERS.
I'M NOT GOING TO WATCH THIS FALL APART WHEN WE'RE SO CLOSE TO SUCCESS!
THE BASIC ELECTRONICS ARE SIMILAR TO EARTH'S, SO I JUST NEED TO FIGURE OUT WHAT THE COMPONENTS ARE.
I THINK THIS MAY BE THE POWER SOURCE FOR THE RADIATION EMISSION...
ARGHH!
GUESS THAT'S A YES.
SORRY.
I QUIT
REX... I THINK WE HAVE OUR ANSWER.
JOKER JR.'S A TRAITOR!
NEVER TRUST A GUY WHO CHOOSES TO DRESS LIKE A CLOWN!
WE'RE ALMOST AT THE PRISON BAY--

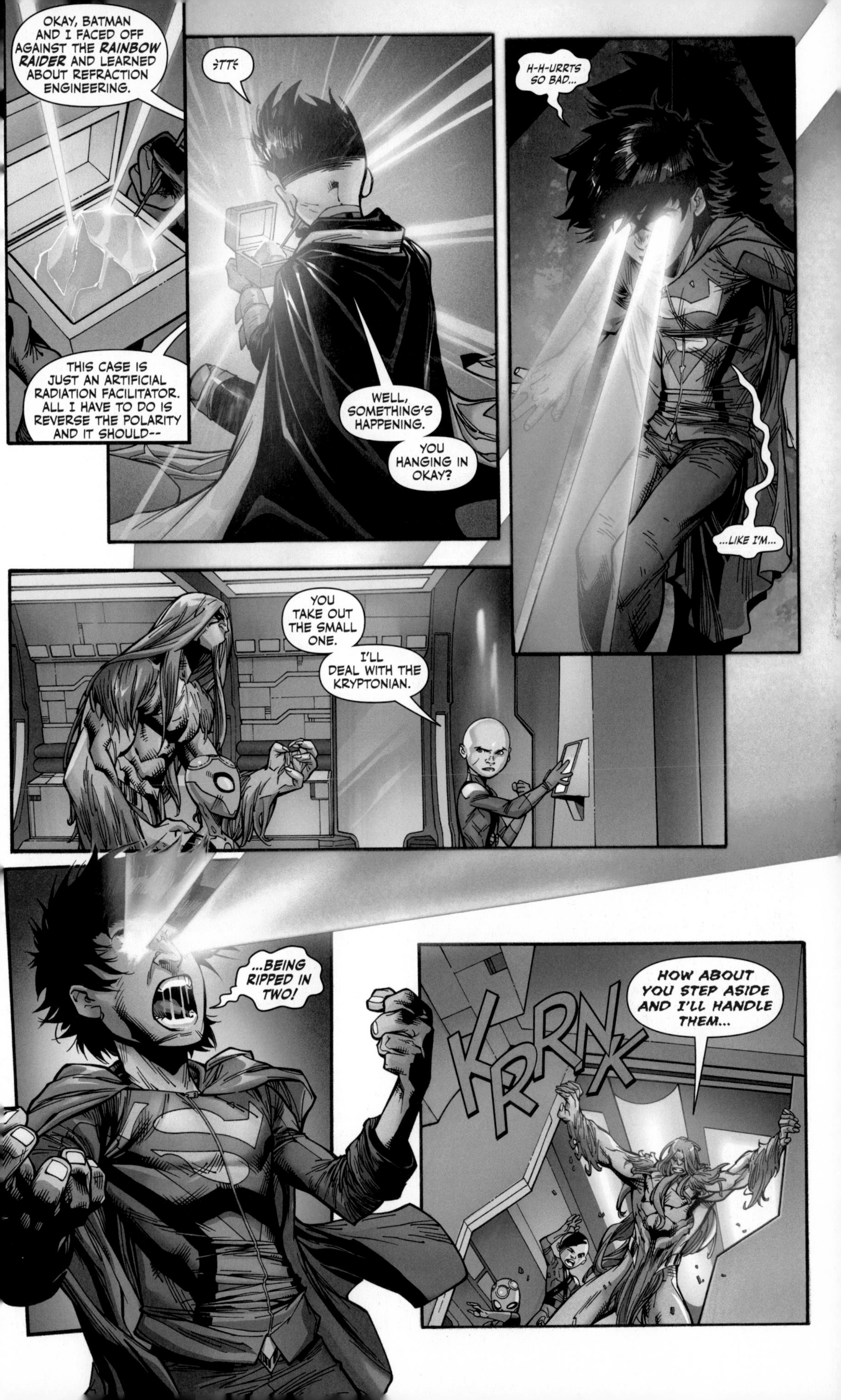

OKAY, BATMAN AND I FACED OFF AGAINST THE *RAINBOW RAIDER* AND LEARNED ABOUT REFRACTION ENGINEERING.
TT
THIS CASE IS JUST AN ARTIFICIAL RADIATION FACILITATOR. ALL I HAVE TO DO IS REVERSE THE POLARITY AND IT SHOULD--
WELL, SOMETHING'S HAPPENING.
YOU HANGING IN OKAY?
H-H-URRTS SO BAD...
...LIKE I'M...
YOU TAKE OUT THE SMALL ONE.
I'LL DEAL WITH THE KRYPTONIAN.
...BEING RIPPED IN TWO!
KRRNK
HOW ABOUT YOU STEP ASIDE AND I'LL HANDLE THEM...

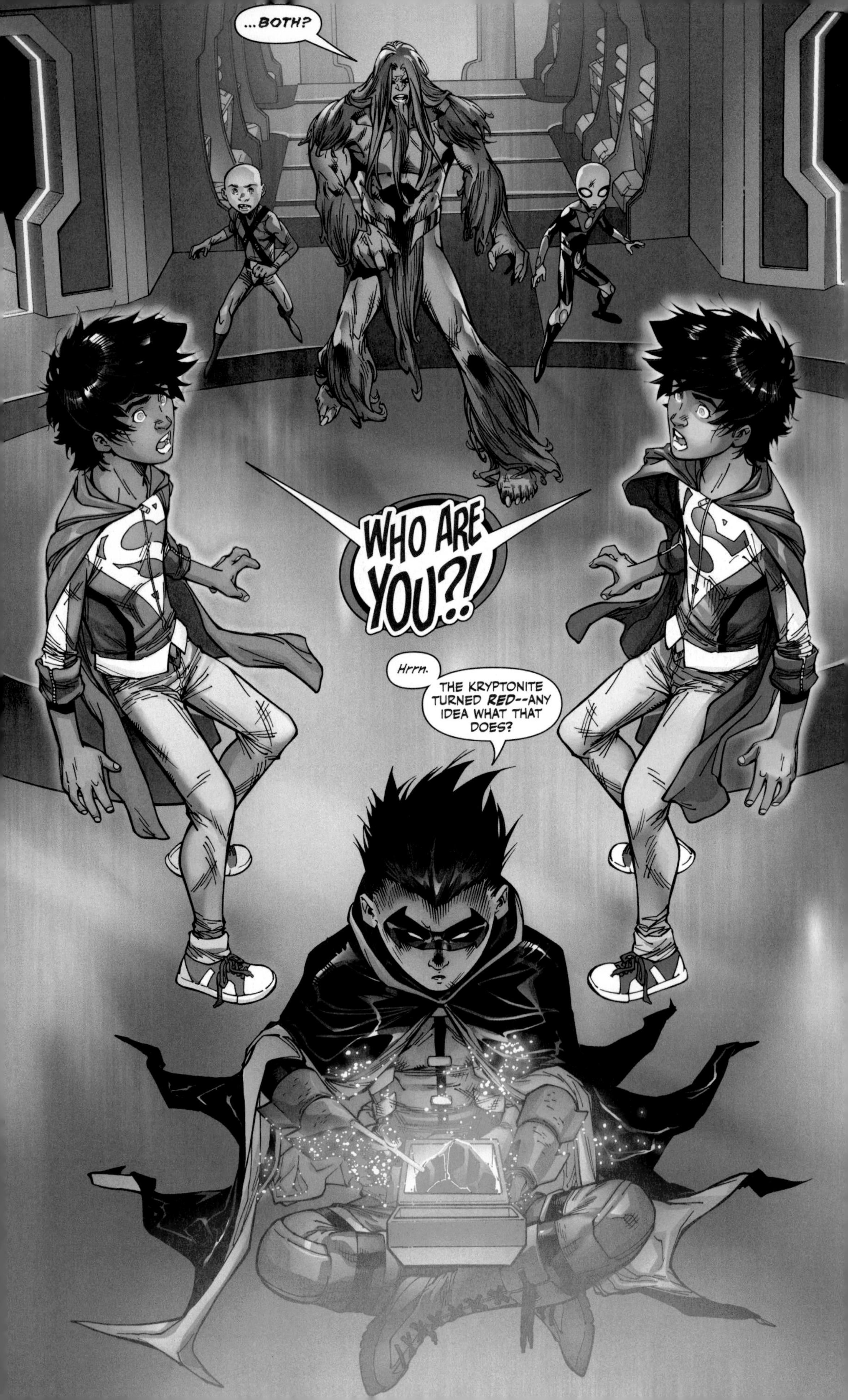
...BOTH?
WHO ARE YOU?!
Hrrn.
THE KRYPTONITE TURNED RED--ANY IDEA WHAT THAT DOES?

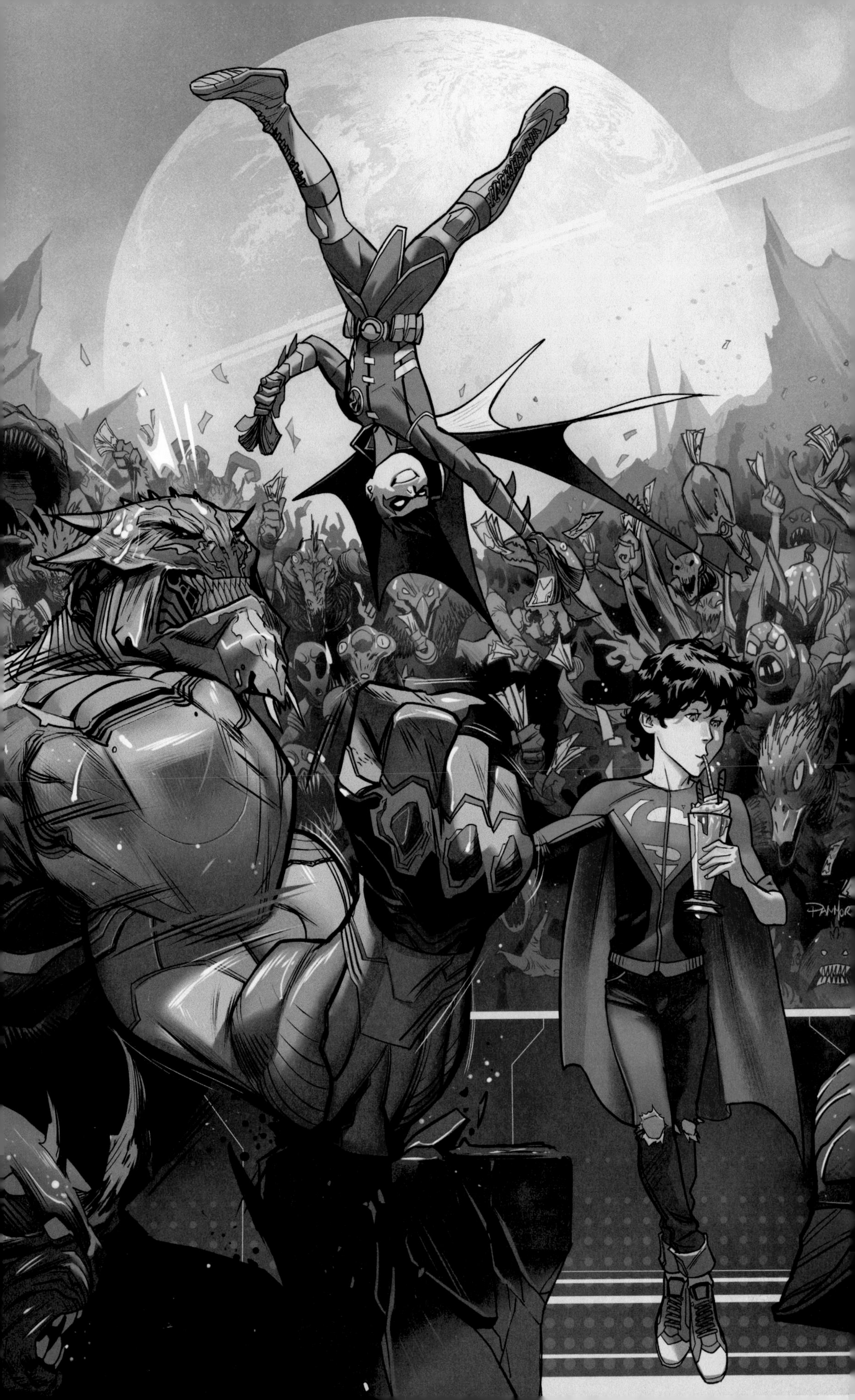

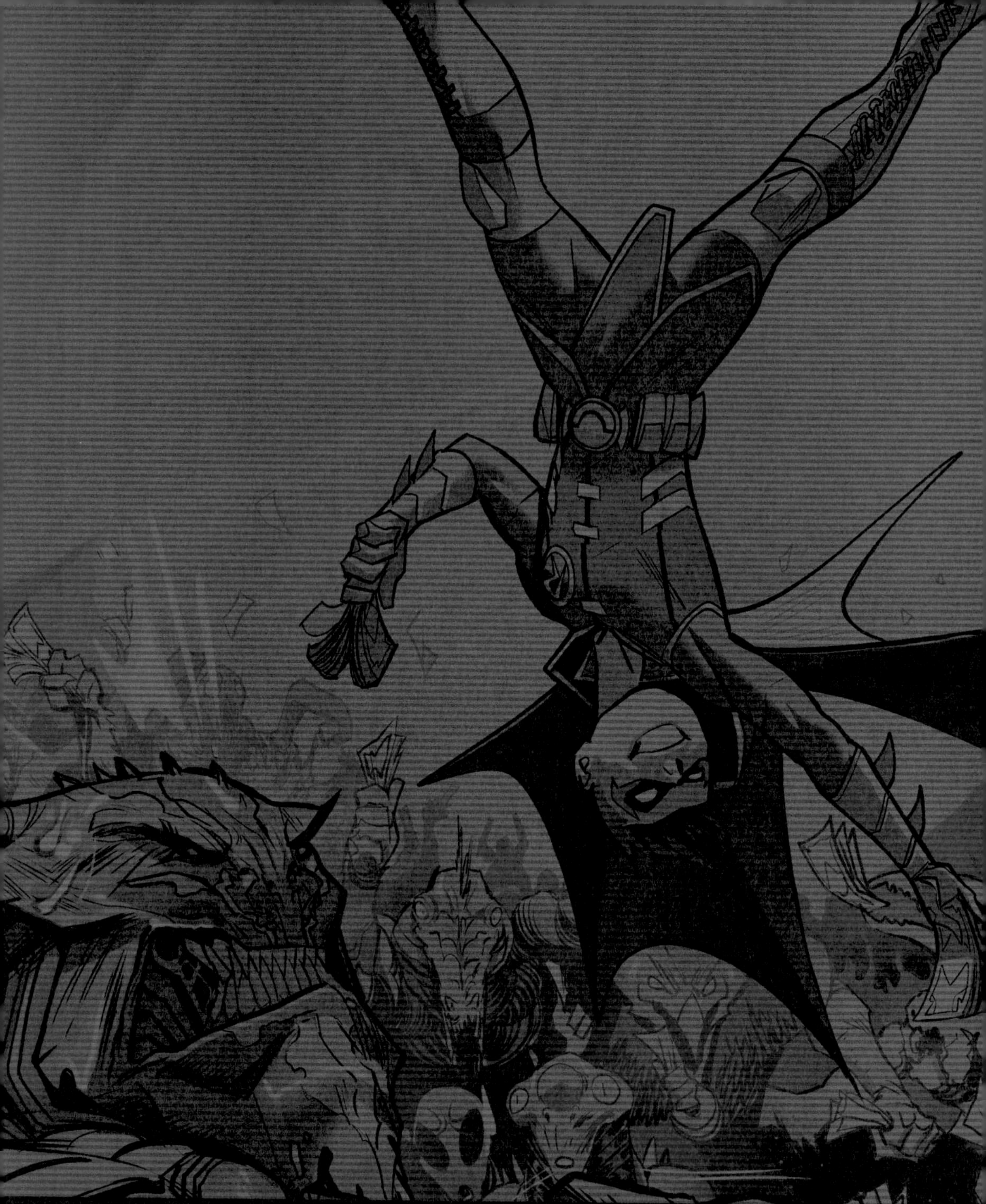

ADVENTURES OF THE SUPER SONS
#3

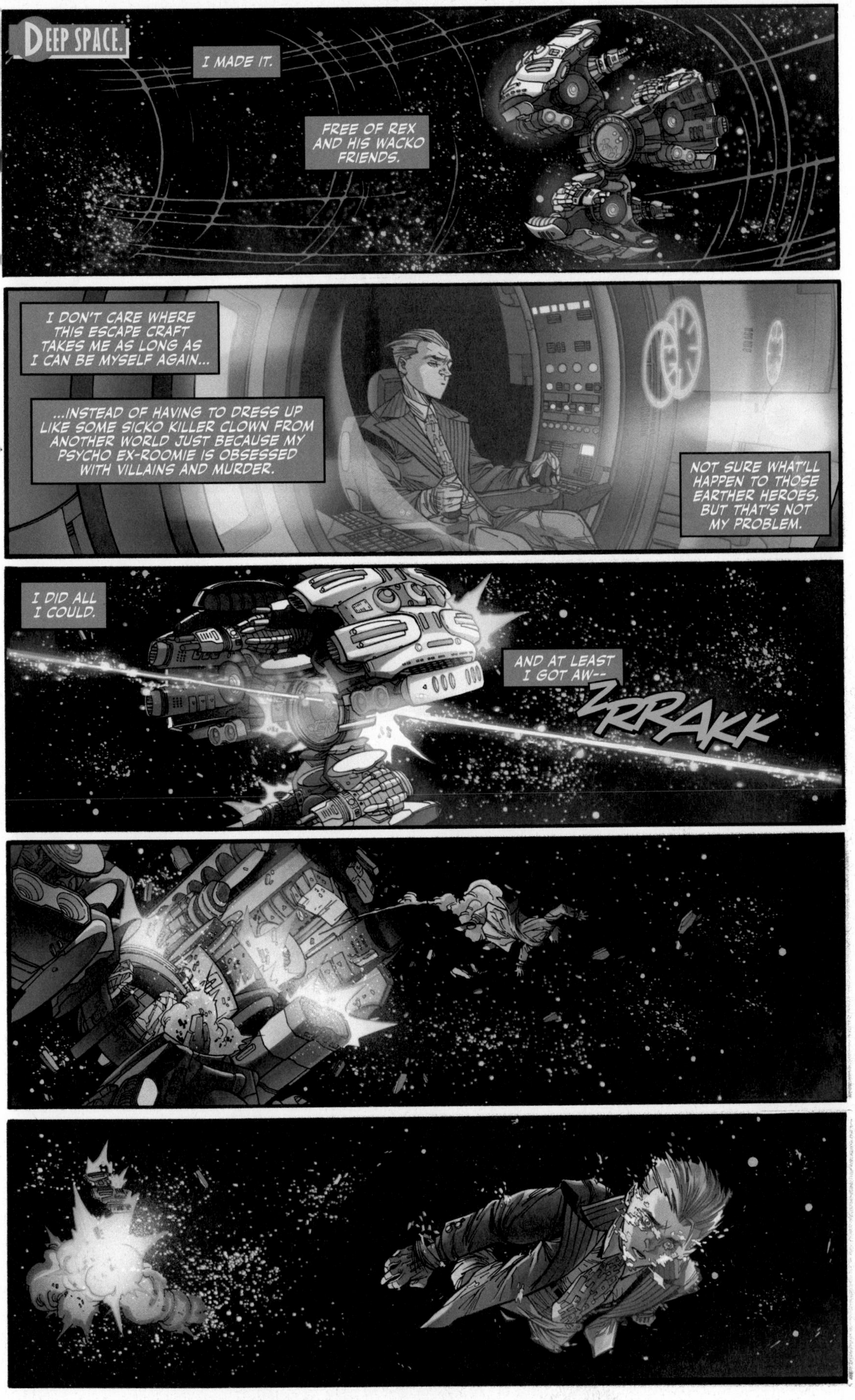
DEEP SPACE.
I MADE IT.
FREE OF REX AND HIS WACKO FRIENDS.
I DON'T CARE WHERE THIS ESCAPE CRAFT TAKES ME AS LONG AS I CAN BE MYSELF AGAIN...
...INSTEAD OF HAVING TO DRESS UP LIKE SOME SICKO KILLER CLOWN FROM ANOTHER WORLD JUST BECAUSE MY PSYCHO EX-ROOMIE IS OBSESSED WITH VILLAINS AND MURDER.
NOT SURE WHAT'LL HAPPEN TO THOSE EARTHER HEROES, BUT THAT'S NOT MY PROBLEM.
I DID ALL I COULD.
AND AT LEAST I GOT AW--
ZRRAKK

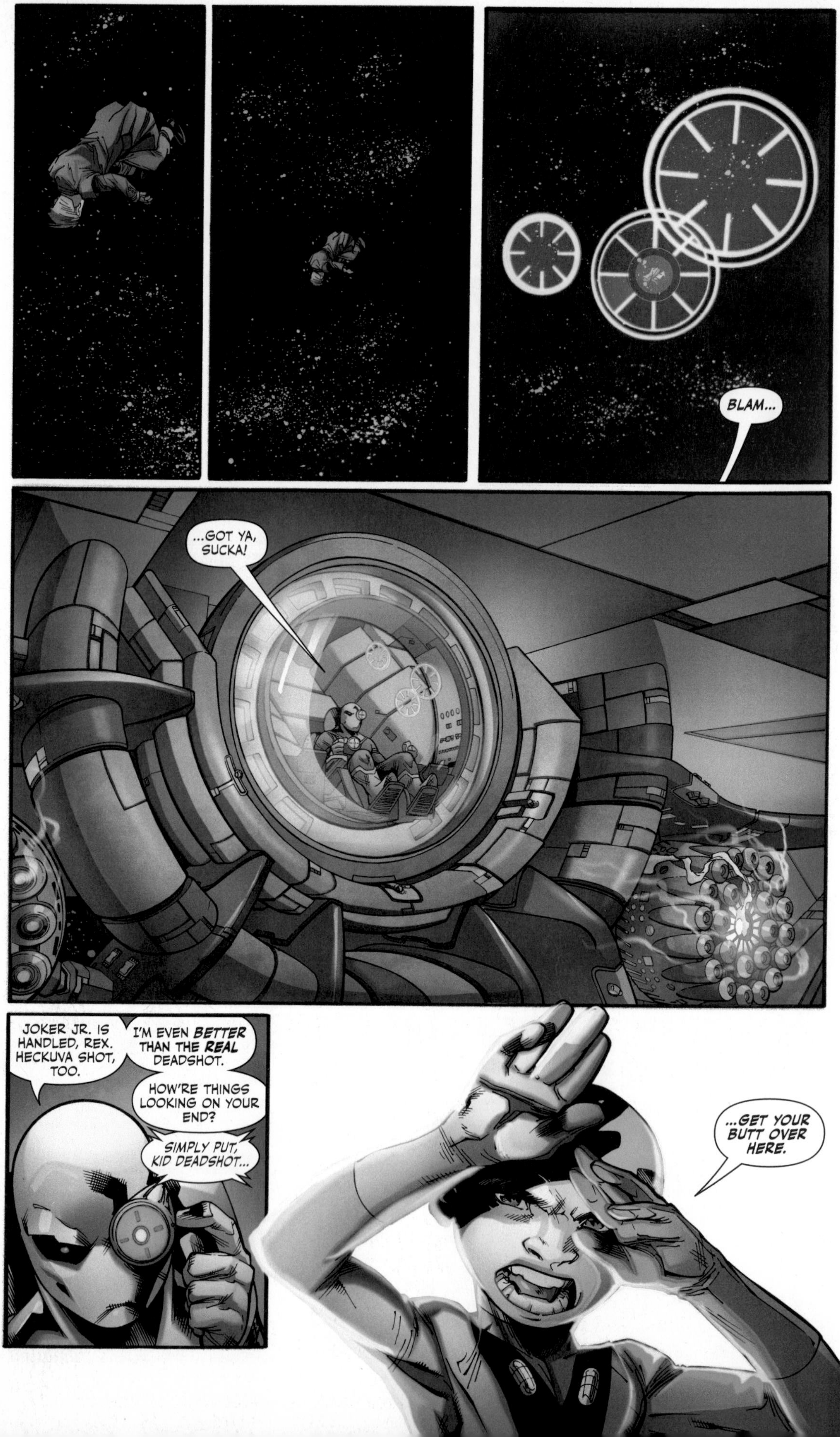

BLAM...
...GOT YA, SUCKA!
JOKER JR. IS HANDLED, REX. HECKUVA SHOT, TOO.
I'M EVEN BETTER THAN THE REAL DEADSHOT.
HOW'RE THINGS LOOKING ON YOUR END?
SIMPLY PUT, KID DEADSHOT...
...GET YOUR BUTT OVER HERE.

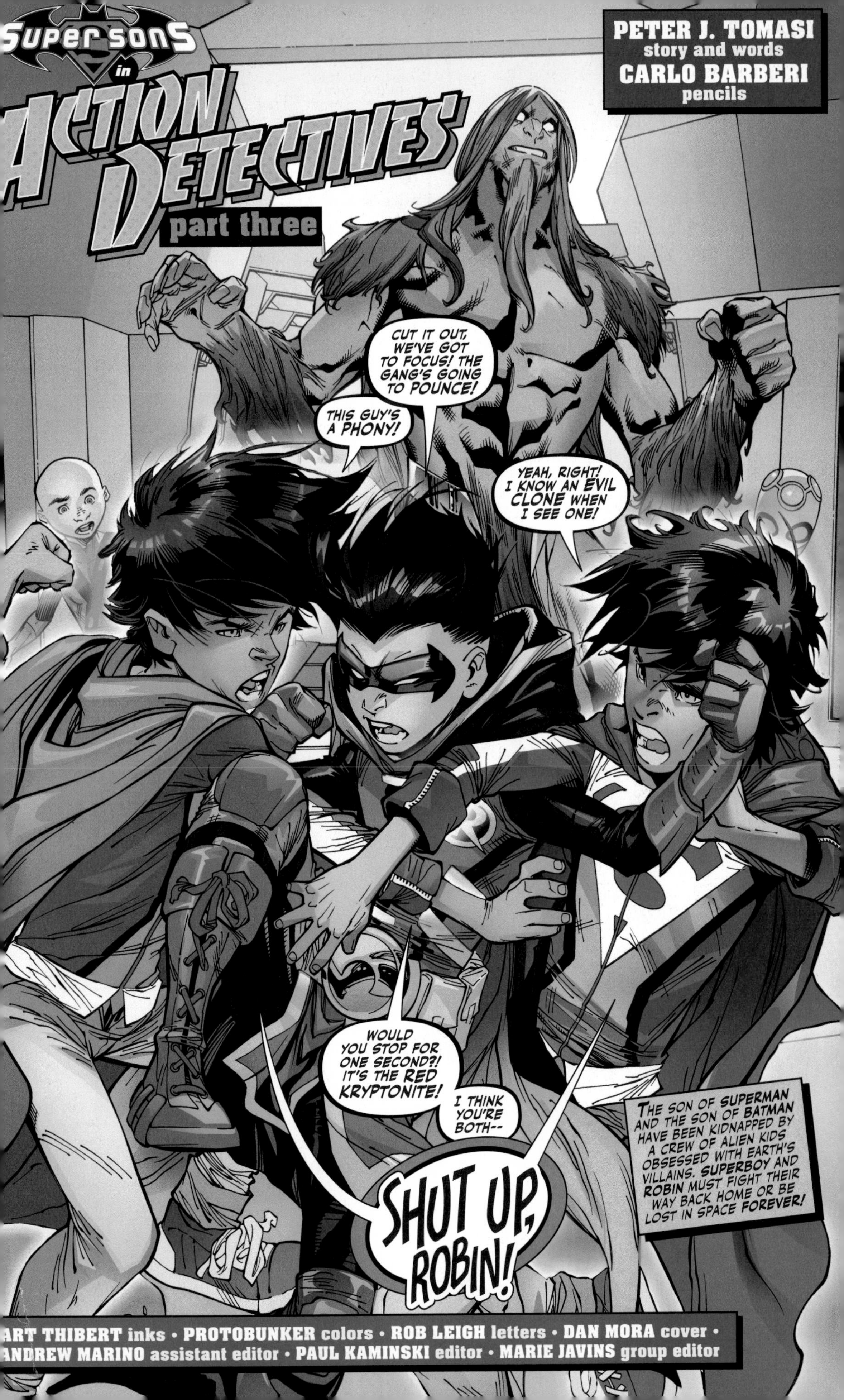

Super Sons in
ACTION DETECTIVES part three
PETER J. TOMASI story and words
CARLO BARBERI pencils
CUT IT OUT, WE'VE GOT TO FOCUS! THE GANG'S GOING TO POUNCE!
THIS GUY'S A PHONY!
YEAH, RIGHT! I KNOW AN EVIL CLONE WHEN I SEE ONE!
WOULD YOU STOP FOR ONE SECOND?! IT'S THE RED KRYPTONITE!
I THINK YOU'RE BOTH--
SHUT UP, ROBIN!
THE SON OF SUPERMAN AND THE SON OF BATMAN HAVE BEEN KIDNAPPED BY A CREW OF ALIEN KIDS OBSESSED WITH EARTH'S VILLAINS. SUPERBOY AND ROBIN MUST FIGHT THEIR WAY BACK HOME OR BE LOST IN SPACE FOREVER!
ART THIBERT inks • PROTOBUNKER colors • ROB LEIGH letters • DAN MORA cover •
ANDREW MARINO assistant editor • PAUL KAMINSKI editor • MARIE JAVINS group editor

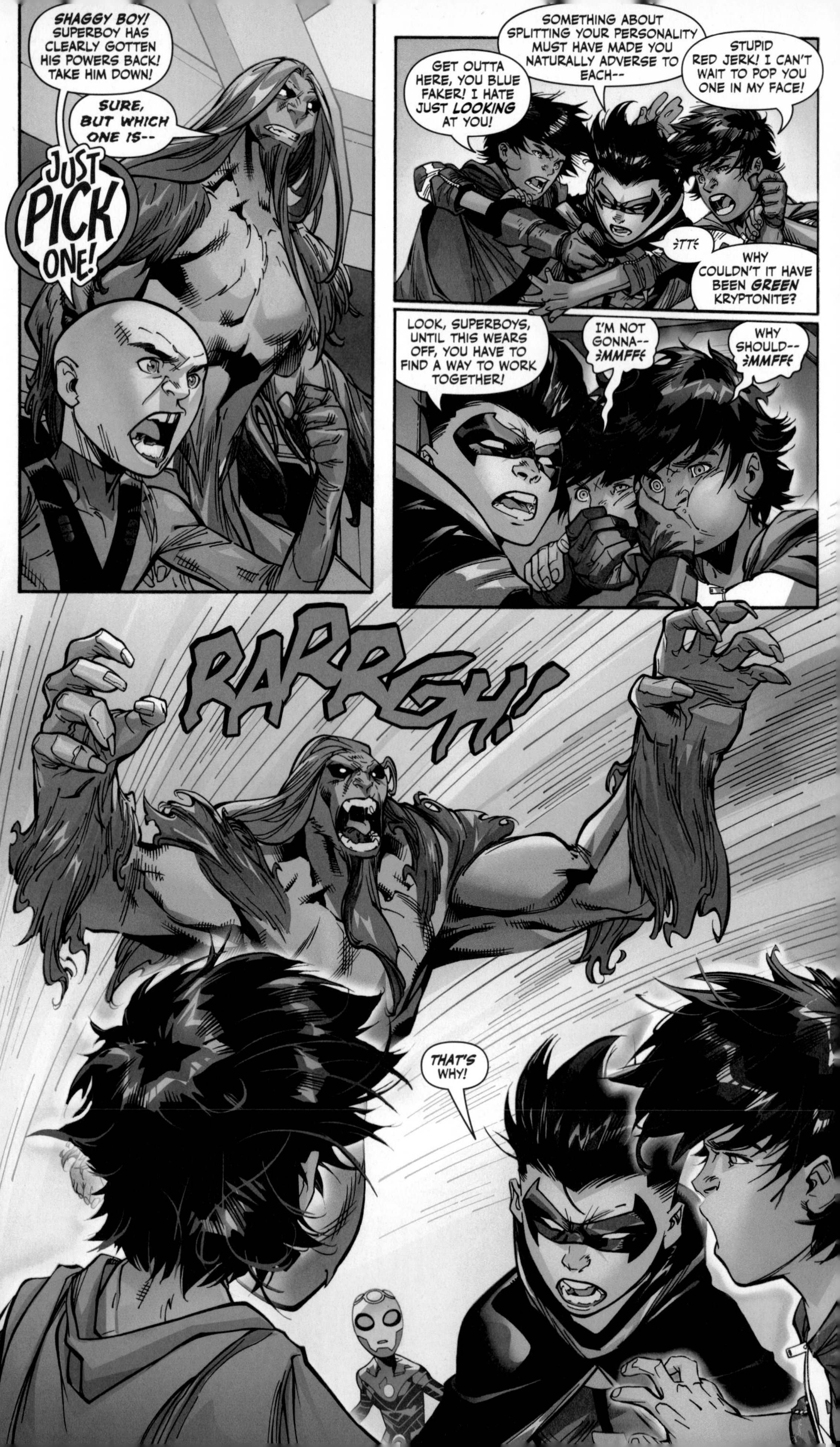
SHAGGY BOY! SUPERBOY HAS CLEARLY GOTTEN HIS POWERS BACK! TAKE HIM DOWN!
SURE, BUT WHICH ONE IS--
JUST PICK ONE!
SOMETHING ABOUT SPLITTING YOUR PERSONALITY MUST HAVE MADE YOU NATURALLY ADVERSE TO EACH--
GET OUTTA HERE, YOU BLUE FAKER! I HATE JUST LOOKING AT YOU!
STUPID RED JERK! I CAN'T WAIT TO POP YOU ONE IN MY FACE!
TT
WHY COULDN'T IT HAVE BEEN GREEN KRYPTONITE?
LOOK, SUPERBOYS, UNTIL THIS WEARS OFF, YOU HAVE TO FIND A WAY TO WORK TOGETHER!
I'M NOT GONNA-- MMFF
WHY SHOULD-- MMFF
RARRGH!
THAT'S WHY!

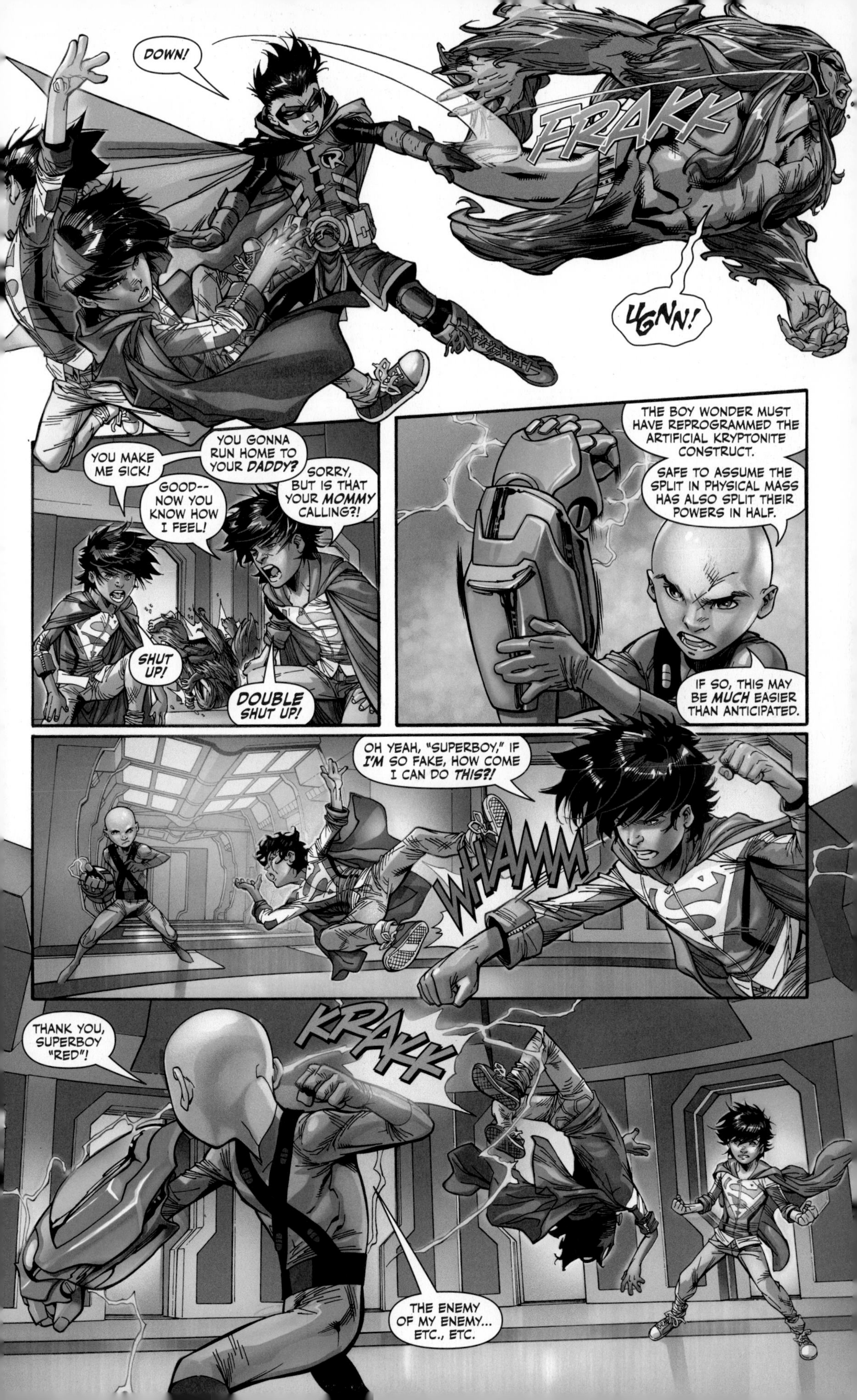
DOWN!
FRAKK
UGNN!
YOU MAKE ME SICK!
YOU GONNA RUN HOME TO YOUR DADDY?
GOOD-- NOW YOU KNOW HOW I FEEL!
SORRY, BUT IS THAT YOUR MOMMY CALLING?!
SHUT UP!
DOUBLE SHUT UP!
THE BOY WONDER MUST HAVE REPROGRAMMED THE ARTIFICIAL KRYPTONITE CONSTRUCT.
SAFE TO ASSUME THE SPLIT IN PHYSICAL MASS HAS ALSO SPLIT THEIR POWERS IN HALF.
IF SO, THIS MAY BE MUCH EASIER THAN ANTICIPATED.
OH YEAH, "SUPERBOY," IF I'M SO FAKE, HOW COME I CAN DO THIS?!
WHAMM
THANK YOU, SUPERBOY "RED"!
KRAKK
THE ENEMY OF MY ENEMY... ETC., ETC.

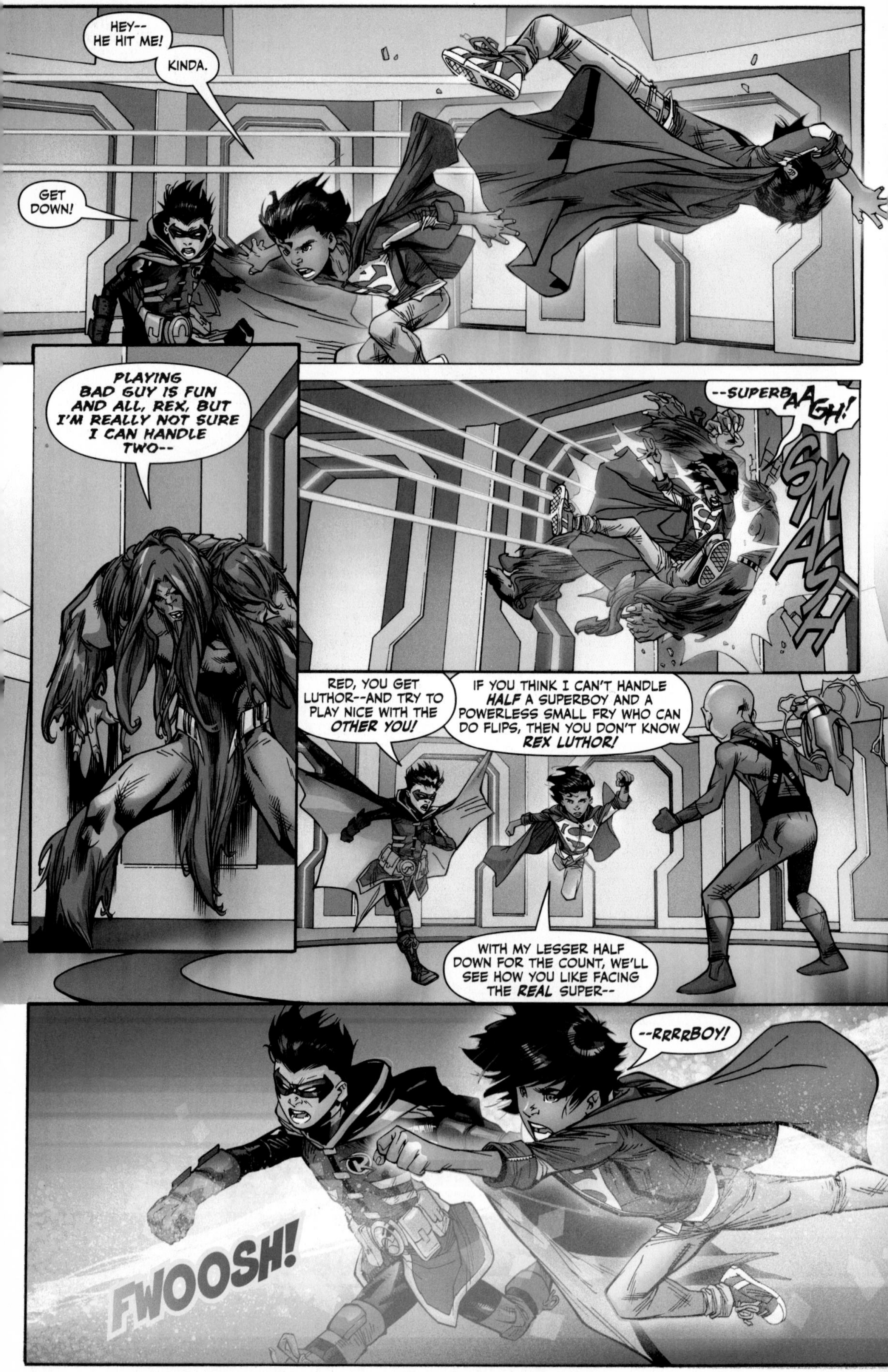
HEY--
HE HIT ME!
KINDA.
GET DOWN!
PLAYING BAD GUY IS FUN AND ALL, REX, BUT I'M REALLY NOT SURE I CAN HANDLE TWO--
--SUPERBAAGH!
SMASH
RED, YOU GET LUTHOR--AND TRY TO PLAY NICE WITH THE OTHER YOU!
IF YOU THINK I CAN'T HANDLE HALF A SUPERBOY AND A POWERLESS SMALL FRY WHO CAN DO FLIPS, THEN YOU DON'T KNOW REX LUTHOR!
WITH MY LESSER HALF DOWN FOR THE COUNT, WE'LL SEE HOW YOU LIKE FACING THE REAL SUPER--
--RRRRBOY!
FWOOSH!

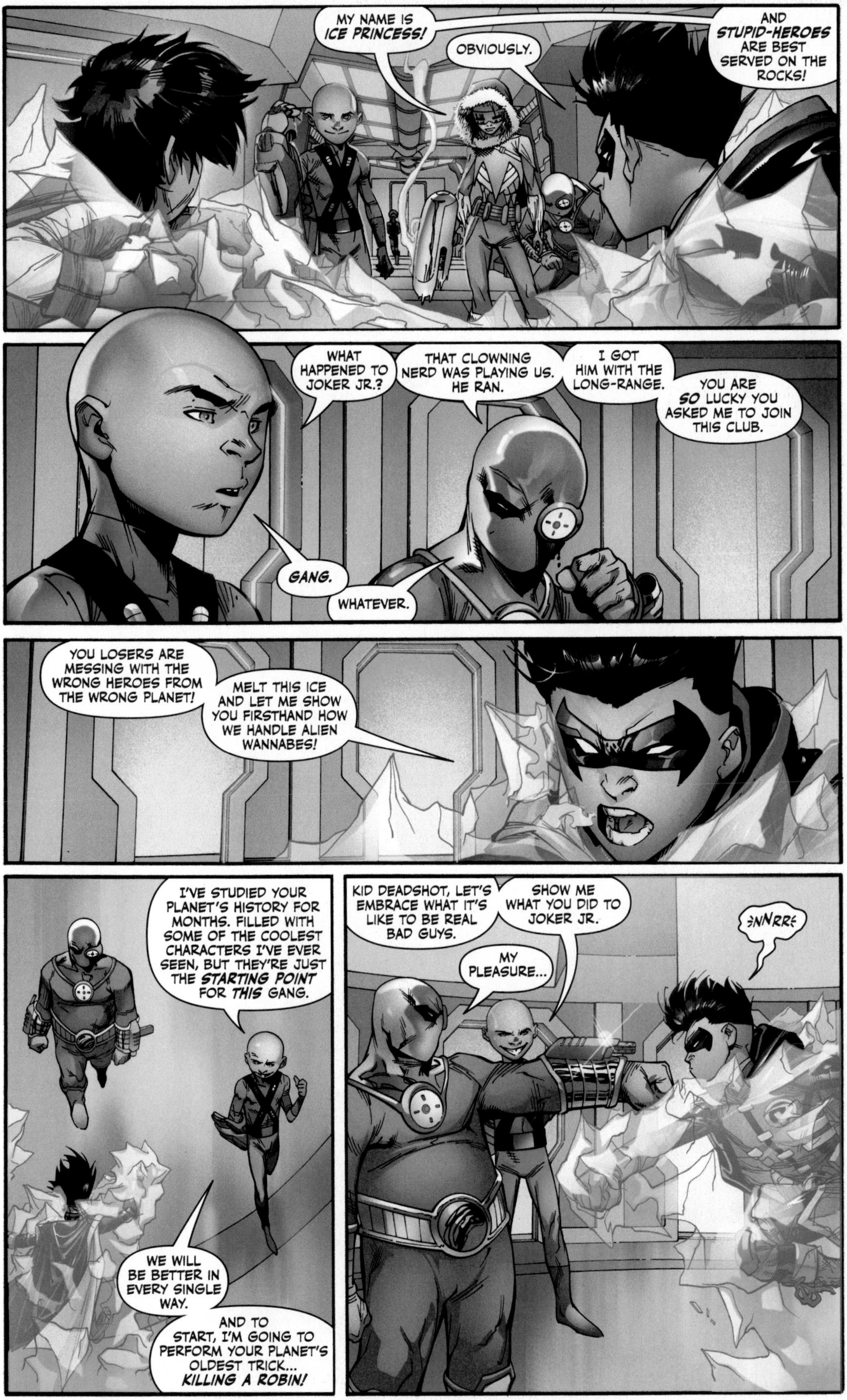
MY NAME IS ICE PRINCESS!
AND STUPID-HEROES ARE BEST SERVED ON THE ROCKS!
OBVIOUSLY.
WHAT HAPPENED TO JOKER JR.?
THAT CLOWNING NERD WAS PLAYING US. HE RAN.
I GOT HIM WITH THE LONG-RANGE.
YOU ARE SO LUCKY YOU ASKED ME TO JOIN THIS CLUB.
GANG.
WHATEVER.
YOU LOSERS ARE MESSING WITH THE WRONG HEROES FROM THE WRONG PLANET!
MELT THIS ICE AND LET ME SHOW YOU FIRSTHAND HOW WE HANDLE ALIEN WANNABES!
I'VE STUDIED YOUR PLANET'S HISTORY FOR MONTHS. FILLED WITH SOME OF THE COOLEST CHARACTERS I'VE EVER SEEN, BUT THEY'RE JUST THE STARTING POINT FOR THIS GANG.
WE WILL BE BETTER IN EVERY SINGLE WAY.
AND TO START, I'M GOING TO PERFORM YOUR PLANET'S OLDEST TRICK... KILLING A ROBIN!
KID DEADSHOT, LET'S EMBRACE WHAT IT'S LIKE TO BE REAL BAD GUYS.
SHOW ME WHAT YOU DID TO JOKER JR.
MY PLEASURE...
ƎNNRR⸗

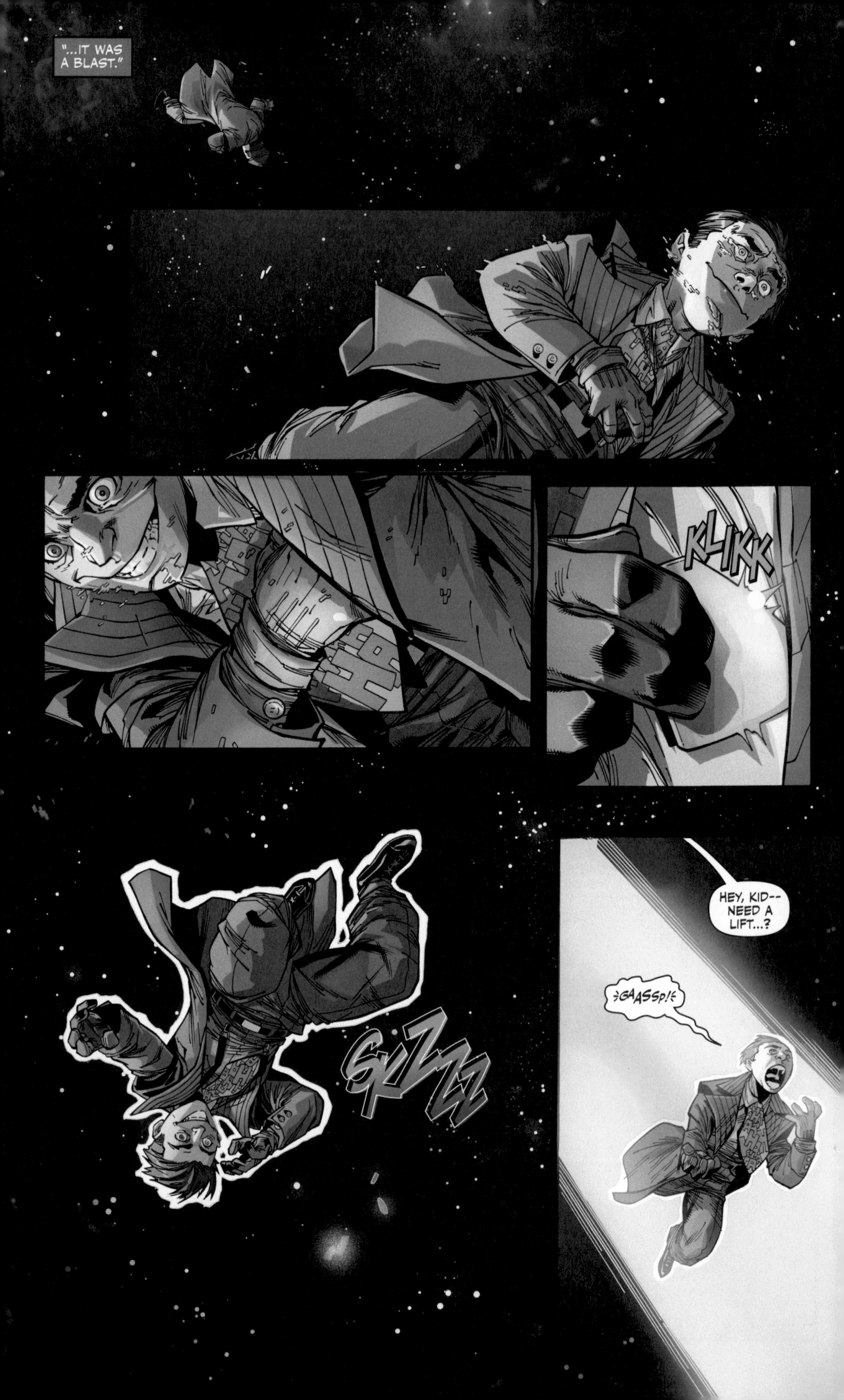
"...IT WAS A BLAST."
KLIKK
SKZZZZ
HEY, KID-- NEED A LIFT...?
GAASSP!

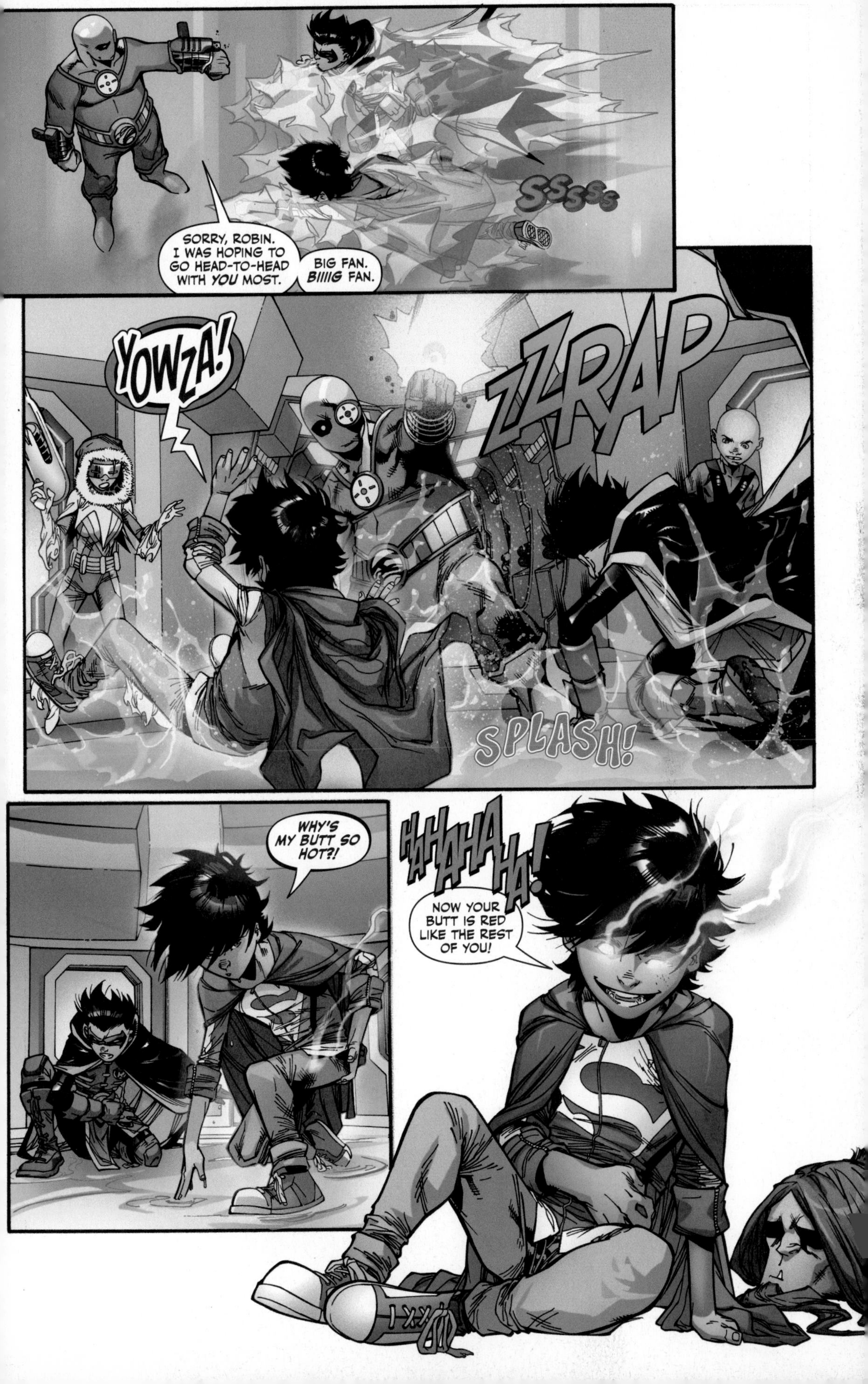
SSSSS
SORRY, ROBIN. I WAS HOPING TO GO HEAD-TO-HEAD WITH YOU MOST.
BIG FAN. BIIIIG FAN.
YOWZA!
ZZRAP
SPLASH!
WHY'S MY BUTT SO HOT?!
HAHAHAHAHA!
NOW YOUR BUTT IS RED LIKE THE REST OF YOU!

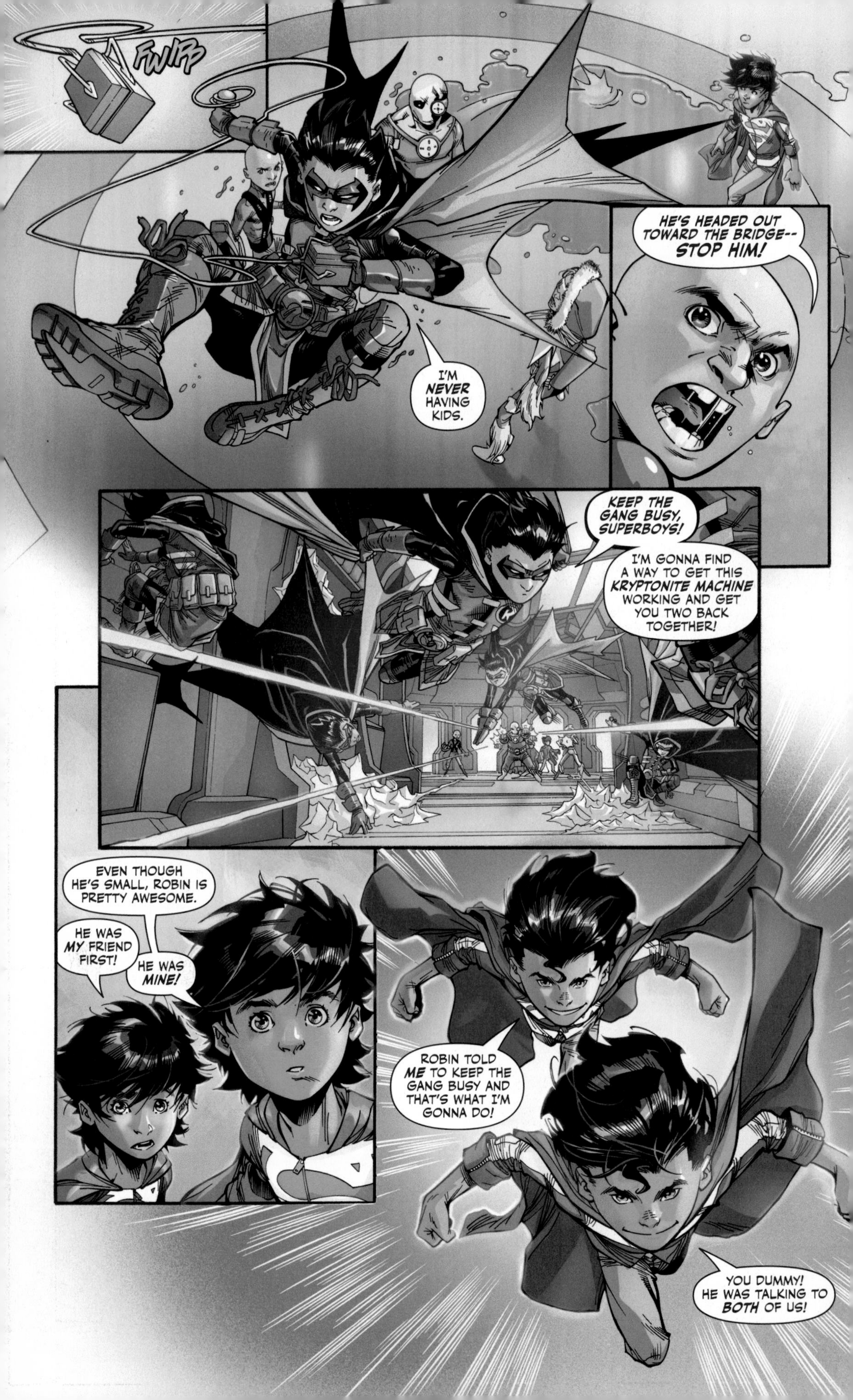
FWIPP
HE'S HEADED OUT TOWARD THE BRIDGE-- STOP HIM!
I'M NEVER HAVING KIDS.
KEEP THE GANG BUSY, SUPERBOYS!
I'M GONNA FIND A WAY TO GET THIS KRYPTONITE MACHINE WORKING AND GET YOU TWO BACK TOGETHER!
EVEN THOUGH HE'S SMALL, ROBIN IS PRETTY AWESOME.
HE WAS MY FRIEND FIRST!
HE WAS MINE!
ROBIN TOLD ME TO KEEP THE GANG BUSY AND THAT'S WHAT I'M GONNA DO!
YOU DUMMY! HE WAS TALKING TO BOTH OF US!

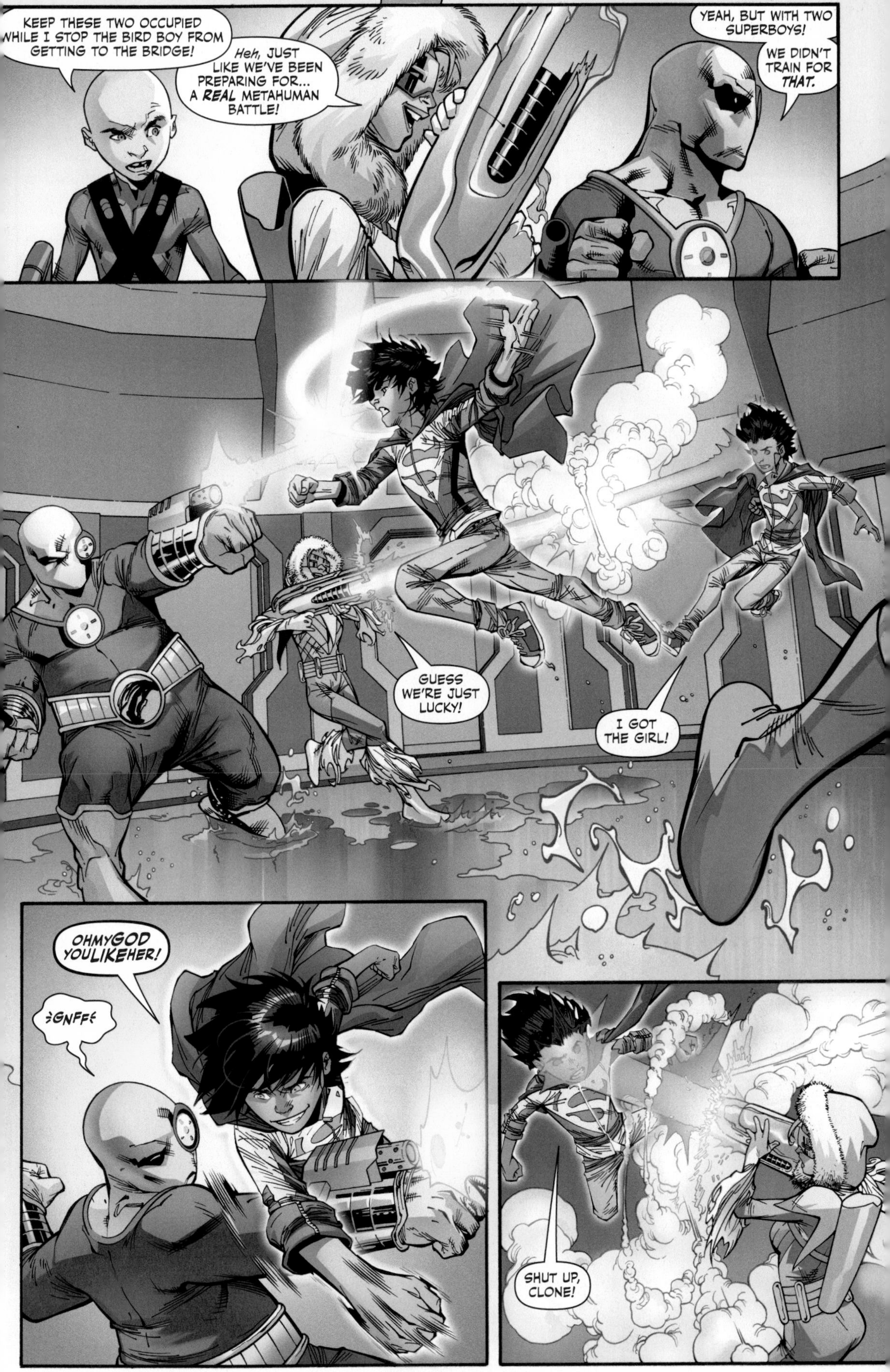
KEEP THESE TWO OCCUPIED WHILE I STOP THE BIRD BOY FROM GETTING TO THE BRIDGE!
Heh, JUST LIKE WE'VE BEEN PREPARING FOR... A *REAL* METAHUMAN BATTLE!
YEAH, BUT WITH TWO SUPERBOYS!
WE DIDN'T TRAIN FOR *THAT.*
GUESS WE'RE JUST LUCKY!
I GOT THE GIRL!
OHMY*GOD* YOU*LIKE*HER!
GNFF
SHUT UP, CLONE!

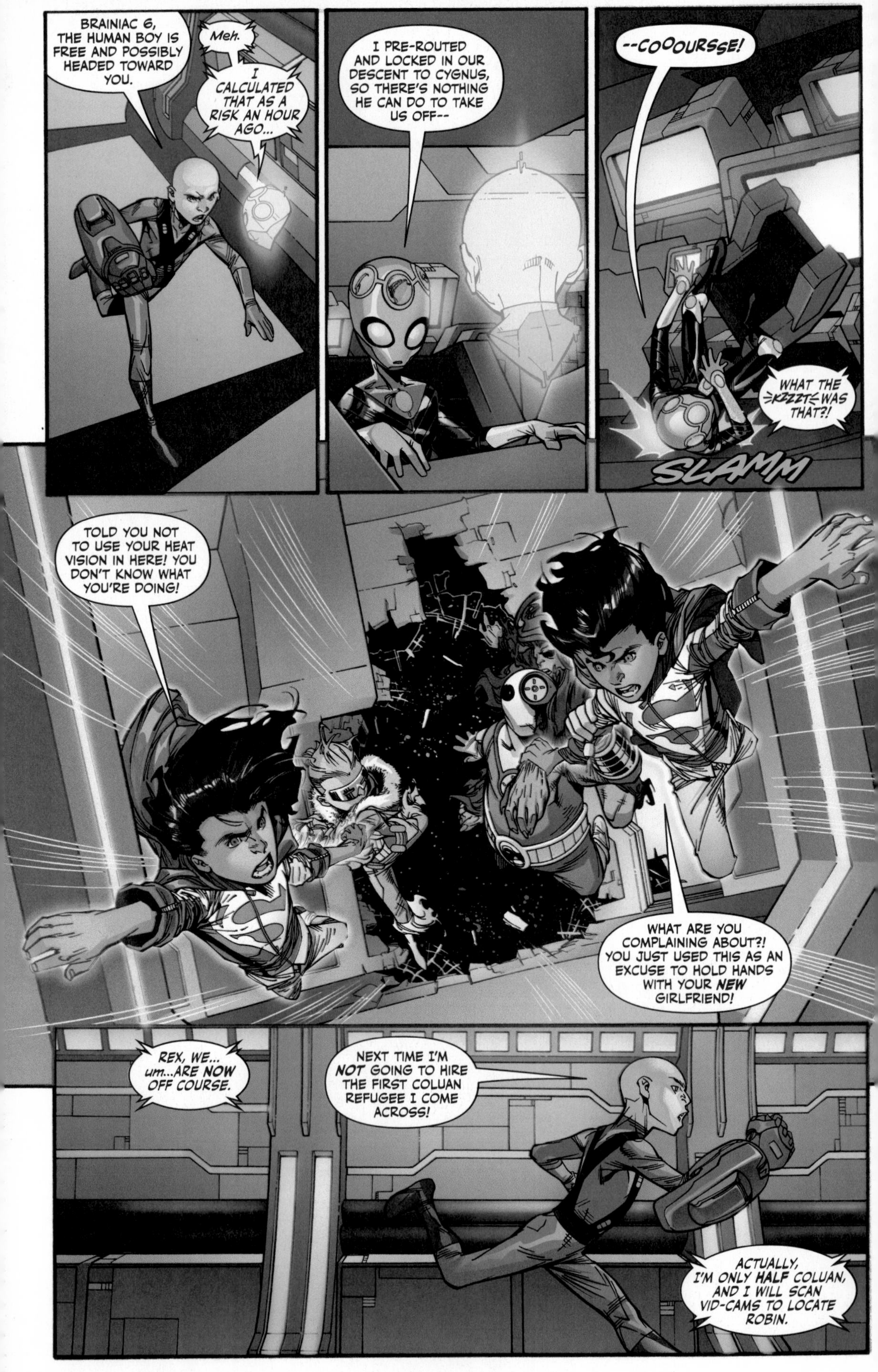
BRAINIAC 6, THE HUMAN BOY IS FREE AND POSSIBLY HEADED TOWARD YOU.
Meh.
I CALCULATED THAT AS A RISK AN HOUR AGO...
I PRE-ROUTED AND LOCKED IN OUR DESCENT TO CYGNUS, SO THERE'S NOTHING HE CAN DO TO TAKE US OFF--
--COOOURSSE!
WHAT THE KZZZT WAS THAT?!
SLAMM
TOLD YOU NOT TO USE YOUR HEAT VISION IN HERE! YOU DON'T KNOW WHAT YOU'RE DOING!
WHAT ARE YOU COMPLAINING ABOUT?! YOU JUST USED THIS AS AN EXCUSE TO HOLD HANDS WITH YOUR NEW GIRLFRIEND!
REX, WE... um...ARE NOW OFF COURSE.
NEXT TIME I'M NOT GOING TO HIRE THE FIRST COLUAN REFUGEE I COME ACROSS!
ACTUALLY, I'M ONLY HALF COLUAN, AND I WILL SCAN VID-CAMS TO LOCATE ROBIN.

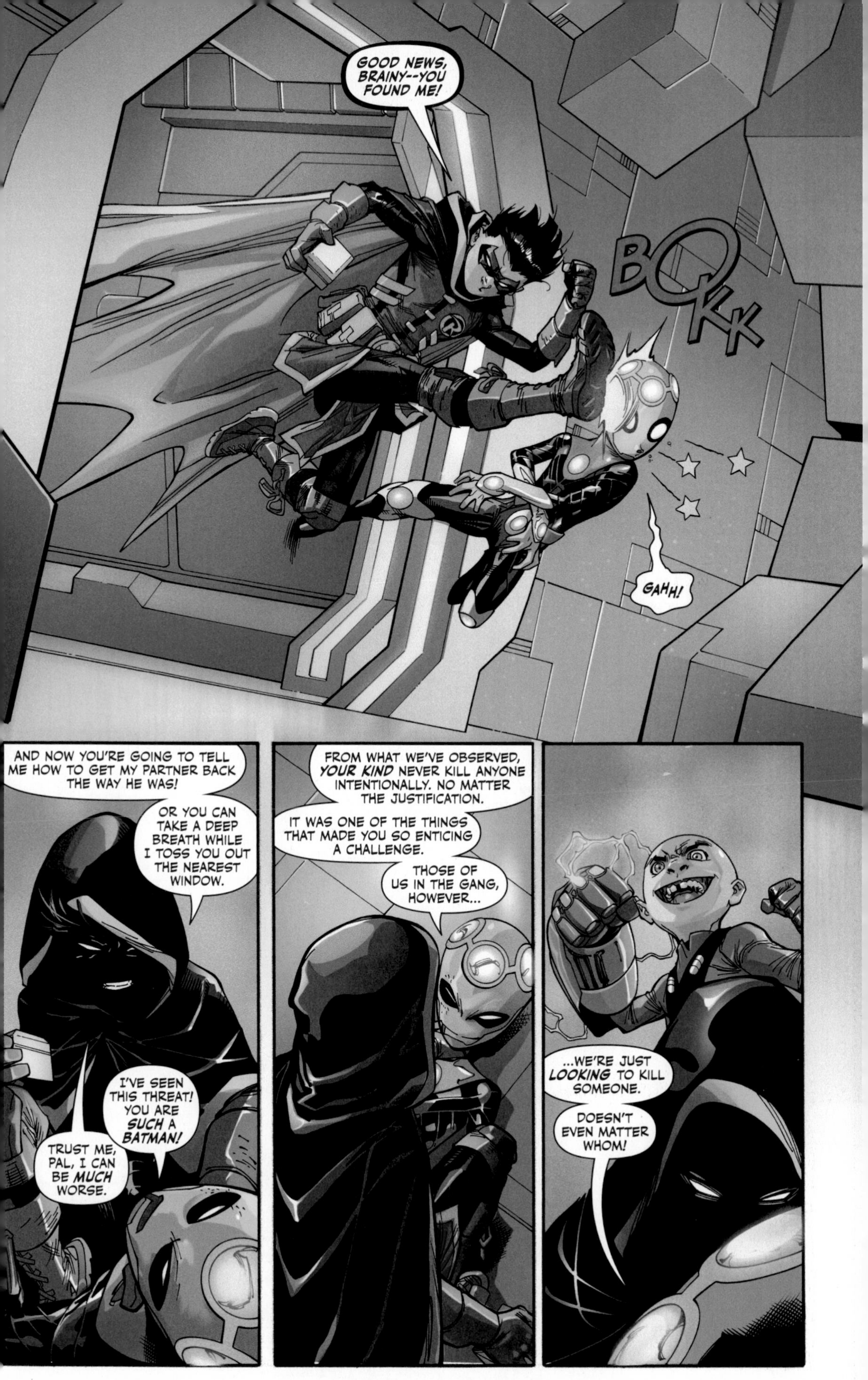
GOOD NEWS, BRAINY--YOU FOUND ME!
BOKK
GAHH!
AND NOW YOU'RE GOING TO TELL ME HOW TO GET MY PARTNER BACK THE WAY HE WAS!
OR YOU CAN TAKE A DEEP BREATH WHILE I TOSS YOU OUT THE NEAREST WINDOW.
I'VE SEEN THIS THREAT! YOU ARE *SUCH* A *BATMAN!*
TRUST ME, PAL, I CAN BE *MUCH* WORSE.
FROM WHAT WE'VE OBSERVED, *YOUR KIND* NEVER KILL ANYONE INTENTIONALLY. NO MATTER THE JUSTIFICATION.
IT WAS ONE OF THE THINGS THAT MADE YOU SO ENTICING A CHALLENGE.
THOSE OF US IN THE GANG, HOWEVER...
...WE'RE JUST *LOOKING* TO KILL SOMEONE.
DOESN'T EVEN MATTER WHOM!

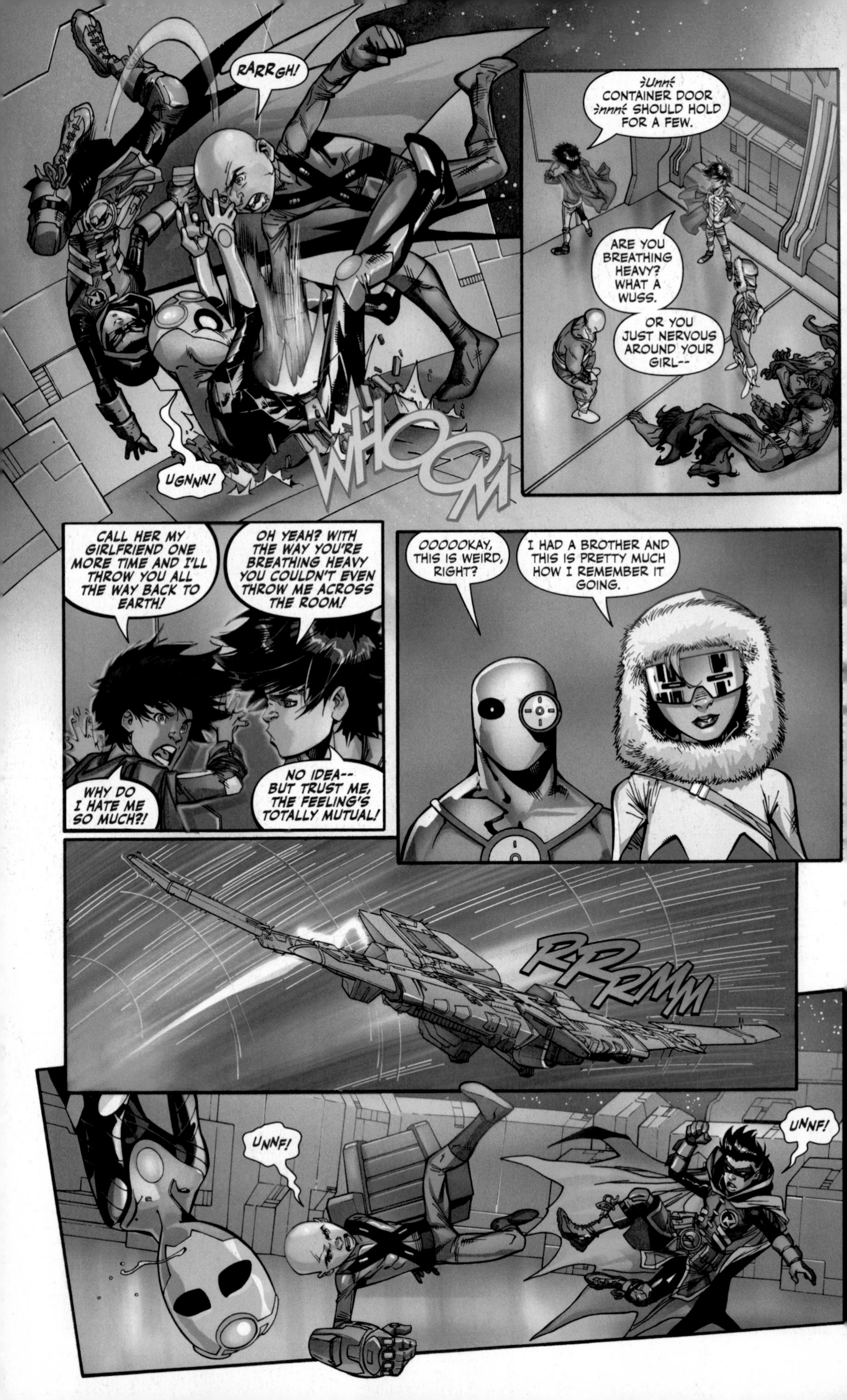
RARRGH!
UGNNN!
WHOOM
Unn CONTAINER DOOR nnn SHOULD HOLD FOR A FEW.
ARE YOU BREATHING HEAVY? WHAT A WUSS.
OR YOU JUST NERVOUS AROUND YOUR GIRL--
CALL HER MY GIRLFRIEND ONE MORE TIME AND I'LL THROW YOU ALL THE WAY BACK TO EARTH!
OH YEAH? WITH THE WAY YOU'RE BREATHING HEAVY YOU COULDN'T EVEN THROW ME ACROSS THE ROOM!
WHY DO I HATE ME SO MUCH?!
NO IDEA-- BUT TRUST ME, THE FEELING'S TOTALLY MUTUAL!
OOOOOKAY, THIS IS WEIRD, RIGHT?
I HAD A BROTHER AND THIS IS PRETTY MUCH HOW I REMEMBER IT GOING.
RRRMM
UNNF!
UNNF!

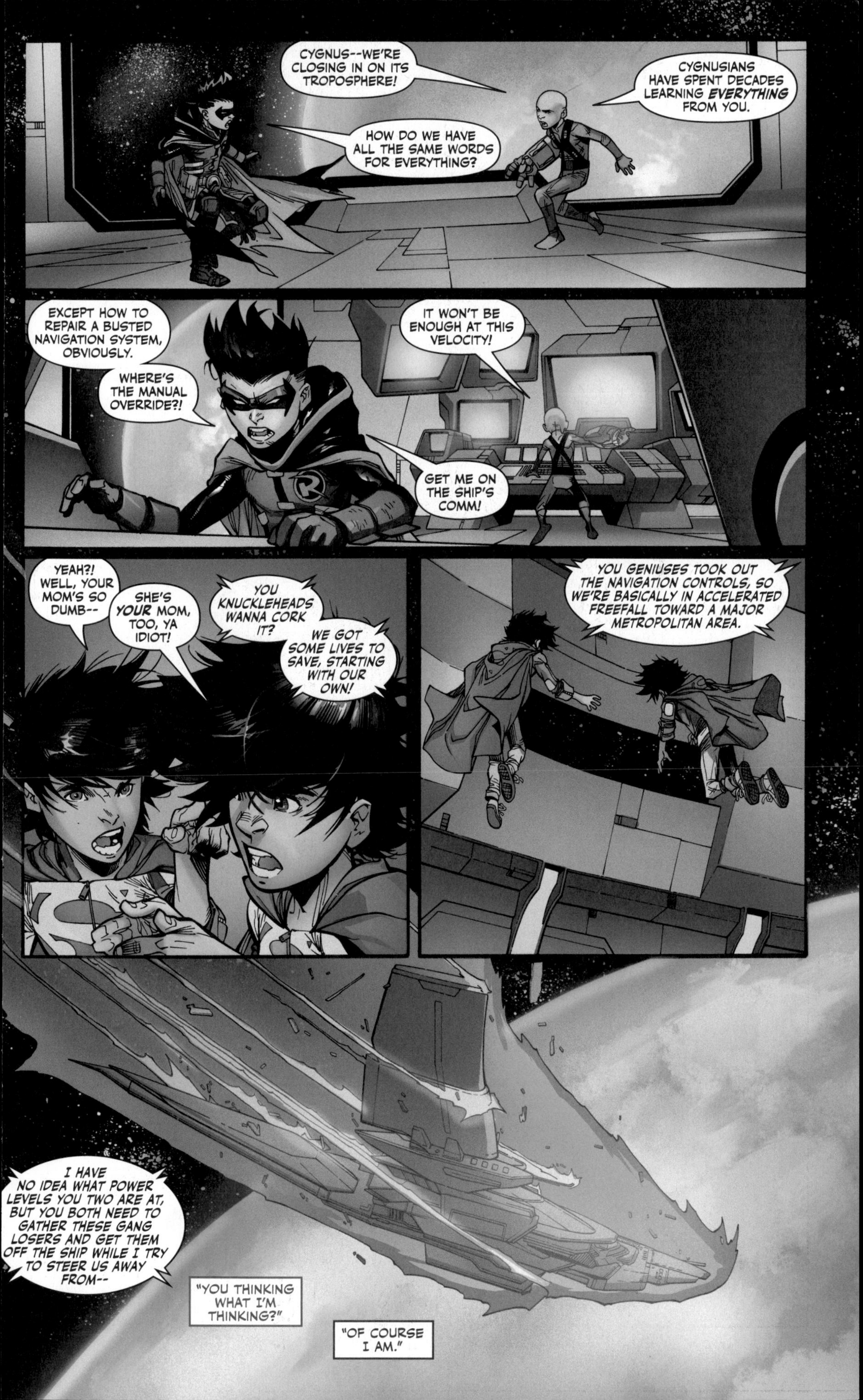
CYGNUS--WE'RE CLOSING IN ON ITS TROPOSPHERE!
HOW DO WE HAVE ALL THE SAME WORDS FOR EVERYTHING?
CYGNUSIANS HAVE SPENT DECADES LEARNING *EVERYTHING* FROM YOU.
EXCEPT HOW TO REPAIR A BUSTED NAVIGATION SYSTEM, OBVIOUSLY.
WHERE'S THE MANUAL OVERRIDE?!
IT WON'T BE ENOUGH AT THIS VELOCITY!
GET ME ON THE SHIP'S COMM!
YEAH?! WELL, YOUR MOM'S SO DUMB--
SHE'S *YOUR* MOM, TOO, YA IDIOT!
YOU KNUCKLEHEADS WANNA CORK IT?
WE GOT SOME LIVES TO SAVE, STARTING WITH OUR OWN!
YOU GENIUSES TOOK OUT THE NAVIGATION CONTROLS, SO WE'RE BASICALLY IN ACCELERATED FREEFALL TOWARD A MAJOR METROPOLITAN AREA.
I HAVE NO IDEA WHAT POWER LEVELS YOU TWO ARE AT, BUT YOU BOTH NEED TO GATHER THESE GANG LOSERS AND GET THEM OFF THE SHIP WHILE I TRY TO STEER US AWAY FROM--
"YOU THINKING WHAT I'M THINKING?"
"OF COURSE I AM."

WE GOTTA PUSH AND PULL.

OPPOSING FORCES!

DON'T EVEN TRY AND TELL ME THIS IS SOME KINDA METAPHOR FOR OUR RELATIONSHIP!

Pfft! YOU READ TOO MANY BOOKS!

SO DO YOU!

WOULD YOU TWO SHUT UP FOR TWO SECONDS? WE NEED TO GET THESE PEOPLE OFF OF--

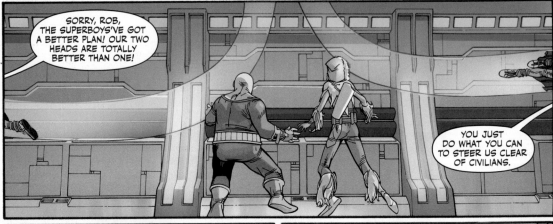

SORRY, ROB, THE SUPERBOYS'VE GOT A BETTER PLAN! OUR TWO HEADS ARE TOTALLY BETTER THAN ONE!

YOU JUST DO WHAT YOU CAN TO STEER US CLEAR OF CIVILIANS.

ROBIN IS *SOOOO* LUCKY TO WORK WITH US, BLUE.

I'M OUT THROUGH THE STERN.

TELL ME ABOUT IT, RED.

AND I'M OUT THROUGH THE BOW.

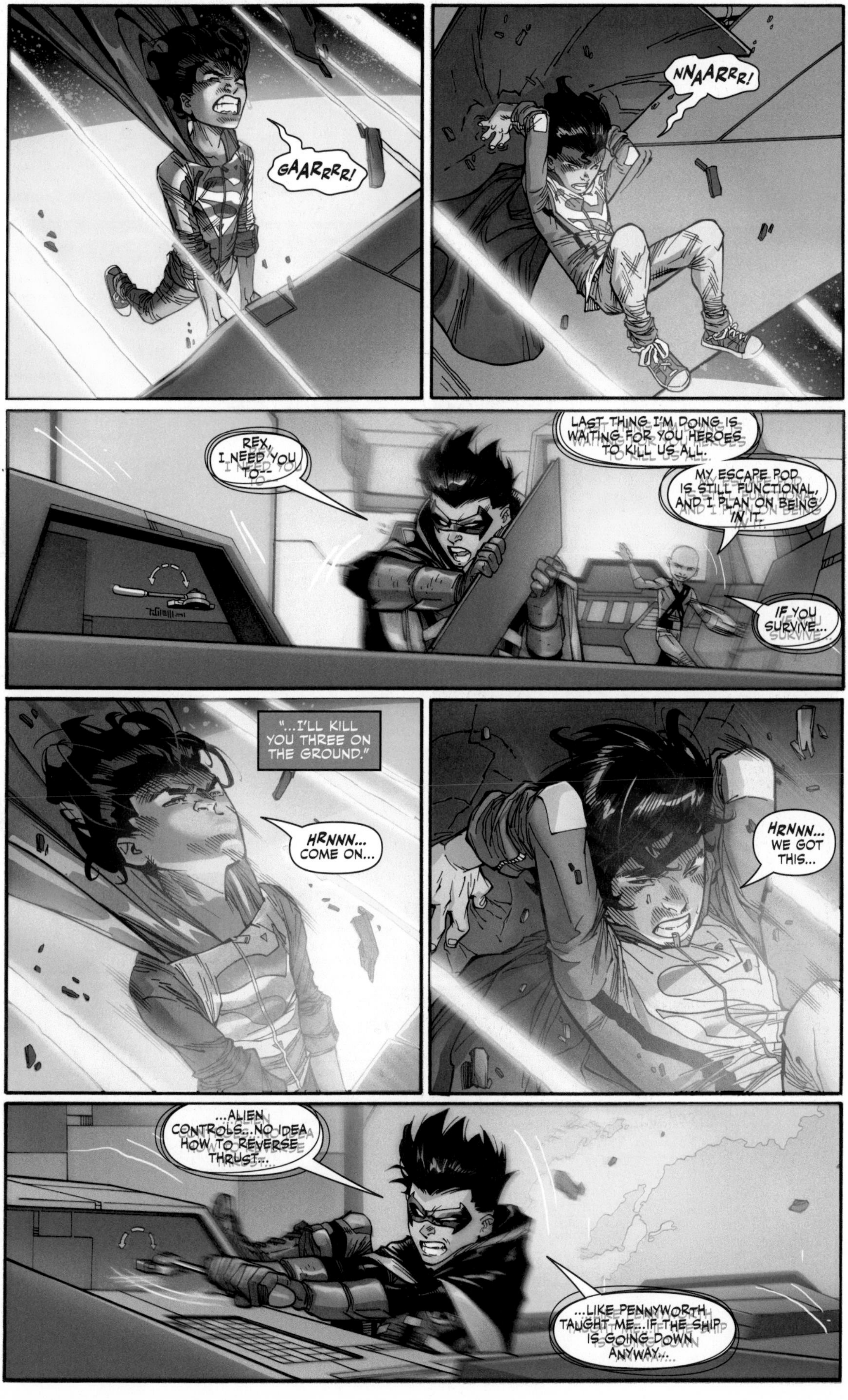
GAARRRR!
NNAARRR!
REX, I NEED YOU TO--
LAST THING I'M DOING IS WAITING FOR YOU HEROES TO KILL US ALL.
MY ESCAPE POD IS STILL FUNCTIONAL, AND I PLAN ON BEING IN IT.
IF YOU SURVIVE...
"...I'LL KILL YOU THREE ON THE GROUND."
HRNNN... COME ON...
HRNNN... WE GOT THIS...
...ALIEN CONTROLS...NO IDEA HOW TO REVERSE THRUST...
...LIKE PENNYWORTH TAUGHT ME...IF THE SHIP IS GOING DOWN ANYWAY...

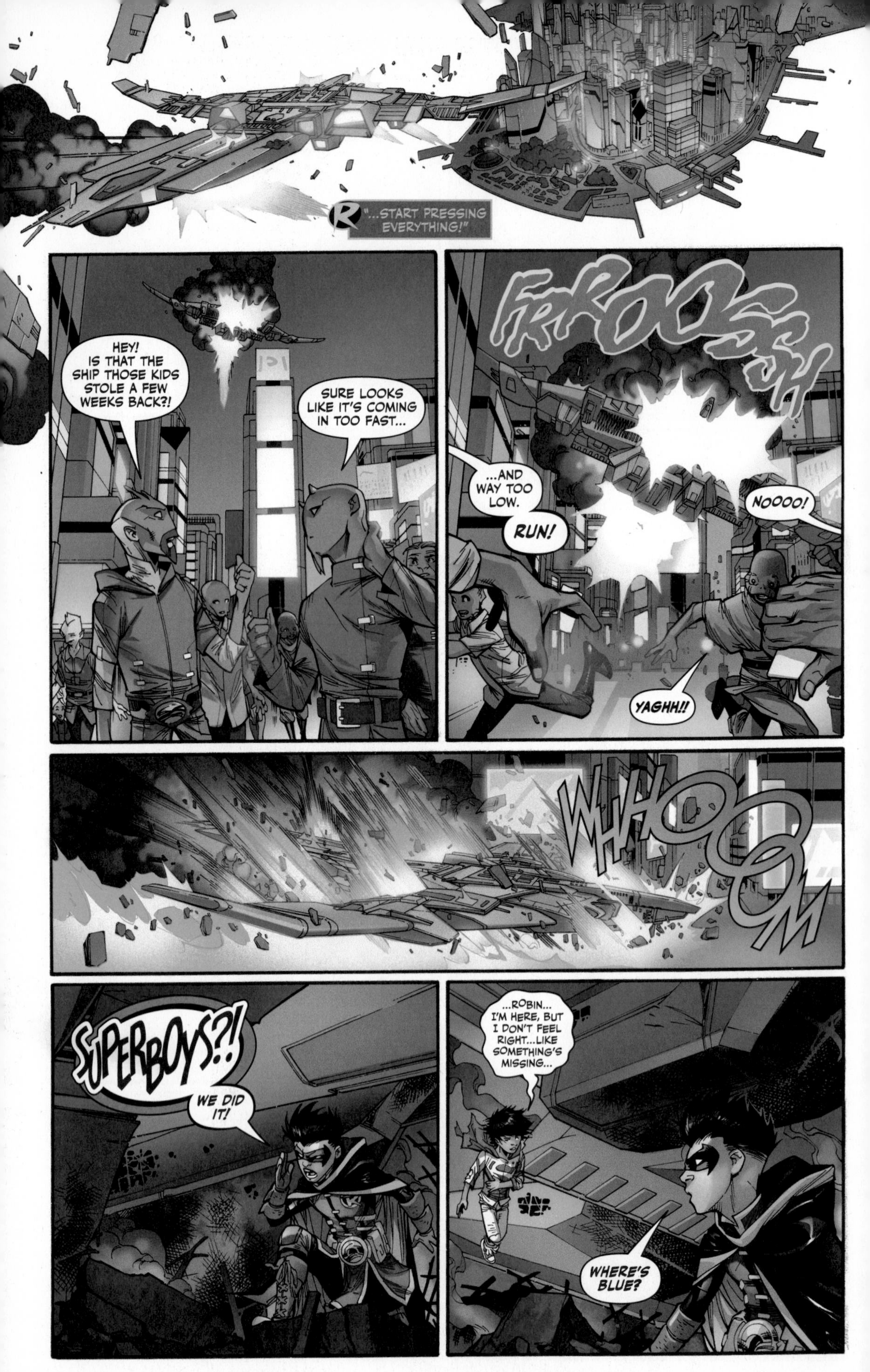
"...START PRESSING EVERYTHING!"
HEY! IS THAT THE SHIP THOSE KIDS STOLE A FEW WEEKS BACK?!
SURE LOOKS LIKE IT'S COMING IN TOO FAST...
FRROOSSH
...AND WAY TOO LOW.
RUN!
NOOOO!
YAGHH!!
WHOOOOM
SUPERBOYS?!
WE DID IT!
...ROBIN... I'M HERE, BUT I DON'T FEEL RIGHT...LIKE SOMETHING'S MISSING...
WHERE'S BLUE?

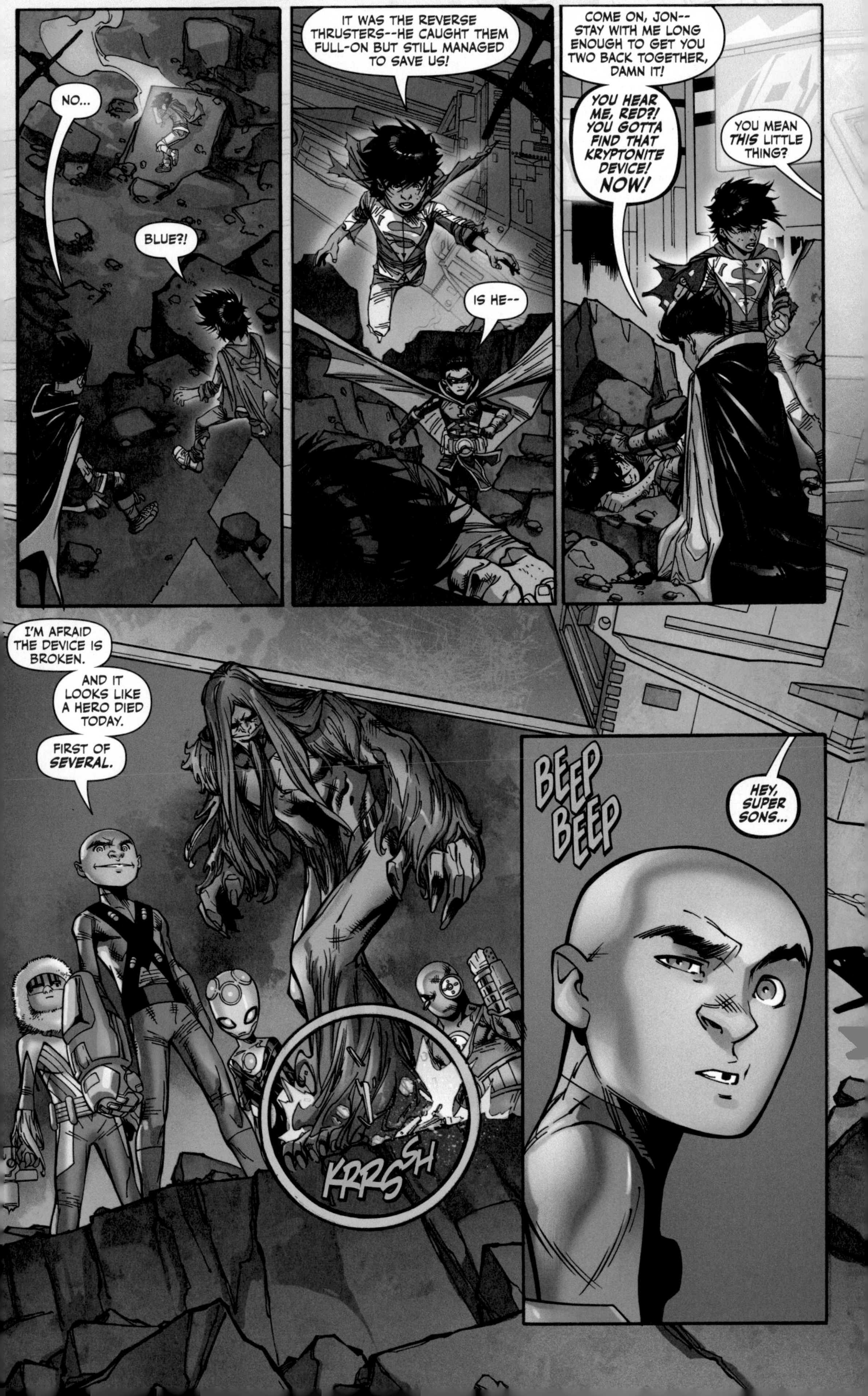
NO...
BLUE?!
IT WAS THE REVERSE THRUSTERS--HE CAUGHT THEM FULL-ON BUT STILL MANAGED TO SAVE US!
IS HE--
COME ON, JON--STAY WITH ME LONG ENOUGH TO GET YOU TWO BACK TOGETHER, DAMN IT!
YOU HEAR ME, RED?! YOU GOTTA FIND THAT KRYPTONITE DEVICE! NOW!
YOU MEAN THIS LITTLE THING?
I'M AFRAID THE DEVICE IS BROKEN.
AND IT LOOKS LIKE A HERO DIED TODAY.
FIRST OF SEVERAL.
KRRGSH
BEEP BEEP
HEY, SUPER SONS...

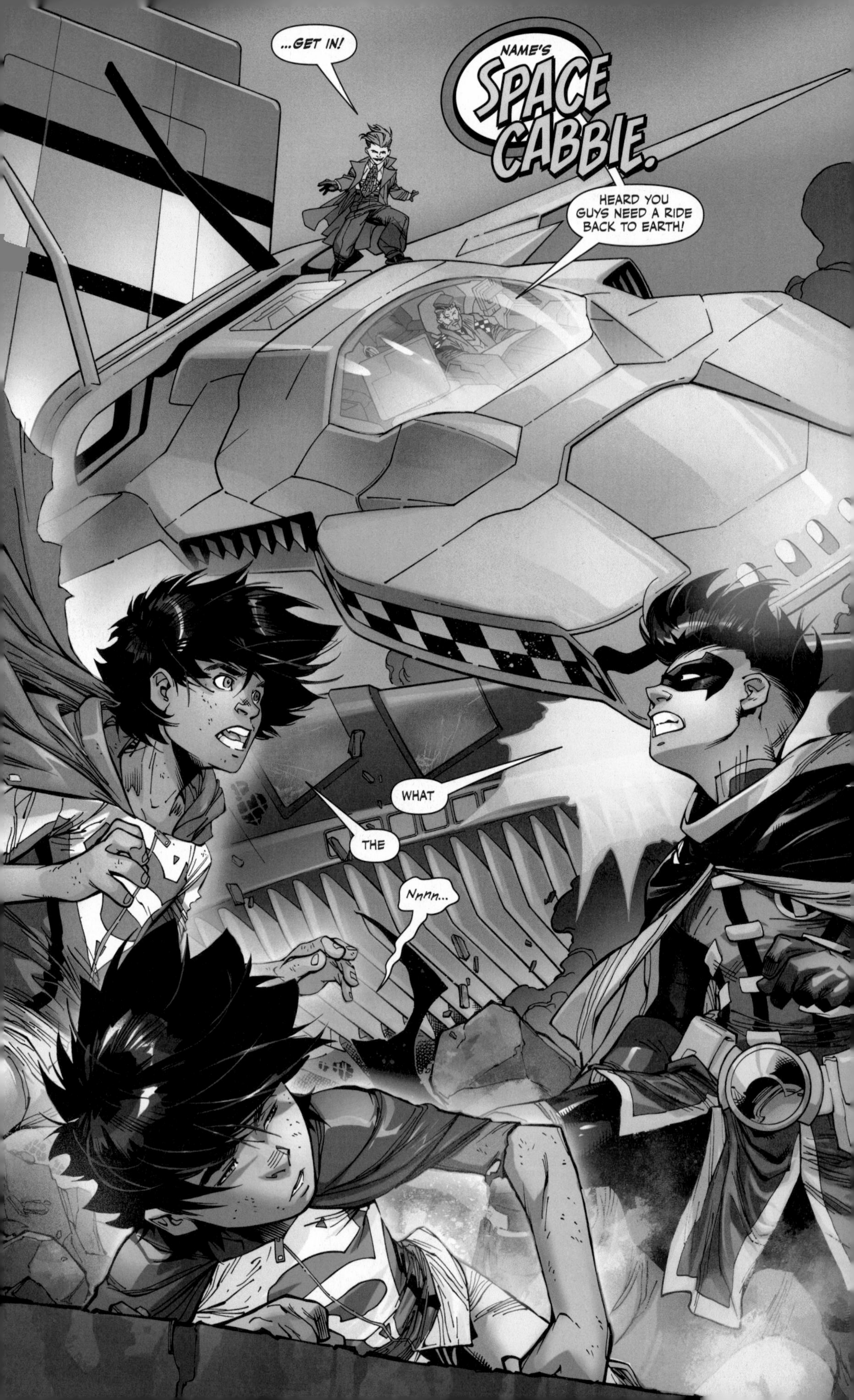
...GET IN!
NAME'S SPACE CABBIE.
HEARD YOU GUYS NEED A RIDE BACK TO EARTH!
WHAT
THE
Nnnn...

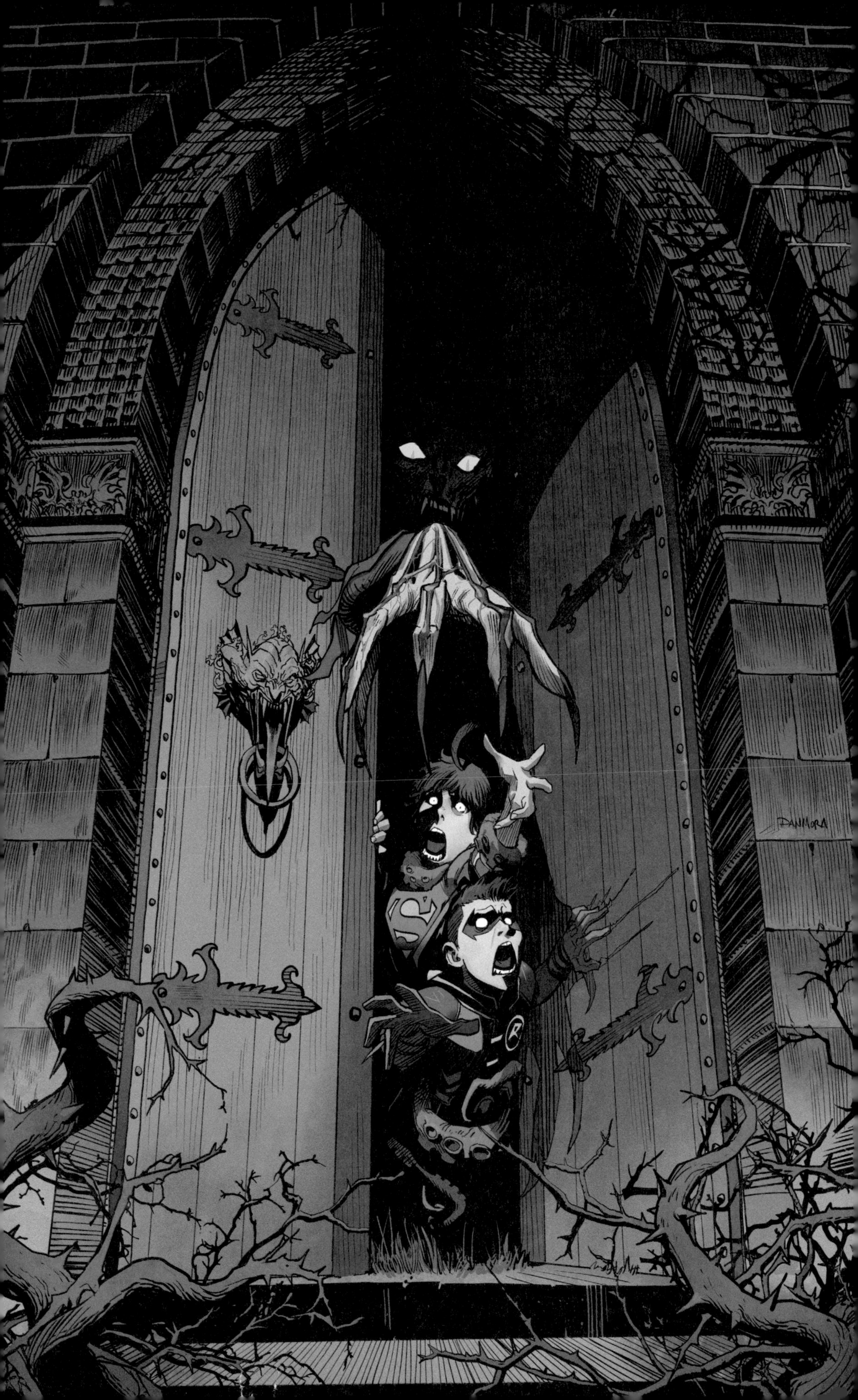
DANMORA

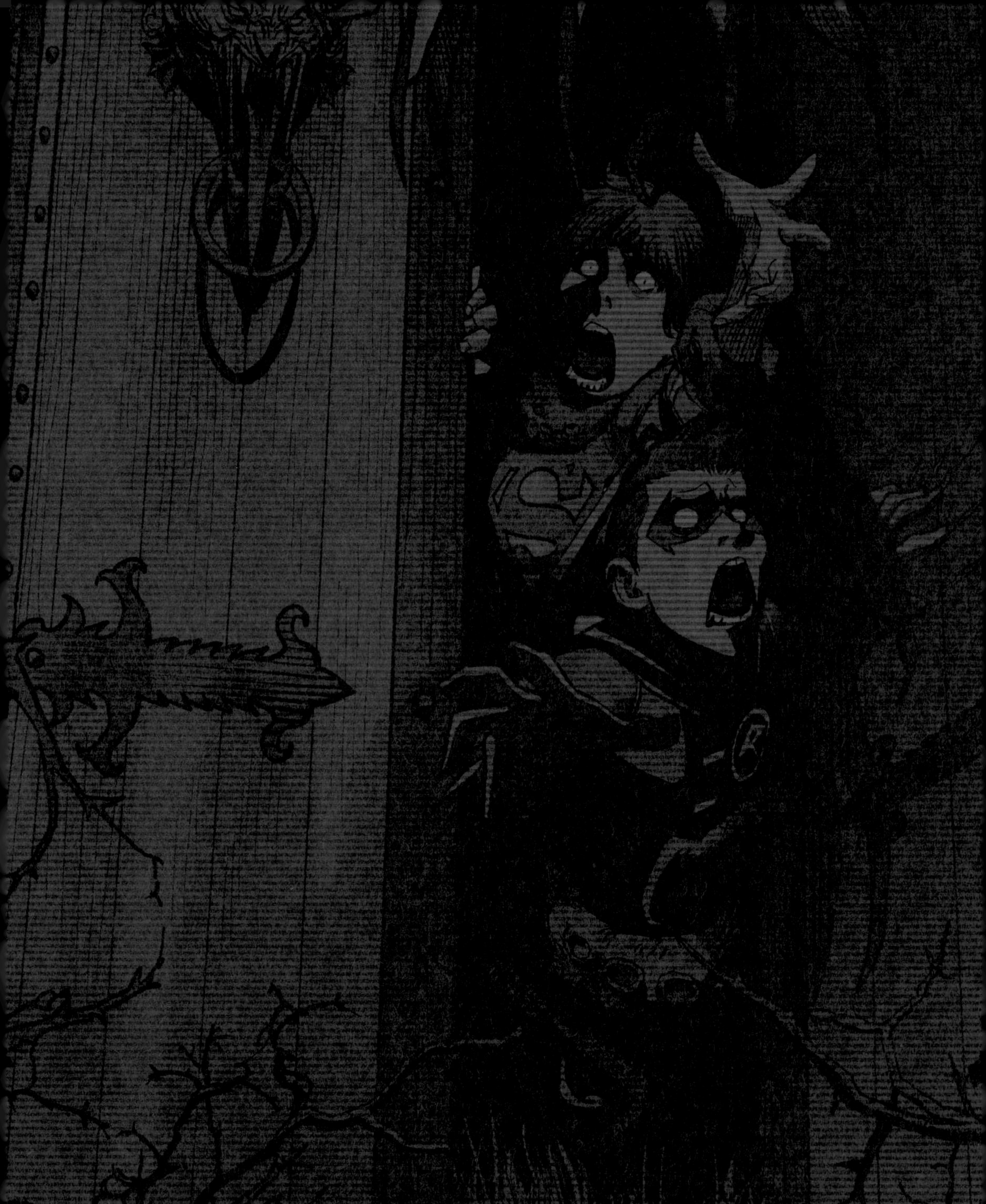

ADVENTURES OF THE SUPER SONS
#4

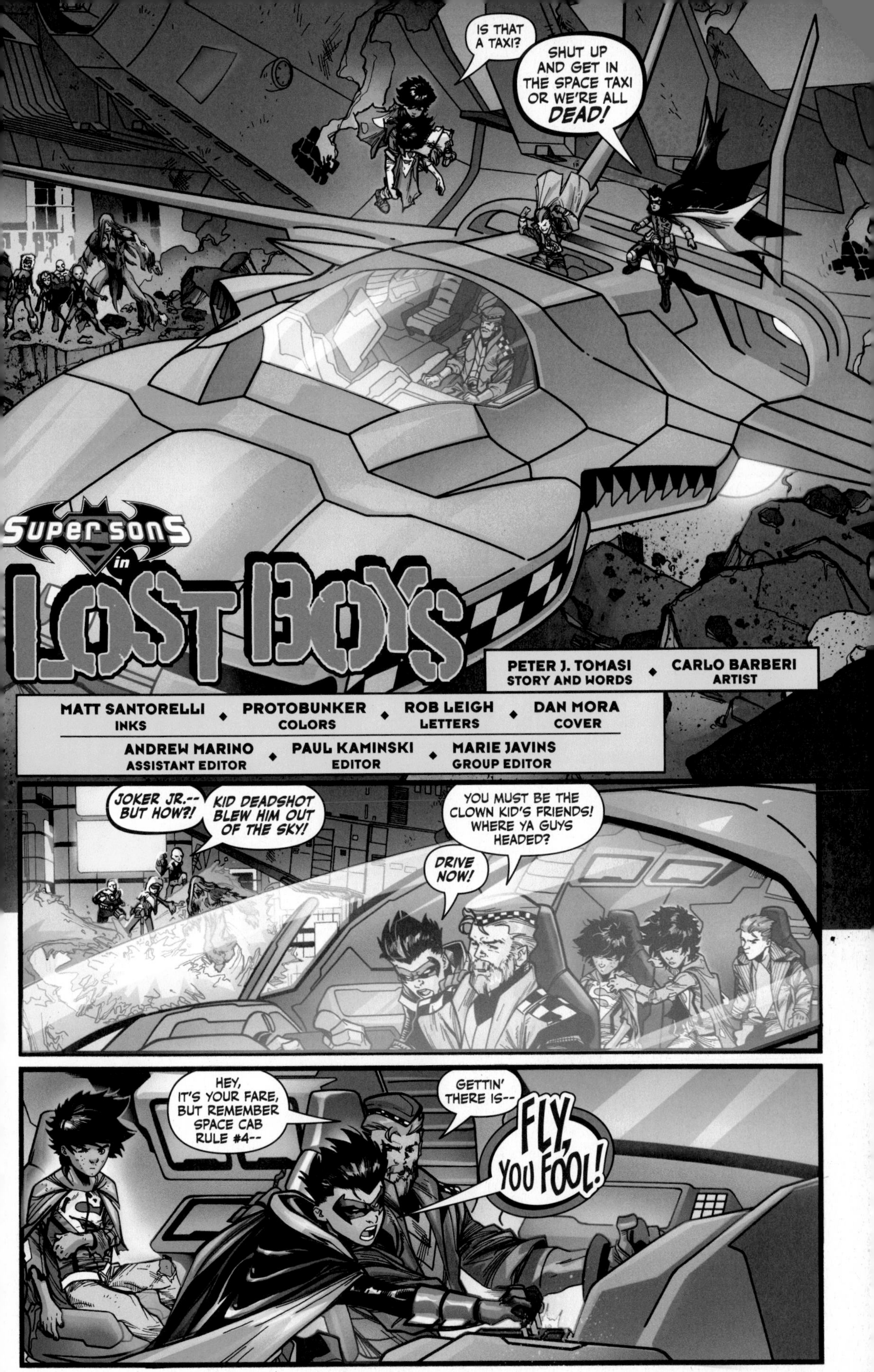
IS THAT A TAXI?
SHUT UP AND GET IN THE SPACE TAXI OR WE'RE ALL DEAD!
Super Sons in
LOST BOYS
PETER J. TOMASI STORY AND WORDS
CARLO BARBERI ARTIST
MATT SANTORELLI INKS
PROTOBUNKER COLORS
ROB LEIGH LETTERS
DAN MORA COVER
ANDREW MARINO ASSISTANT EDITOR
PAUL KAMINSKI EDITOR
MARIE JAVINS GROUP EDITOR
JOKER JR.-- BUT HOW?!
KID DEADSHOT BLEW HIM OUT OF THE SKY!
YOU MUST BE THE CLOWN KID'S FRIENDS! WHERE YA GUYS HEADED?
DRIVE NOW!
HEY, IT'S YOUR FARE, BUT REMEMBER SPACE CAB RULE #4--
GETTIN' THERE IS--
FLY, YOU FOOL!

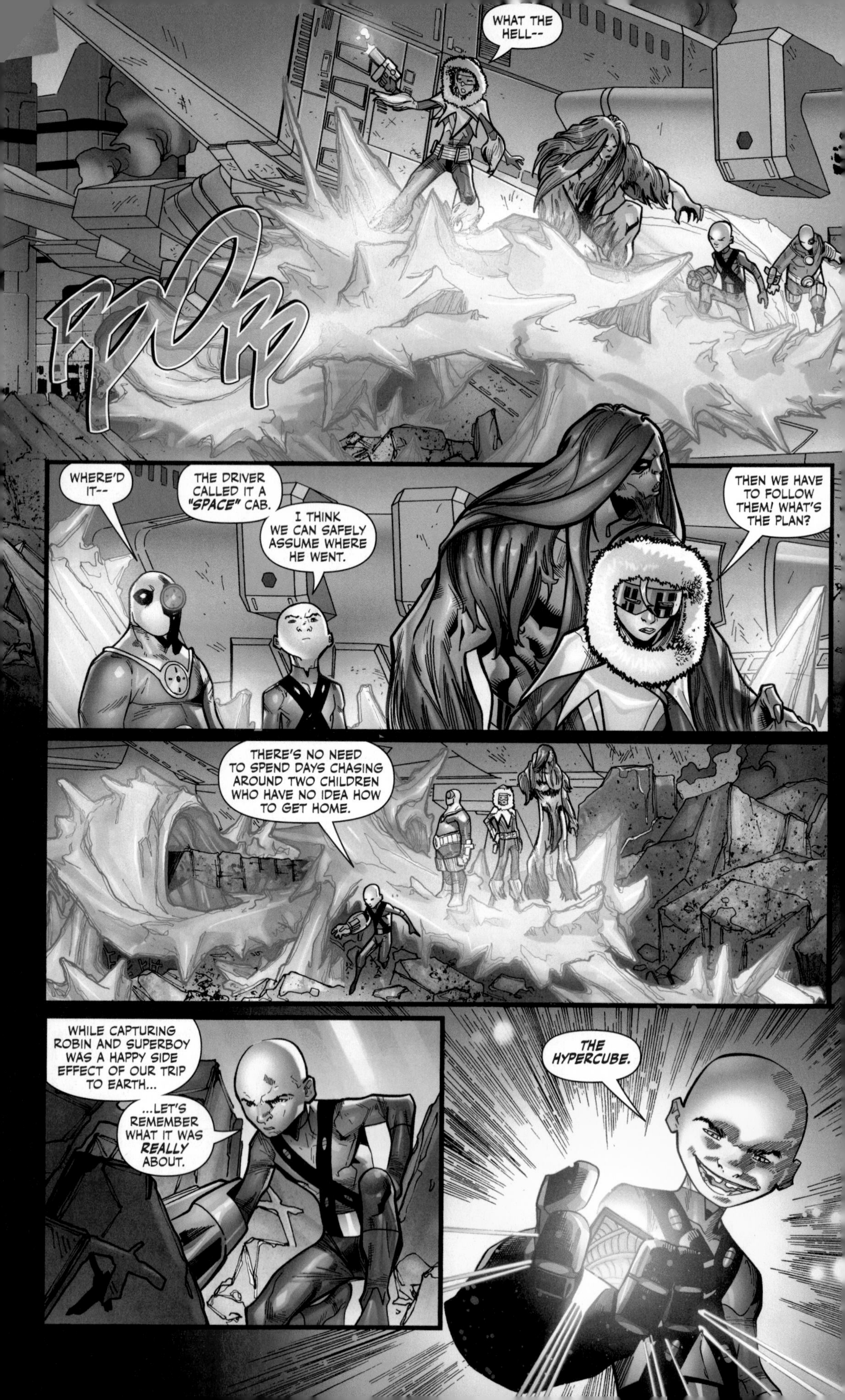

WHAT THE HELL--
BLOOP
WHERE'D IT--
THE DRIVER CALLED IT A "SPACE" CAB.
I THINK WE CAN SAFELY ASSUME WHERE HE WENT.
THEN WE HAVE TO FOLLOW THEM! WHAT'S THE PLAN?
THERE'S NO NEED TO SPEND DAYS CHASING AROUND TWO CHILDREN WHO HAVE NO IDEA HOW TO GET HOME.
WHILE CAPTURING ROBIN AND SUPERBOY WAS A HAPPY SIDE EFFECT OF OUR TRIP TO EARTH...
...LET'S REMEMBER WHAT IT WAS REALLY ABOUT.
THE HYPERCUBE.

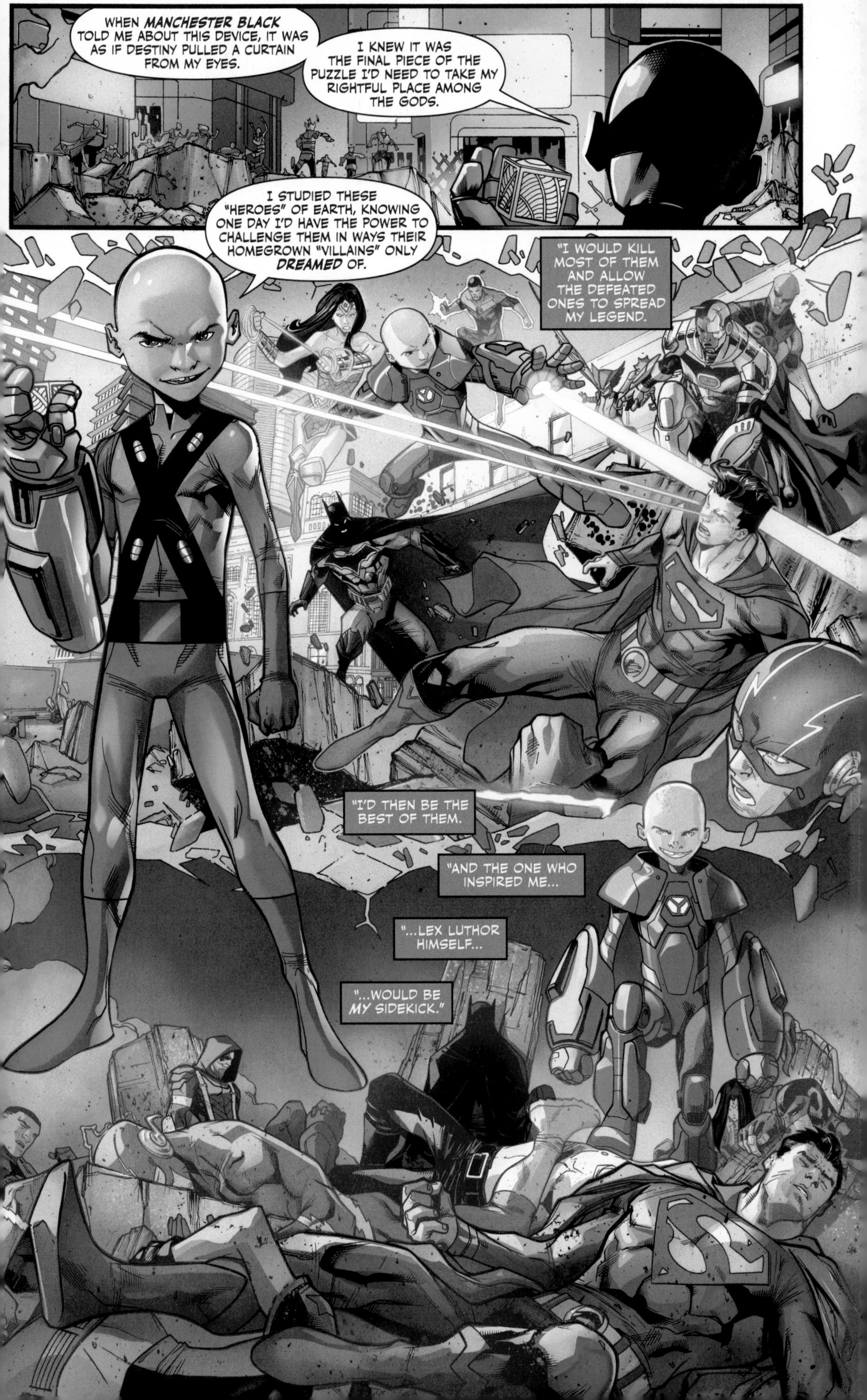

WHEN MANCHESTER BLACK TOLD ME ABOUT THIS DEVICE, IT WAS AS IF DESTINY PULLED A CURTAIN FROM MY EYES.
I KNEW IT WAS THE FINAL PIECE OF THE PUZZLE I'D NEED TO TAKE MY RIGHTFUL PLACE AMONG THE GODS.
I STUDIED THESE "HEROES" OF EARTH, KNOWING ONE DAY I'D HAVE THE POWER TO CHALLENGE THEM IN WAYS THEIR HOMEGROWN "VILLAINS" ONLY DREAMED OF.
"I WOULD KILL MOST OF THEM AND ALLOW THE DEFEATED ONES TO SPREAD MY LEGEND.
"I'D THEN BE THE BEST OF THEM.
"AND THE ONE WHO INSPIRED ME...
"...LEX LUTHOR HIMSELF...
"...WOULD BE MY SIDEKICK."

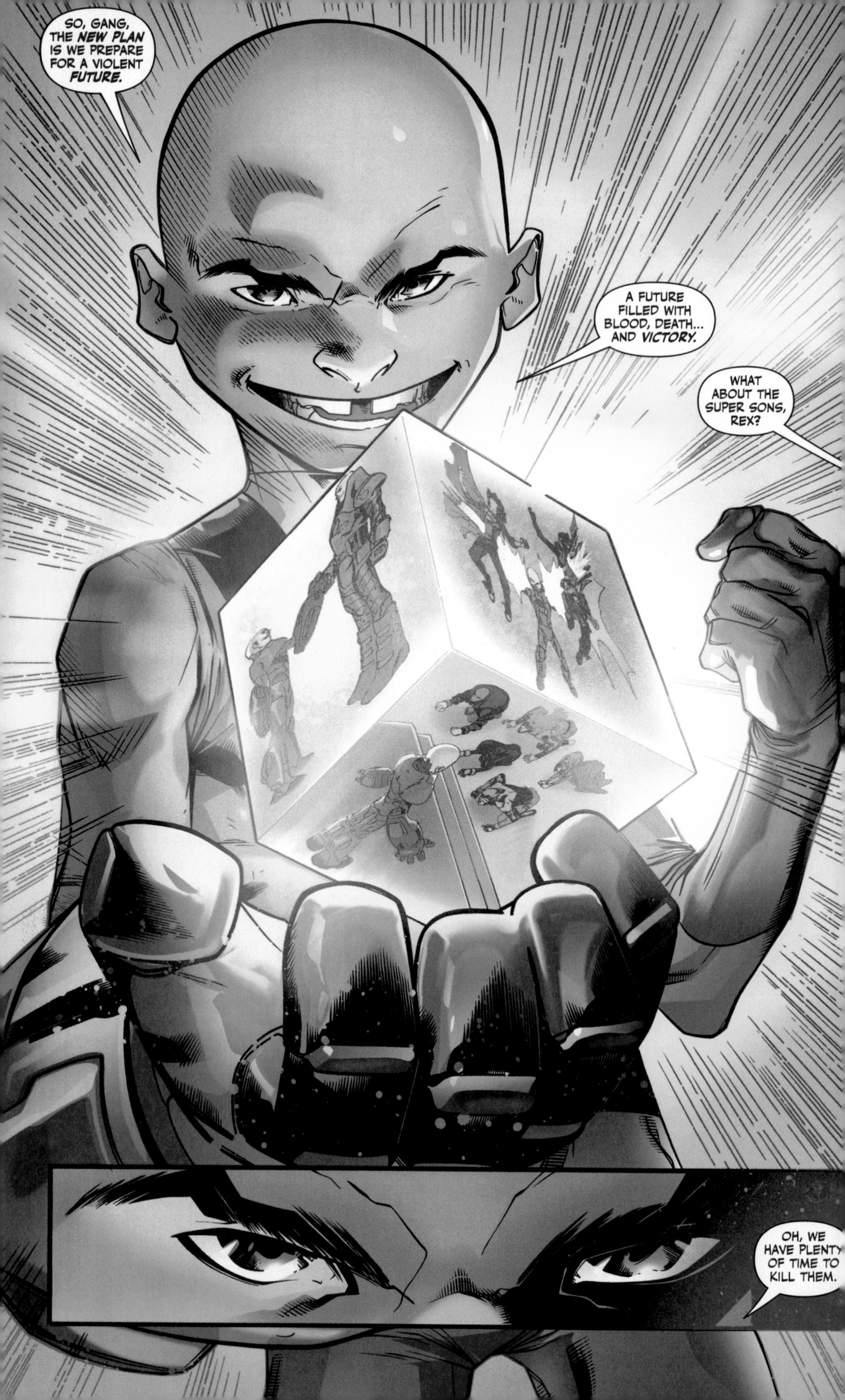
SO, GANG, THE *NEW PLAN* IS WE PREPARE FOR A VIOLENT *FUTURE.*
A FUTURE FILLED WITH BLOOD, DEATH... AND *VICTORY.*
WHAT ABOUT THE SUPER SONS, REX?
OH, WE HAVE PLENTY OF TIME TO KILL THEM.

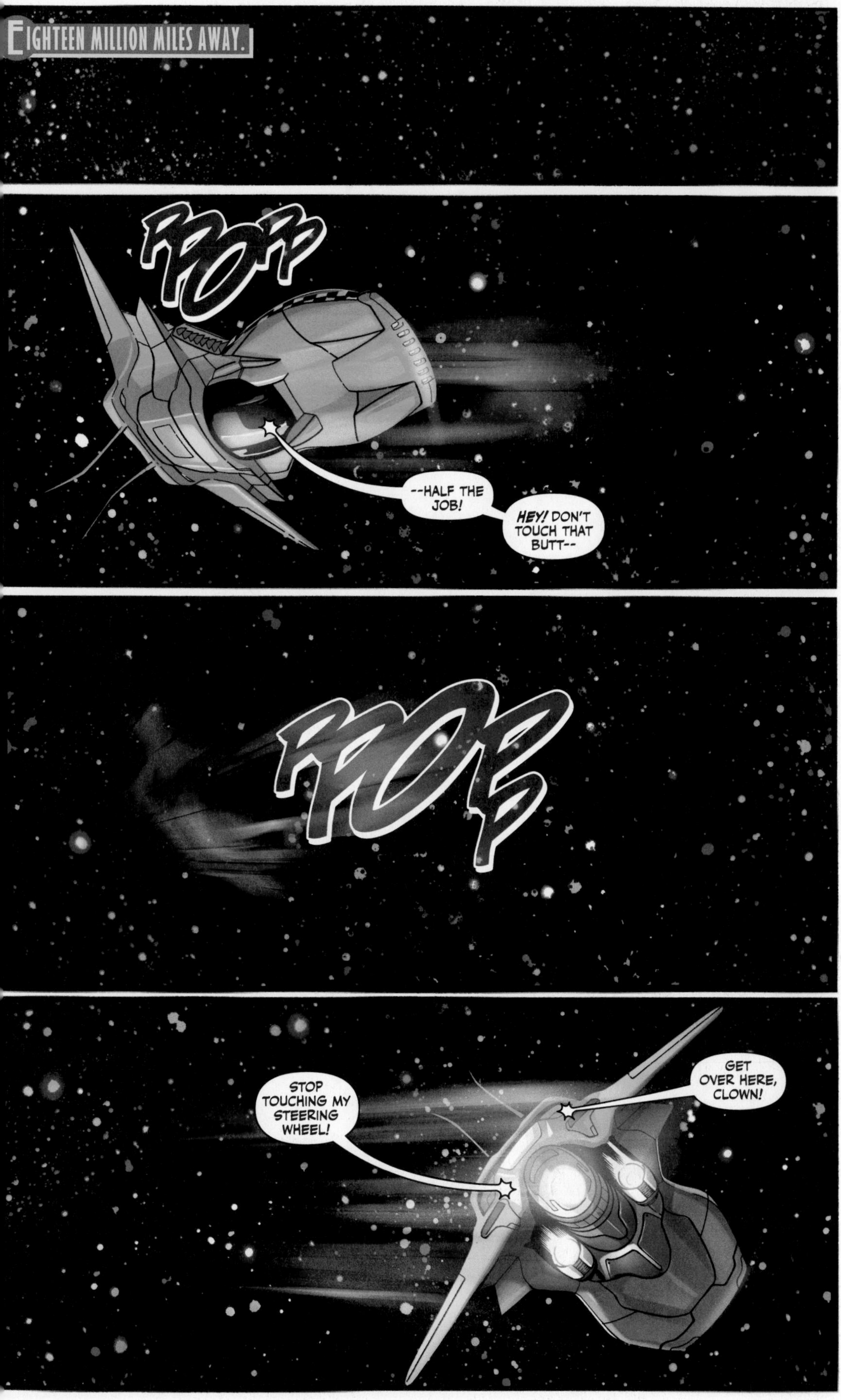
EIGHTEEN MILLION MILES AWAY.
POOP
--HALF THE JOB!
HEY! DON'T TOUCH THAT BUTT--
POOP
STOP TOUCHING MY STEERING WHEEL!
GET OVER HERE, CLOWN!

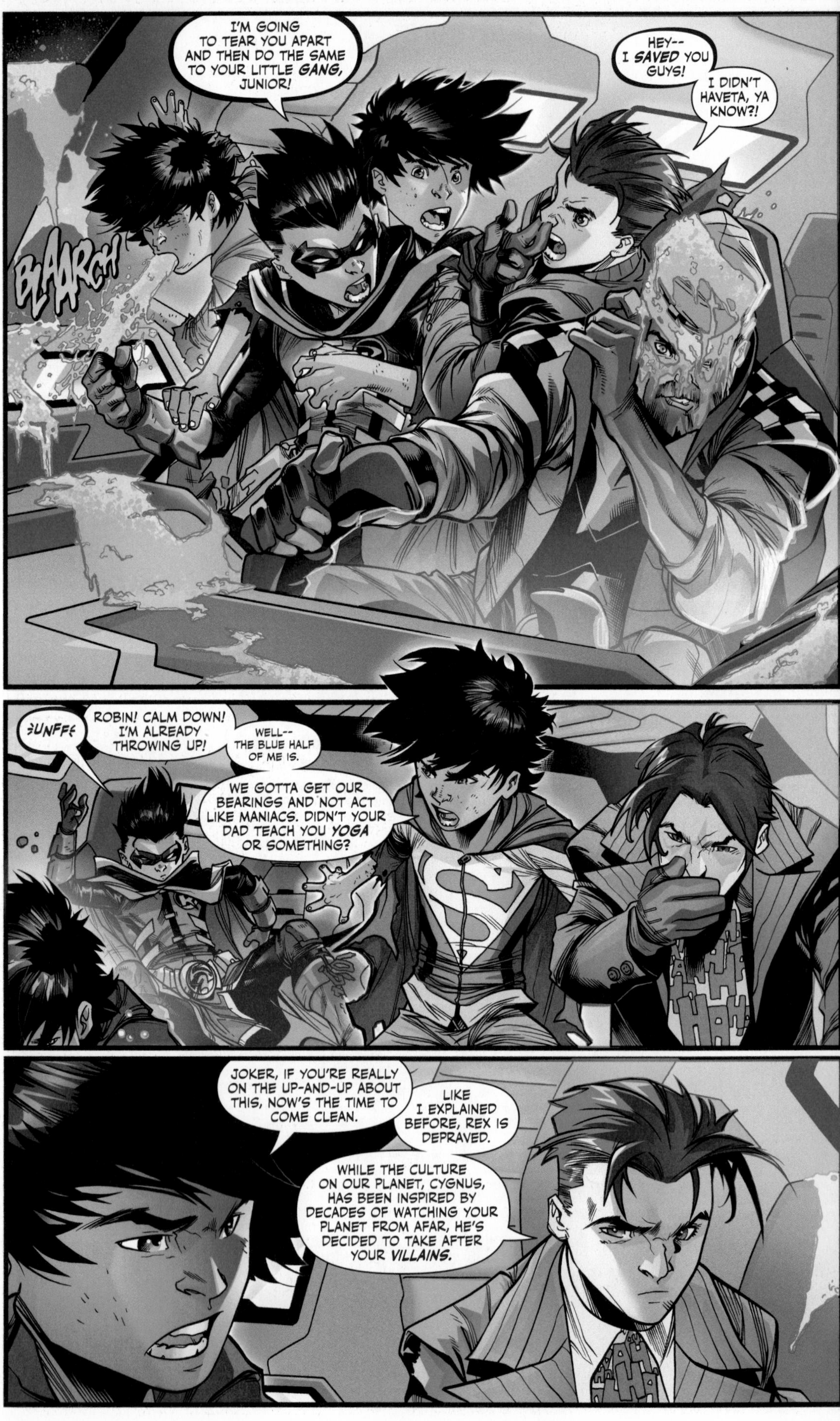
I'M GOING TO TEAR YOU APART AND THEN DO THE SAME TO YOUR LITTLE GANG, JUNIOR!
HEY-- I SAVED YOU GUYS!
I DIDN'T HAVETA, YA KNOW?!
BLAARCH
UNFF
ROBIN! CALM DOWN! I'M ALREADY THROWING UP!
WELL-- THE BLUE HALF OF ME IS.
WE GOTTA GET OUR BEARINGS AND NOT ACT LIKE MANIACS. DIDN'T YOUR DAD TEACH YOU YOGA OR SOMETHING?
JOKER, IF YOU'RE REALLY ON THE UP-AND-UP ABOUT THIS, NOW'S THE TIME TO COME CLEAN.
LIKE I EXPLAINED BEFORE, REX IS DEPRAVED.
WHILE THE CULTURE ON OUR PLANET, CYGNUS, HAS BEEN INSPIRED BY DECADES OF WATCHING YOUR PLANET FROM AFAR, HE'S DECIDED TO TAKE AFTER YOUR VILLAINS.

HE RECRUITED ALL OF US. CHANGED US. GAVE US ALL TWISTED HISTORIES...

...AND SOMEWHERE ALONG THE WAY MET SOME OF THE *REAL* POWERS OF THE UNIVERSE. THAT'S WHAT LED HIM TO THE HYPERCUBE'S LOCATION ON YOUR PLANET.

BUT I DIDN'T WANT ANY OF IT. I NEVER DID. I JUST WANT *OUT*.

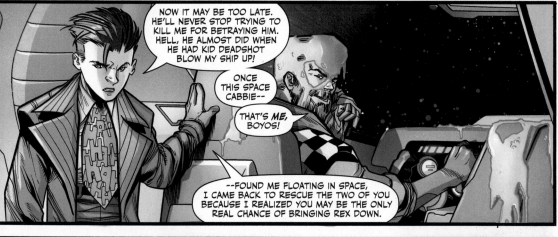

NOW IT MAY BE TOO LATE. HE'LL NEVER STOP TRYING TO KILL ME FOR BETRAYING HIM. HELL, HE ALMOST DID WHEN HE HAD KID DEADSHOT BLOW MY SHIP UP!

ONCE THIS SPACE CABBIE--

THAT'S *ME*, BOYOS!

--FOUND ME FLOATING IN SPACE, I CAME BACK TO RESCUE THE TWO OF YOU BECAUSE I REALIZED YOU MAY BE THE ONLY REAL CHANCE OF BRINGING REX DOWN.

THAT WOULD HAVE BEEN A GREAT IDEA BEFORE MY *FRIEND WAS SPLIT IN TWO!*

CAN'T YOU BUILD ANOTHER OF THOSE KRYPTONITE DEVICES AND PUT ME BACK THE WAY I WAS?

THAT'S WAY BEYOND ME.

REX PROBABLY COULD.

HE'S THE GENIUS.

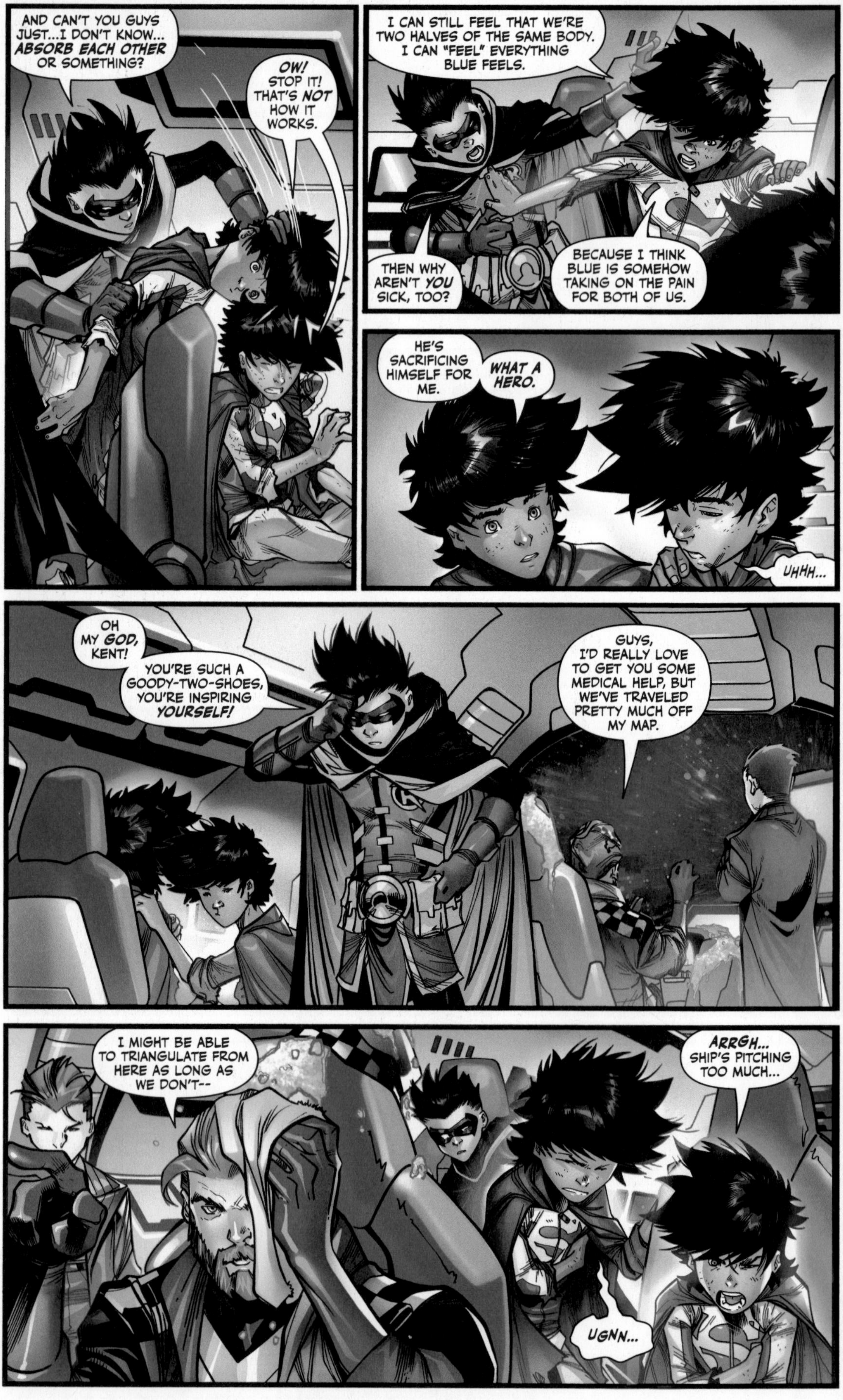
AND CAN'T YOU GUYS JUST...I DON'T KNOW... ABSORB EACH OTHER OR SOMETHING?
OW! STOP IT! THAT'S NOT HOW IT WORKS.
I CAN STILL FEEL THAT WE'RE TWO HALVES OF THE SAME BODY. I CAN "FEEL" EVERYTHING BLUE FEELS.
THEN WHY AREN'T YOU SICK, TOO?
BECAUSE I THINK BLUE IS SOMEHOW TAKING ON THE PAIN FOR BOTH OF US.
HE'S SACRIFICING HIMSELF FOR ME.
WHAT A HERO.
UHHH...
OH MY GOD, KENT!
YOU'RE SUCH A GOODY-TWO-SHOES, YOU'RE INSPIRING YOURSELF!
GUYS, I'D REALLY LOVE TO GET YOU SOME MEDICAL HELP, BUT WE'VE TRAVELED PRETTY MUCH OFF MY MAP.
I MIGHT BE ABLE TO TRIANGULATE FROM HERE AS LONG AS WE DON'T--
ARRGH... SHIP'S PITCHING TOO MUCH...
UGNN...

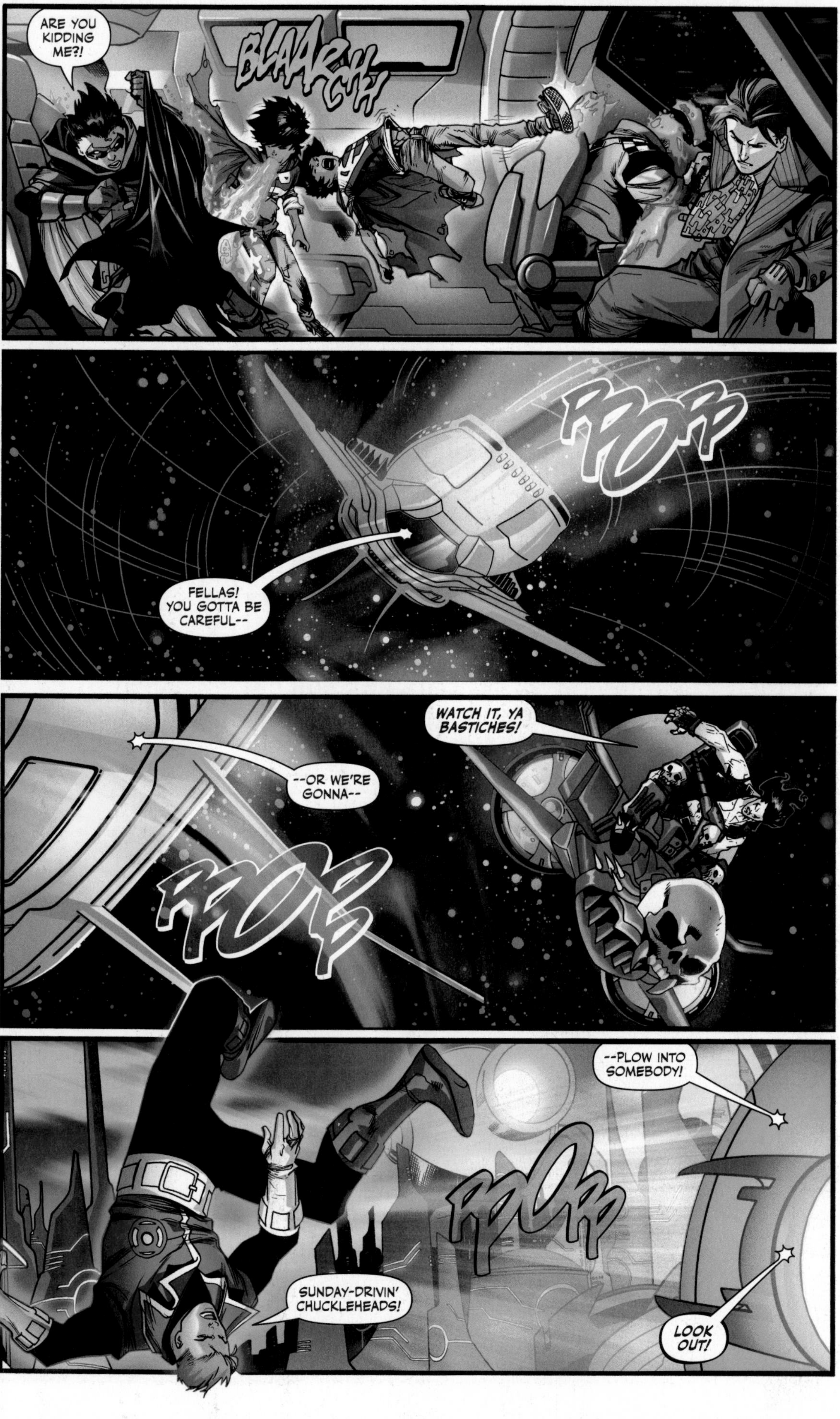
ARE YOU KIDDING ME?!
BLAARCHH
FELLAS! YOU GOTTA BE CAREFUL--
WATCH IT, YA BASTICHES!
--OR WE'RE GONNA--
--PLOW INTO SOMEBODY!
SUNDAY-DRIVIN' CHUCKLEHEADS!
LOOK OUT!

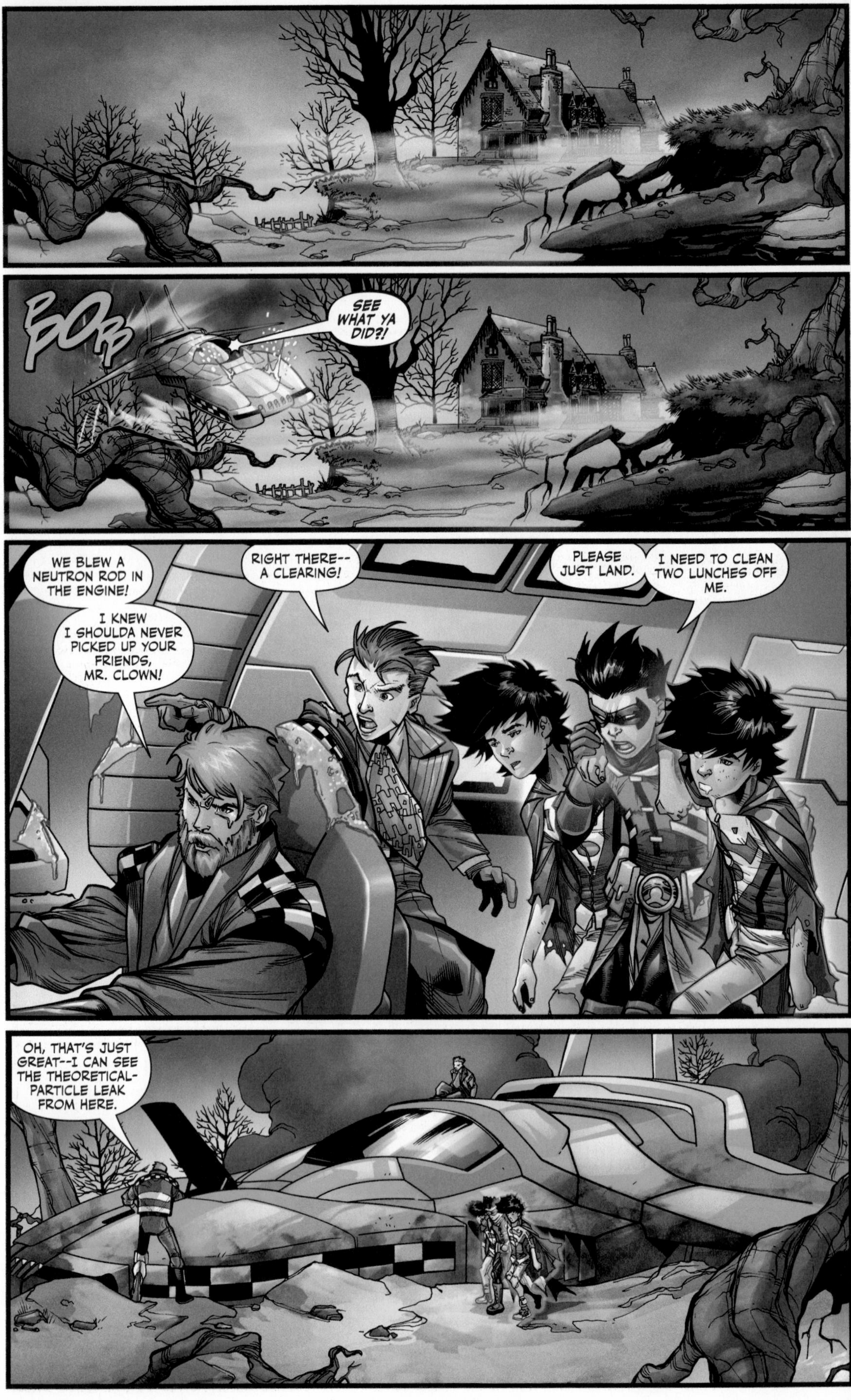
BOOM
SEE WHAT YA DID?!
WE BLEW A NEUTRON ROD IN THE ENGINE!
I KNEW I SHOULDA NEVER PICKED UP YOUR FRIENDS, MR. CLOWN!
RIGHT THERE-- A CLEARING!
PLEASE JUST LAND.
I NEED TO CLEAN TWO LUNCHES OFF ME.
OH, THAT'S JUST GREAT--I CAN SEE THE THEORETICAL-PARTICLE LEAK FROM HERE.

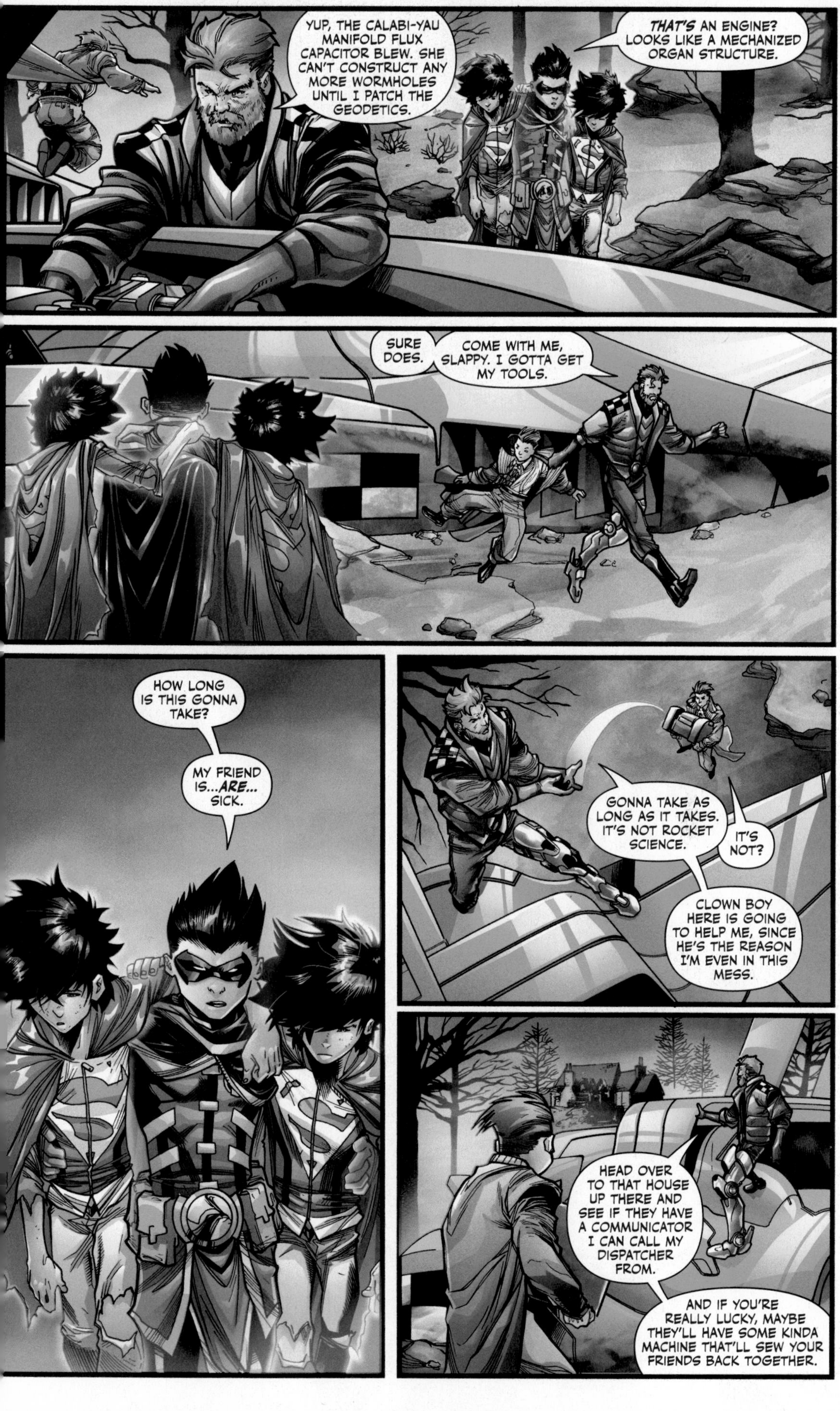
YUP, THE CALABI-YAU MANIFOLD FLUX CAPACITOR BLEW. SHE CAN'T CONSTRUCT ANY MORE WORMHOLES UNTIL I PATCH THE GEODETICS.
THAT'S AN ENGINE? LOOKS LIKE A MECHANIZED ORGAN STRUCTURE.
SURE DOES.
COME WITH ME, SLAPPY. I GOTTA GET MY TOOLS.
HOW LONG IS THIS GONNA TAKE?
MY FRIEND IS...ARE... SICK.
GONNA TAKE AS LONG AS IT TAKES. IT'S NOT ROCKET SCIENCE.
IT'S NOT?
CLOWN BOY HERE IS GOING TO HELP ME, SINCE HE'S THE REASON I'M EVEN IN THIS MESS.
HEAD OVER TO THAT HOUSE UP THERE AND SEE IF THEY HAVE A COMMUNICATOR I CAN CALL MY DISPATCHER FROM.
AND IF YOU'RE REALLY LUCKY, MAYBE THEY'LL HAVE SOME KINDA MACHINE THAT'LL SEW YOUR FRIENDS BACK TOGETHER.

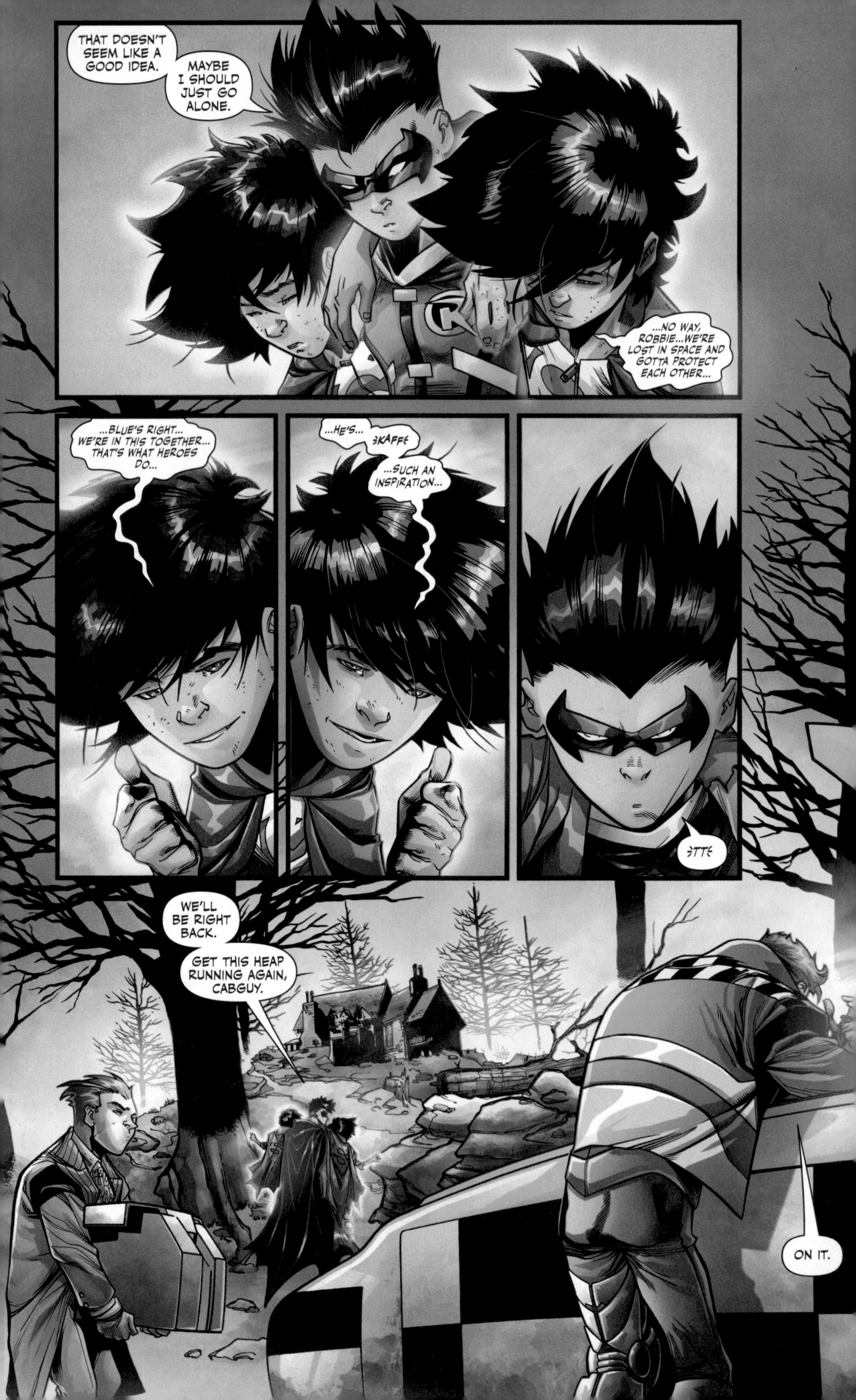
THAT DOESN'T SEEM LIKE A GOOD IDEA.
MAYBE I SHOULD JUST GO ALONE.
...NO WAY, ROBBIE...WE'RE LOST IN SPACE AND GOTTA PROTECT EACH OTHER...
...BLUE'S RIGHT... WE'RE IN THIS TOGETHER... THAT'S WHAT HEROES DO...
...HE'S...
KAFF
...SUCH AN INSPIRATION...
TT
WE'LL BE RIGHT BACK.
GET THIS HEAP RUNNING AGAIN, CABGUY.
ON IT.

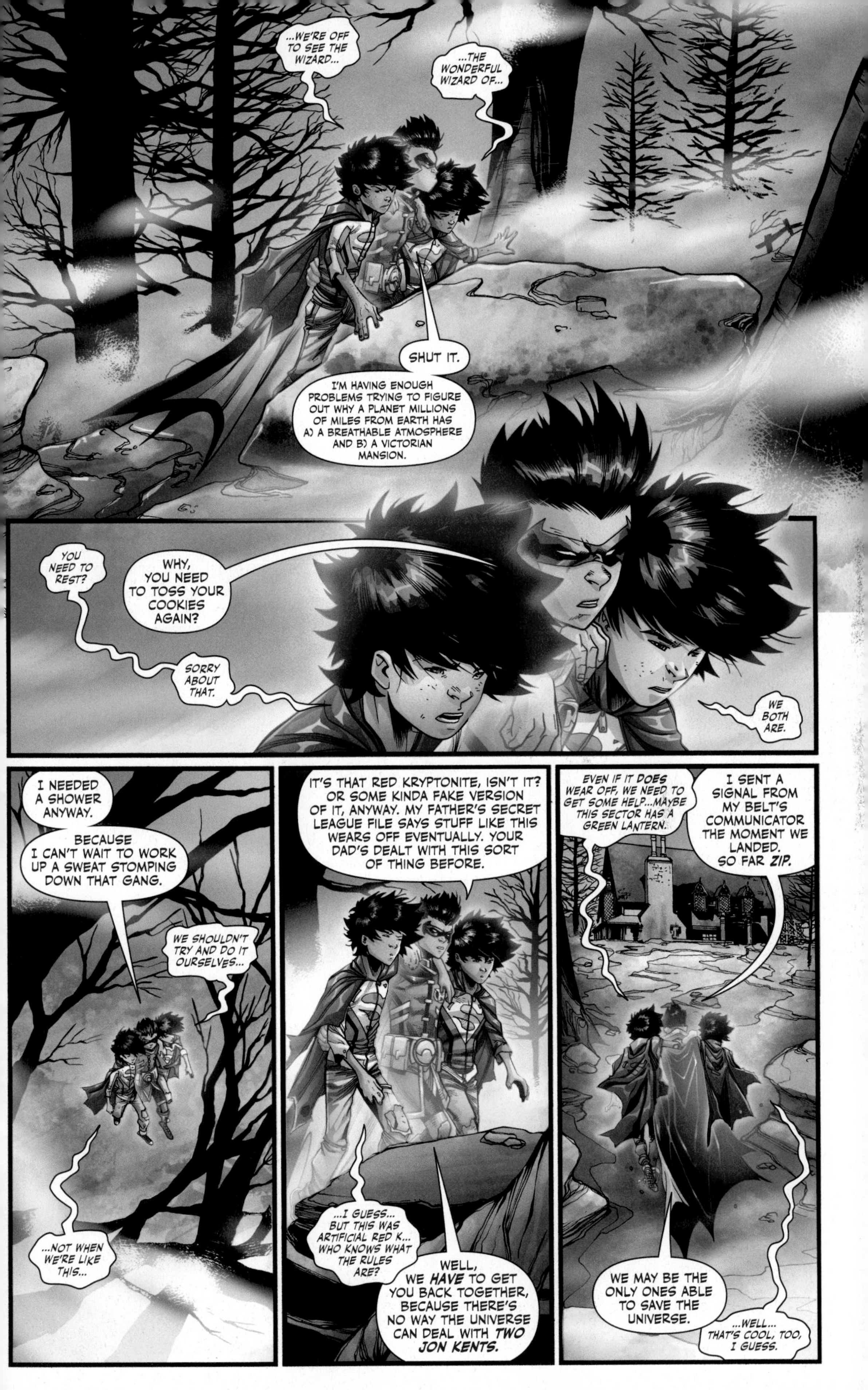
...WE'RE OFF TO SEE THE WIZARD...
...THE WONDERFUL WIZARD OF...
SHUT IT.
I'M HAVING ENOUGH PROBLEMS TRYING TO FIGURE OUT WHY A PLANET MILLIONS OF MILES FROM EARTH HAS A) A BREATHABLE ATMOSPHERE AND B) A VICTORIAN MANSION.
YOU NEED TO REST?
WHY, YOU NEED TO TOSS YOUR COOKIES AGAIN?
SORRY ABOUT THAT.
WE BOTH ARE.
I NEEDED A SHOWER ANYWAY.
BECAUSE I CAN'T WAIT TO WORK UP A SWEAT STOMPING DOWN THAT GANG.
WE SHOULDN'T TRY AND DO IT OURSELVES...
...NOT WHEN WE'RE LIKE THIS...
IT'S THAT RED KRYPTONITE, ISN'T IT? OR SOME KINDA FAKE VERSION OF IT, ANYWAY. MY FATHER'S SECRET LEAGUE FILE SAYS STUFF LIKE THIS WEARS OFF EVENTUALLY. YOUR DAD'S DEALT WITH THIS SORT OF THING BEFORE.
...I GUESS... BUT THIS WAS ARTIFICIAL RED K... WHO KNOWS WHAT THE RULES ARE?
WELL, WE HAVE TO GET YOU BACK TOGETHER, BECAUSE THERE'S NO WAY THE UNIVERSE CAN DEAL WITH TWO JON KENTS.
EVEN IF IT DOES WEAR OFF, WE NEED TO GET SOME HELP...MAYBE THIS SECTOR HAS A GREEN LANTERN.
I SENT A SIGNAL FROM MY BELT'S COMMUNICATOR THE MOMENT WE LANDED. SO FAR ZIP.
WE MAY BE THE ONLY ONES ABLE TO SAVE THE UNIVERSE.
...WELL... THAT'S COOL, TOO, I GUESS.

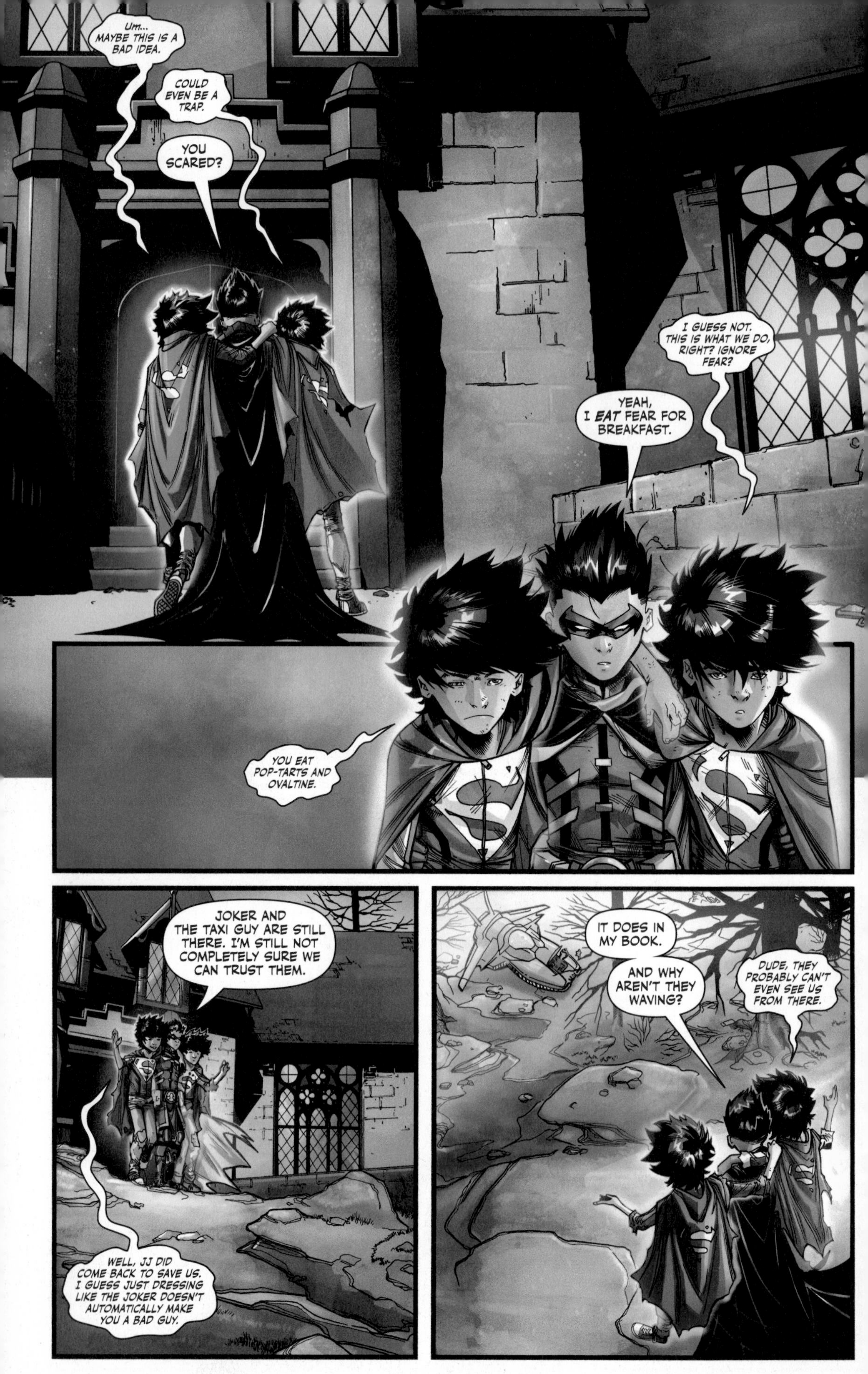
Um... MAYBE THIS IS A BAD IDEA.
COULD EVEN BE A TRAP.
YOU SCARED?
I GUESS NOT. THIS IS WHAT WE DO, RIGHT? IGNORE FEAR?
YEAH, I EAT FEAR FOR BREAKFAST.
YOU EAT POP-TARTS AND OVALTINE.
JOKER AND THE TAXI GUY ARE STILL THERE. I'M STILL NOT COMPLETELY SURE WE CAN TRUST THEM.
WELL, JJ DID COME BACK TO SAVE US. I GUESS JUST DRESSING LIKE THE JOKER DOESN'T AUTOMATICALLY MAKE YOU A BAD GUY.
IT DOES IN MY BOOK.
AND WHY AREN'T THEY WAVING?
DUDE, THEY PROBABLY CAN'T EVEN SEE US FROM THERE.

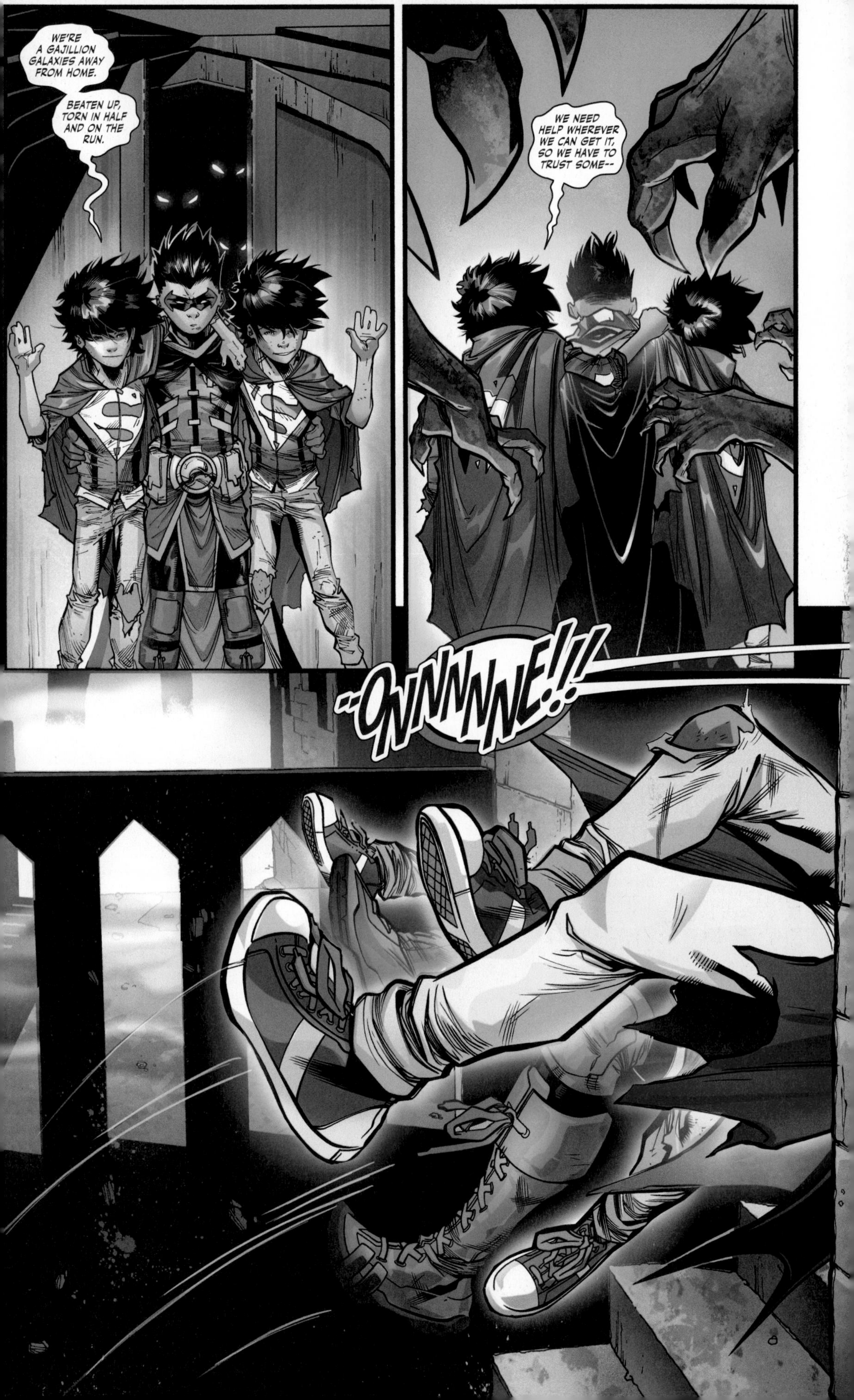
WE'RE A GAJILLION GALAXIES AWAY FROM HOME.
BEATEN UP, TORN IN HALF AND ON THE RUN.
WE NEED HELP WHEREVER WE CAN GET IT, SO WE HAVE TO TRUST SOME--
--ONNNNNE!!!

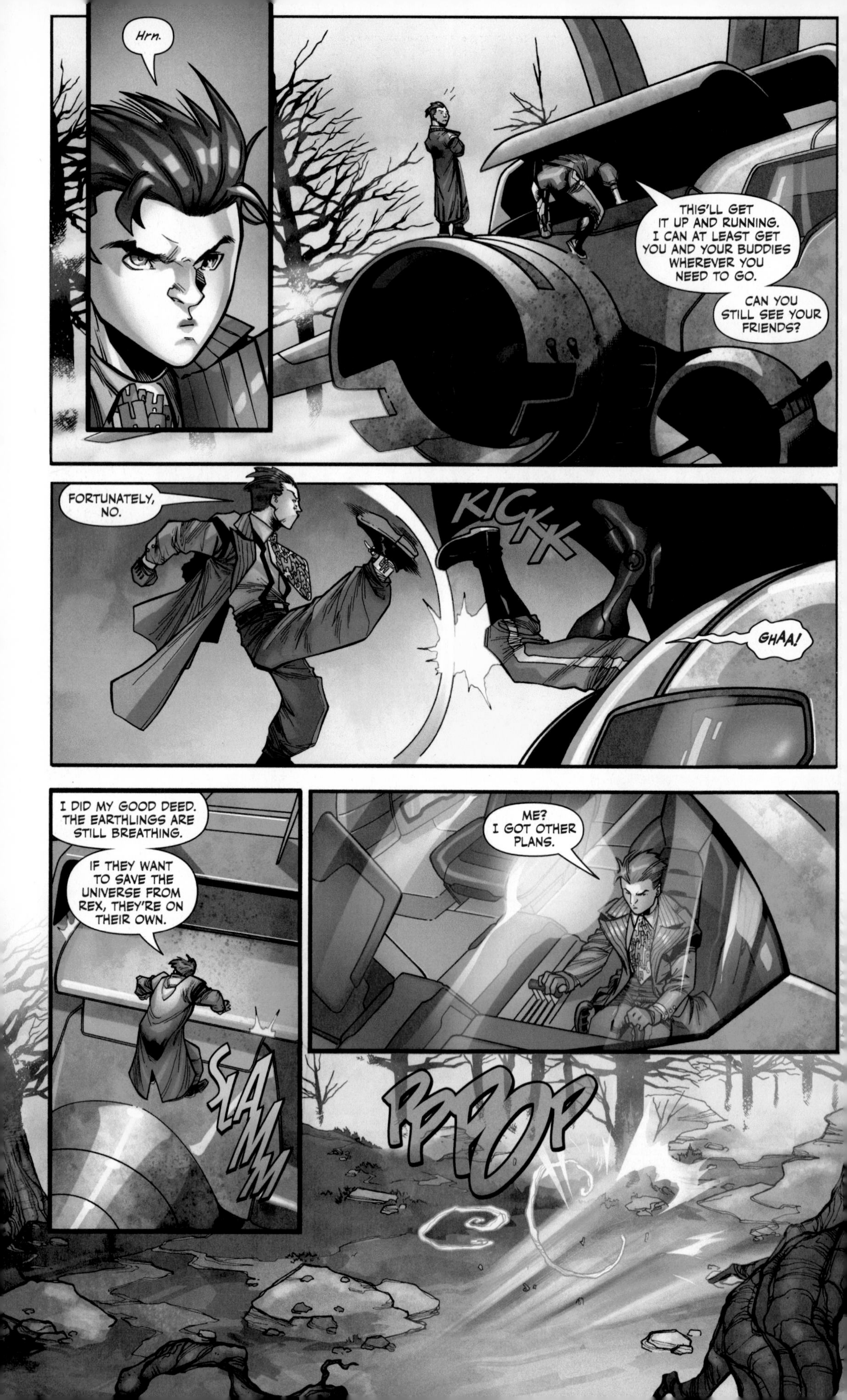
Hrn.
THIS'LL GET IT UP AND RUNNING. I CAN AT LEAST GET YOU AND YOUR BUDDIES WHEREVER YOU NEED TO GO.
CAN YOU STILL SEE YOUR FRIENDS?
FORTUNATELY, NO.
KICKK
GHAA!
I DID MY GOOD DEED. THE EARTHLINGS ARE STILL BREATHING.
IF THEY WANT TO SAVE THE UNIVERSE FROM REX, THEY'RE ON THEIR OWN.
SLAMM
ME? I GOT OTHER PLANS.
BOOOP

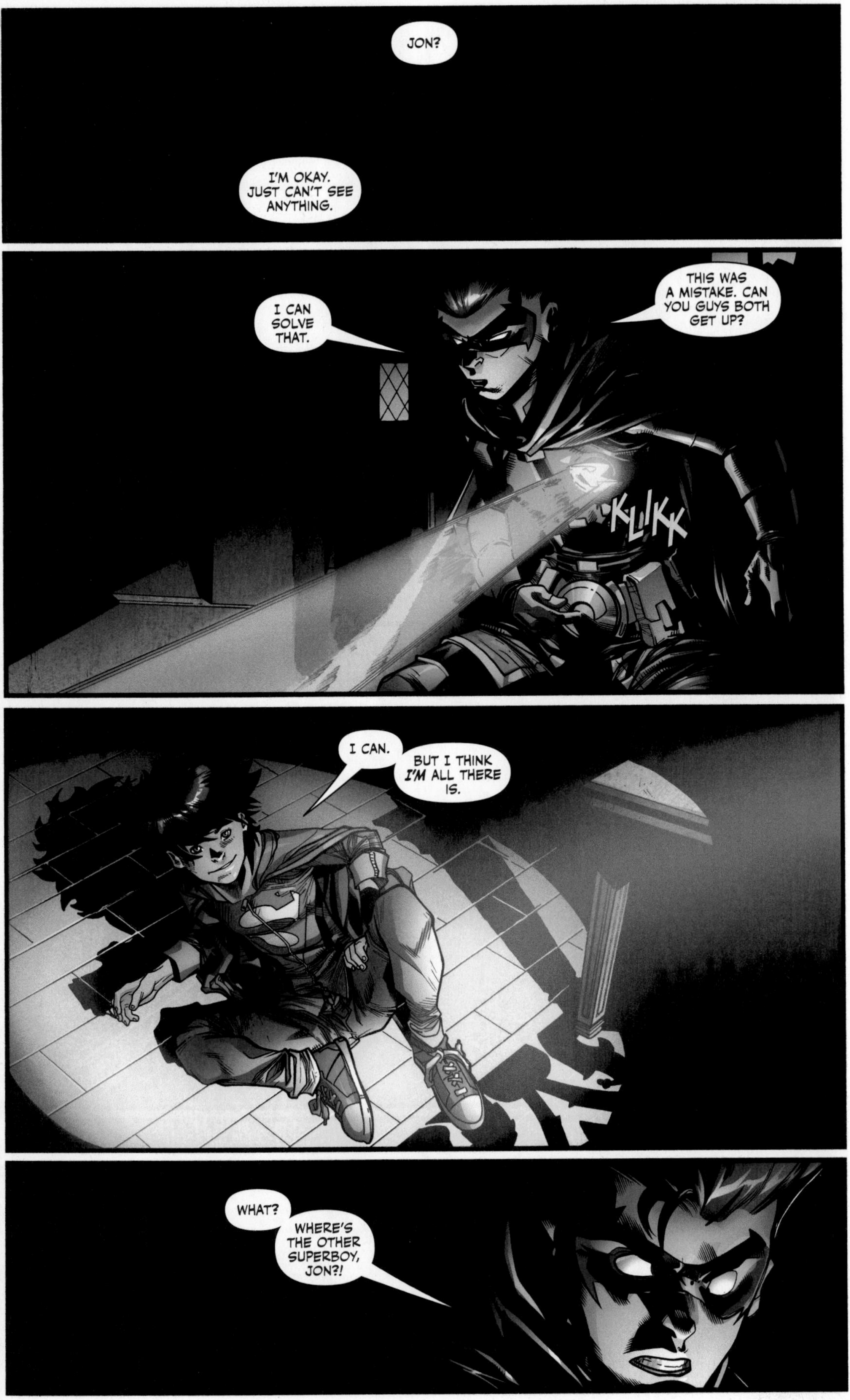
JON?
I'M OKAY. JUST CAN'T SEE ANYTHING.
THIS WAS A MISTAKE. CAN YOU GUYS BOTH GET UP?
I CAN SOLVE THAT.
KLIKK
I CAN.
BUT I THINK I'M ALL THERE IS.
WHAT?
WHERE'S THE OTHER SUPERBOY, JON?!

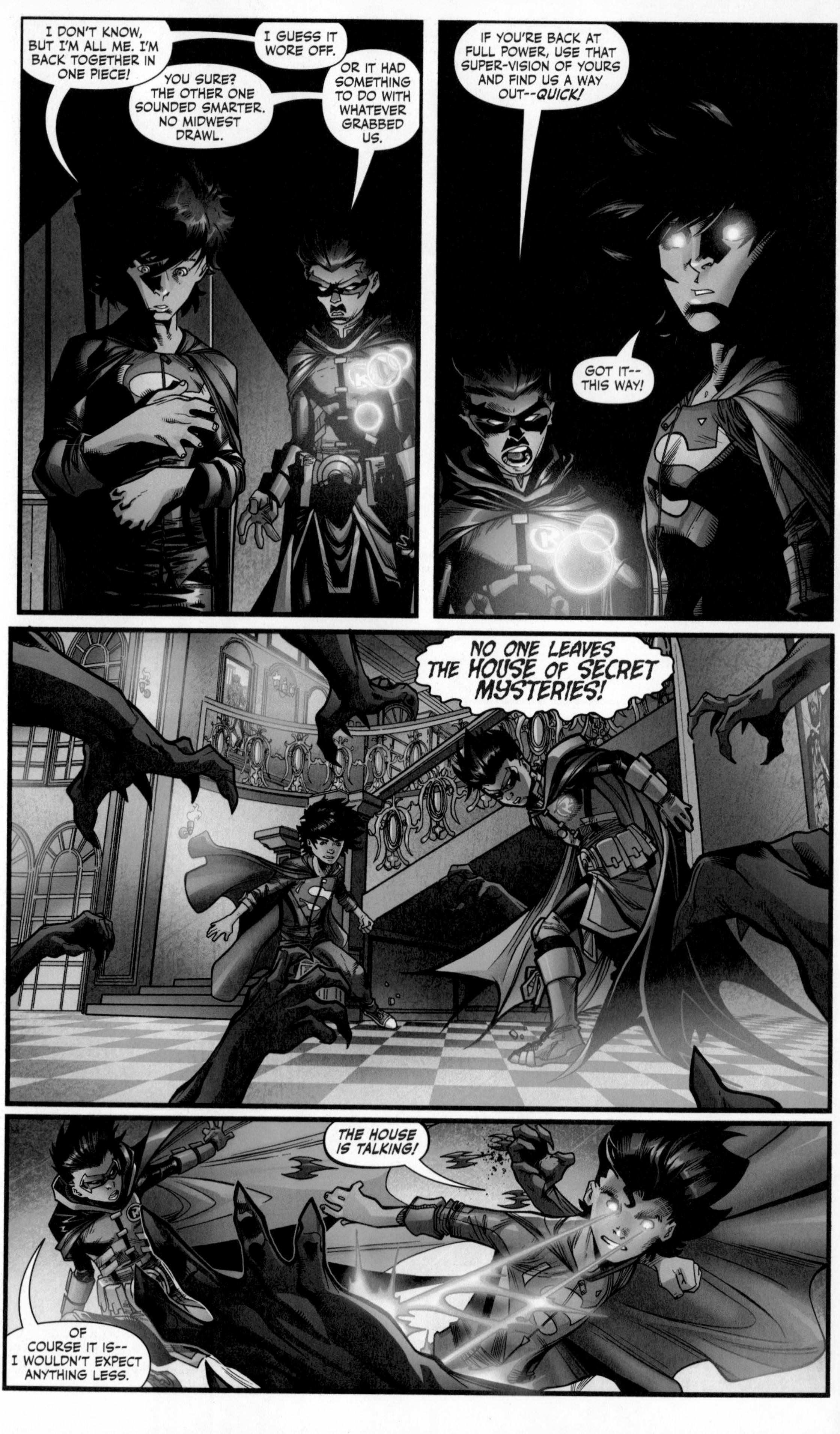
I DON'T KNOW, BUT I'M ALL ME. I'M BACK TOGETHER IN ONE PIECE!
I GUESS IT WORE OFF.
YOU SURE? THE OTHER ONE SOUNDED SMARTER. NO MIDWEST DRAWL.
OR IT HAD SOMETHING TO DO WITH WHATEVER GRABBED US.
IF YOU'RE BACK AT FULL POWER, USE THAT SUPER-VISION OF YOURS AND FIND US A WAY OUT--QUICK!
GOT IT-- THIS WAY!
NO ONE LEAVES THE HOUSE OF SECRET MYSTERIES!
THE HOUSE IS TALKING!
OF COURSE IT IS-- I WOULDN'T EXPECT ANYTHING LESS.

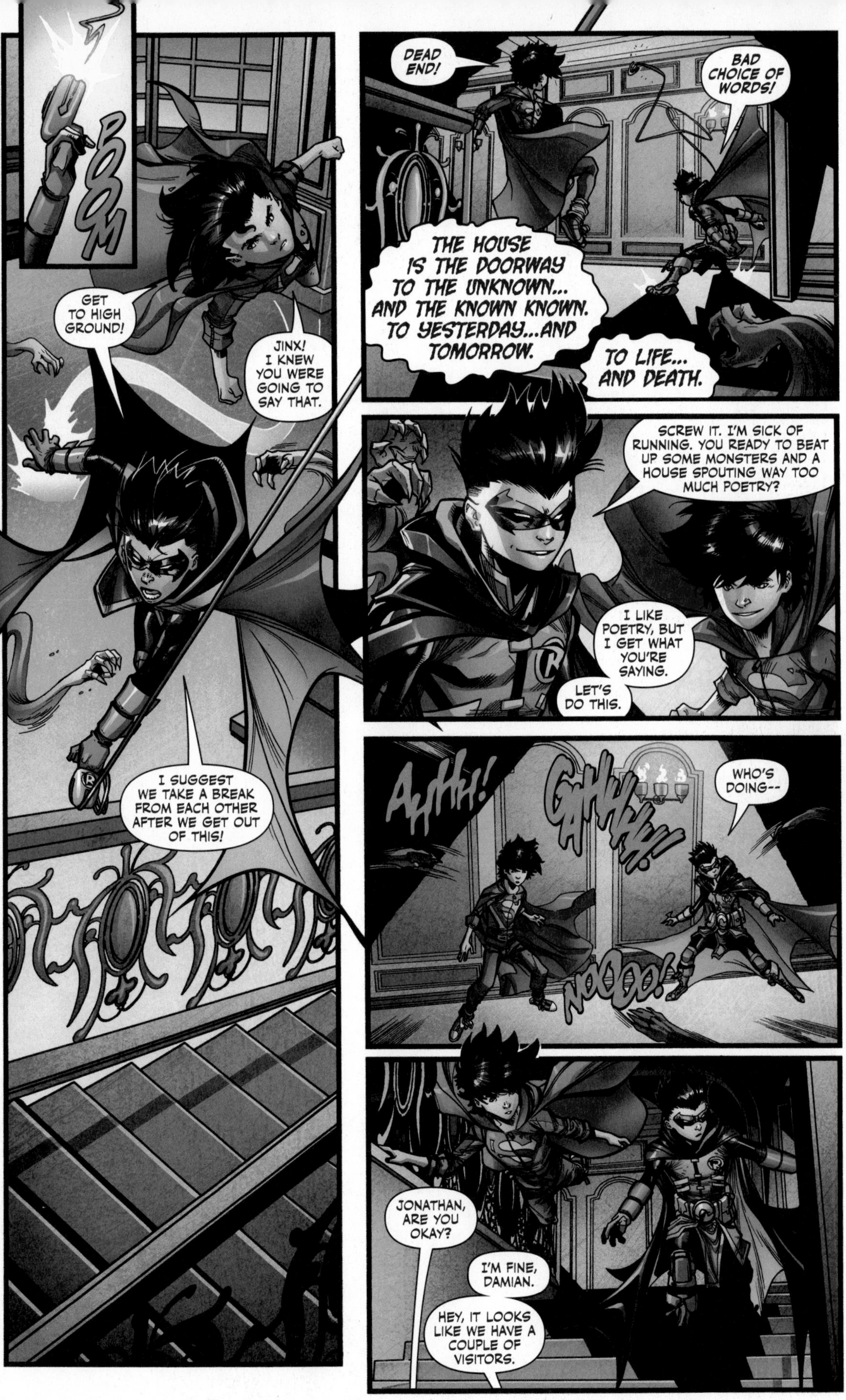
BOOM
GET TO HIGH GROUND!
JINX! I KNEW YOU WERE GOING TO SAY THAT.
I SUGGEST WE TAKE A BREAK FROM EACH OTHER AFTER WE GET OUT OF THIS!
DEAD END!
BAD CHOICE OF WORDS!
THE HOUSE IS THE DOORWAY TO THE UNKNOWN... AND THE KNOWN KNOWN. TO YESTERDAY...AND TOMORROW.
TO LIFE... AND DEATH.
SCREW IT. I'M SICK OF RUNNING. YOU READY TO BEAT UP SOME MONSTERS AND A HOUSE SPOUTING WAY TOO MUCH POETRY?
I LIKE POETRY, BUT I GET WHAT YOU'RE SAYING.
LET'S DO THIS.
AHHH!
GAHHHH!!
WHO'S DOING--
NOOOO!
JONATHAN, ARE YOU OKAY?
I'M FINE, DAMIAN.
HEY, IT LOOKS LIKE WE HAVE A COUPLE OF VISITORS.

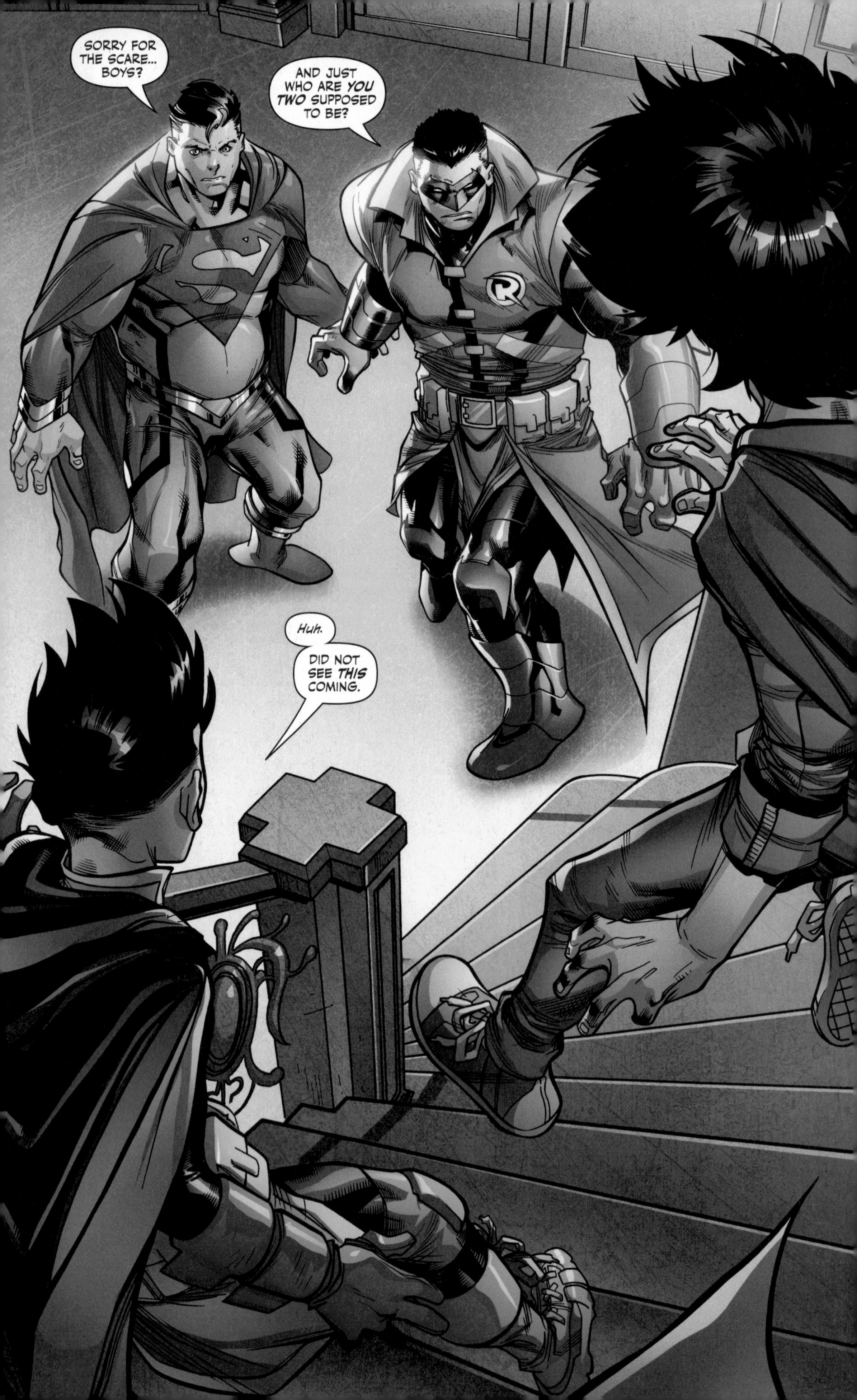

SORRY FOR THE SCARE... BOYS?
AND JUST WHO ARE *YOU TWO* SUPPOSED TO BE?
Huh.
DID NOT SEE *THIS* COMING.

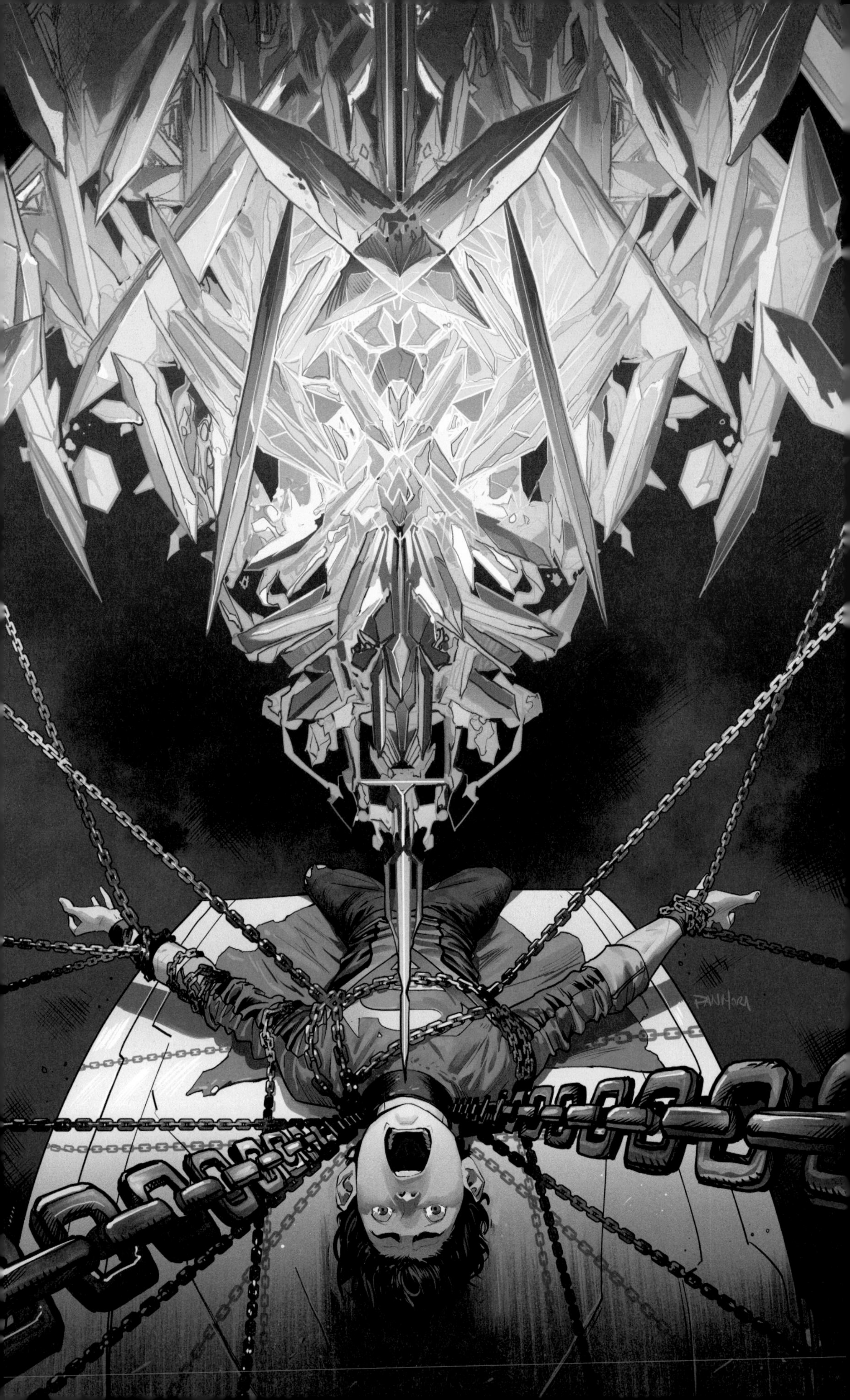

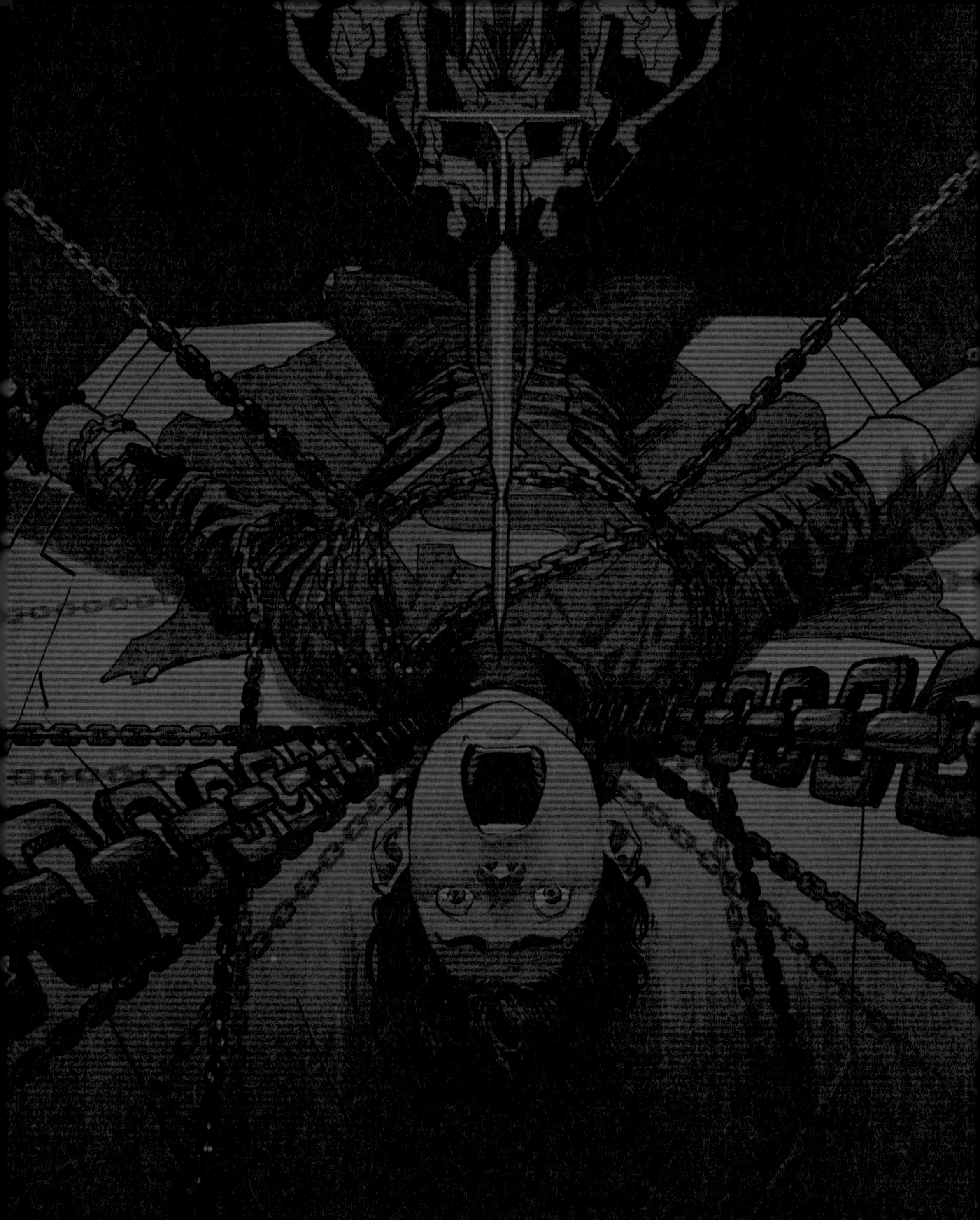

ADVENTURES OF THE SUPER SONS

#5

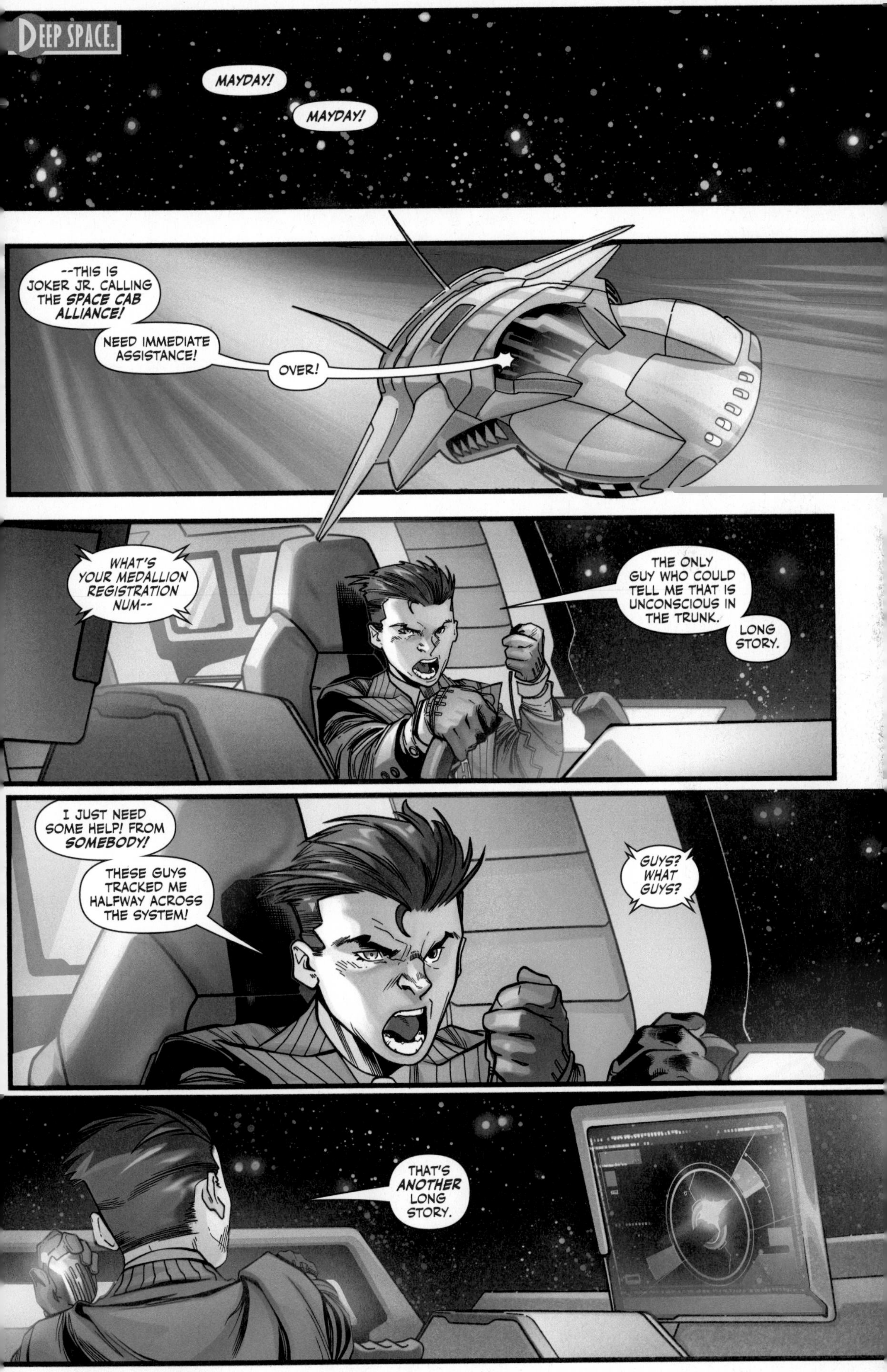
DEEP SPACE.
MAYDAY!
MAYDAY!
--THIS IS JOKER JR. CALLING THE SPACE CAB ALLIANCE!
NEED IMMEDIATE ASSISTANCE!
OVER!
WHAT'S YOUR MEDALLION REGISTRATION NUM--
THE ONLY GUY WHO COULD TELL ME THAT IS UNCONSCIOUS IN THE TRUNK.
LONG STORY.
I JUST NEED SOME HELP! FROM SOMEBODY!
THESE GUYS TRACKED ME HALFWAY ACROSS THE SYSTEM!
GUYS? WHAT GUYS?
THAT'S ANOTHER LONG STORY.

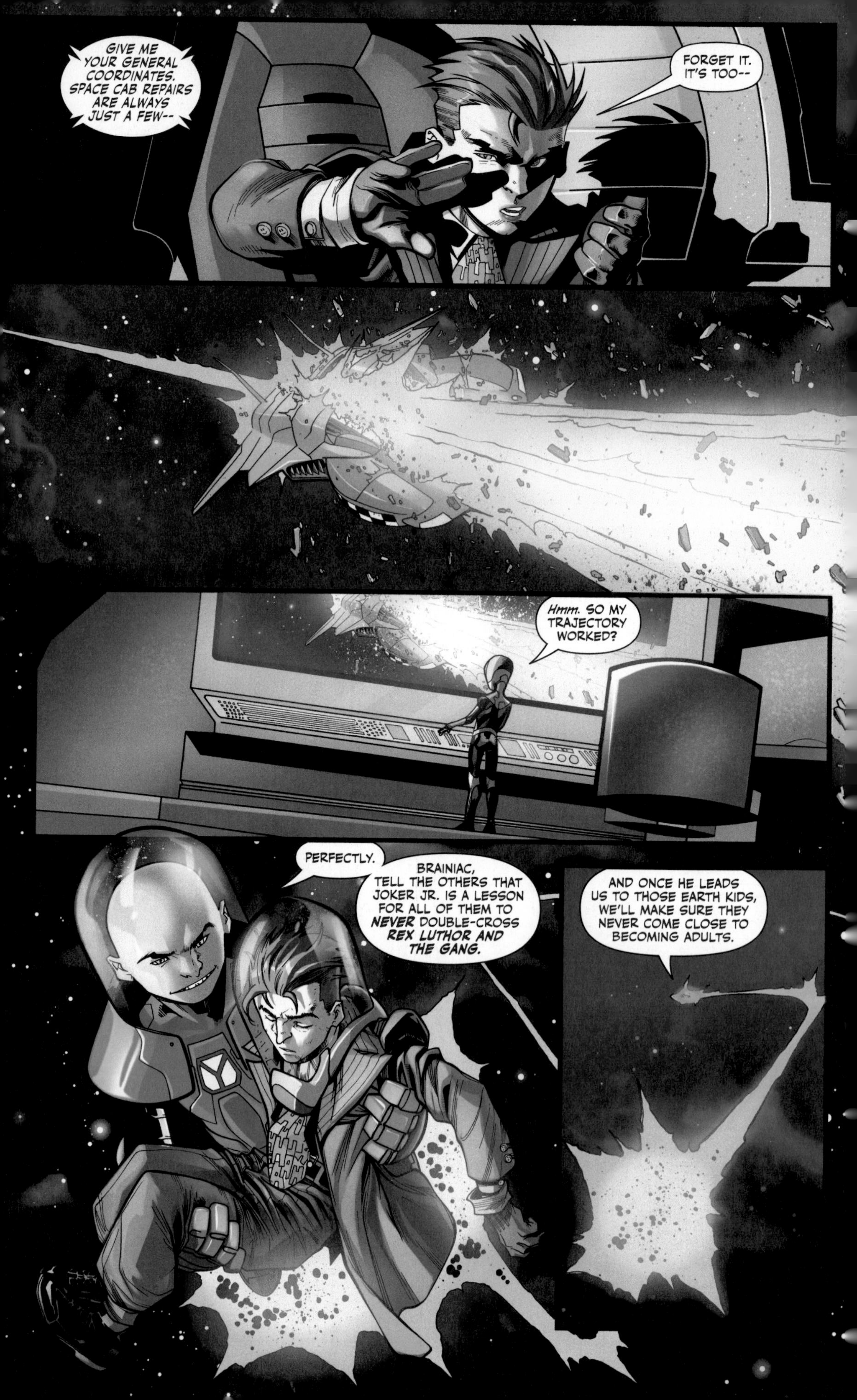
GIVE ME YOUR GENERAL COORDINATES. SPACE CAB REPAIRS ARE ALWAYS JUST A FEW--
FORGET IT. IT'S TOO--
Hmm. SO MY TRAJECTORY WORKED?
PERFECTLY.
BRAINIAC, TELL THE OTHERS THAT JOKER JR. IS A LESSON FOR ALL OF THEM TO ***NEVER*** DOUBLE-CROSS ***REX LUTHOR AND THE GANG.***
AND ONCE HE LEADS US TO THOSE EARTH KIDS, WE'LL MAKE SURE THEY NEVER COME CLOSE TO BECOMING ADULTS.

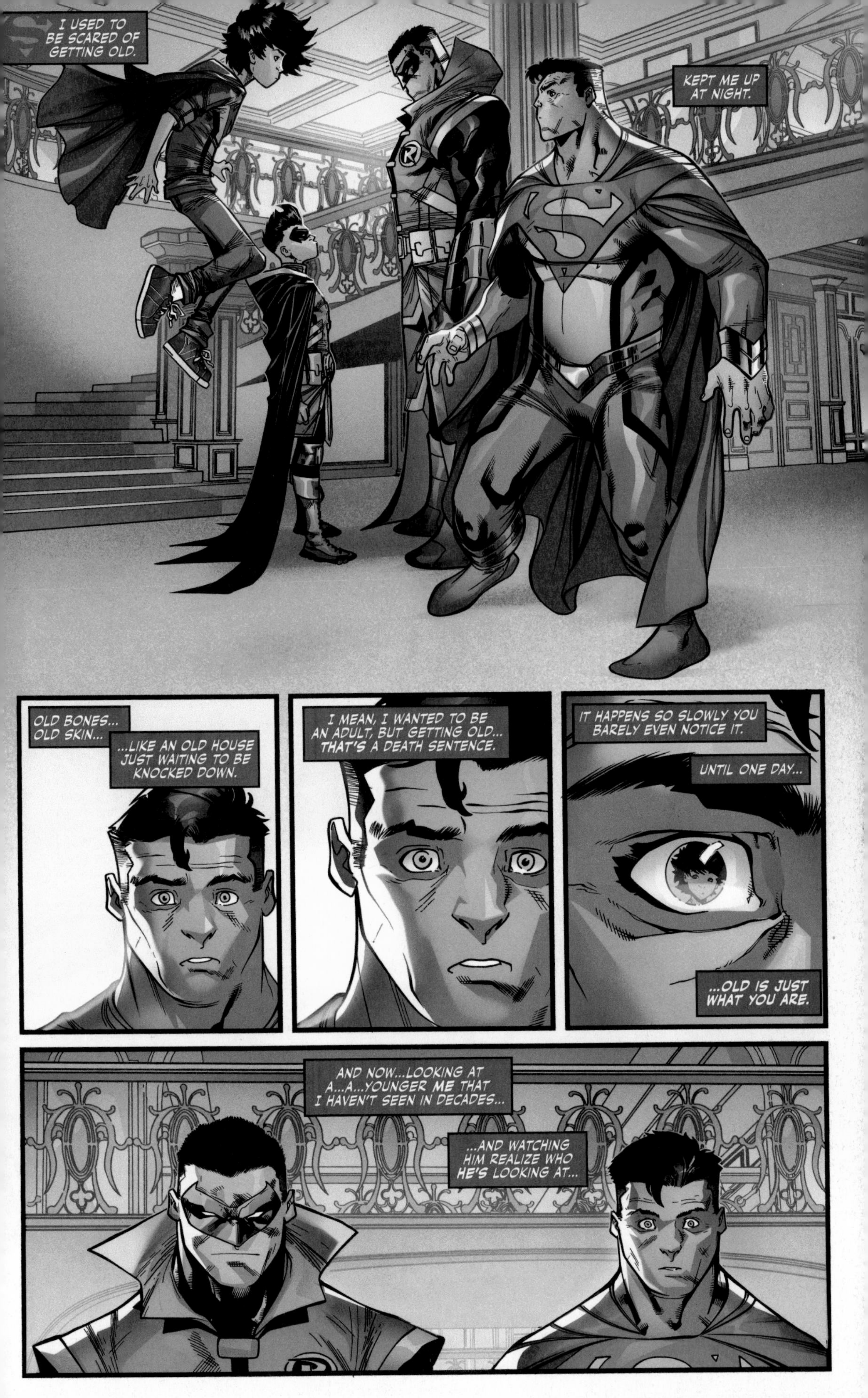

I USED TO BE SCARED OF GETTING OLD.
KEPT ME UP AT NIGHT.
OLD BONES... OLD SKIN...
...LIKE AN OLD HOUSE JUST WAITING TO BE KNOCKED DOWN.
I MEAN, I WANTED TO BE AN ADULT, BUT GETTING OLD... THAT'S A DEATH SENTENCE.
IT HAPPENS SO SLOWLY YOU BARELY EVEN NOTICE IT.
UNTIL ONE DAY...
...OLD IS JUST WHAT YOU ARE.
AND NOW...LOOKING AT A...A...YOUNGER ME THAT I HAVEN'T SEEN IN DECADES...
...AND WATCHING HIM REALIZE WHO HE'S LOOKING AT...

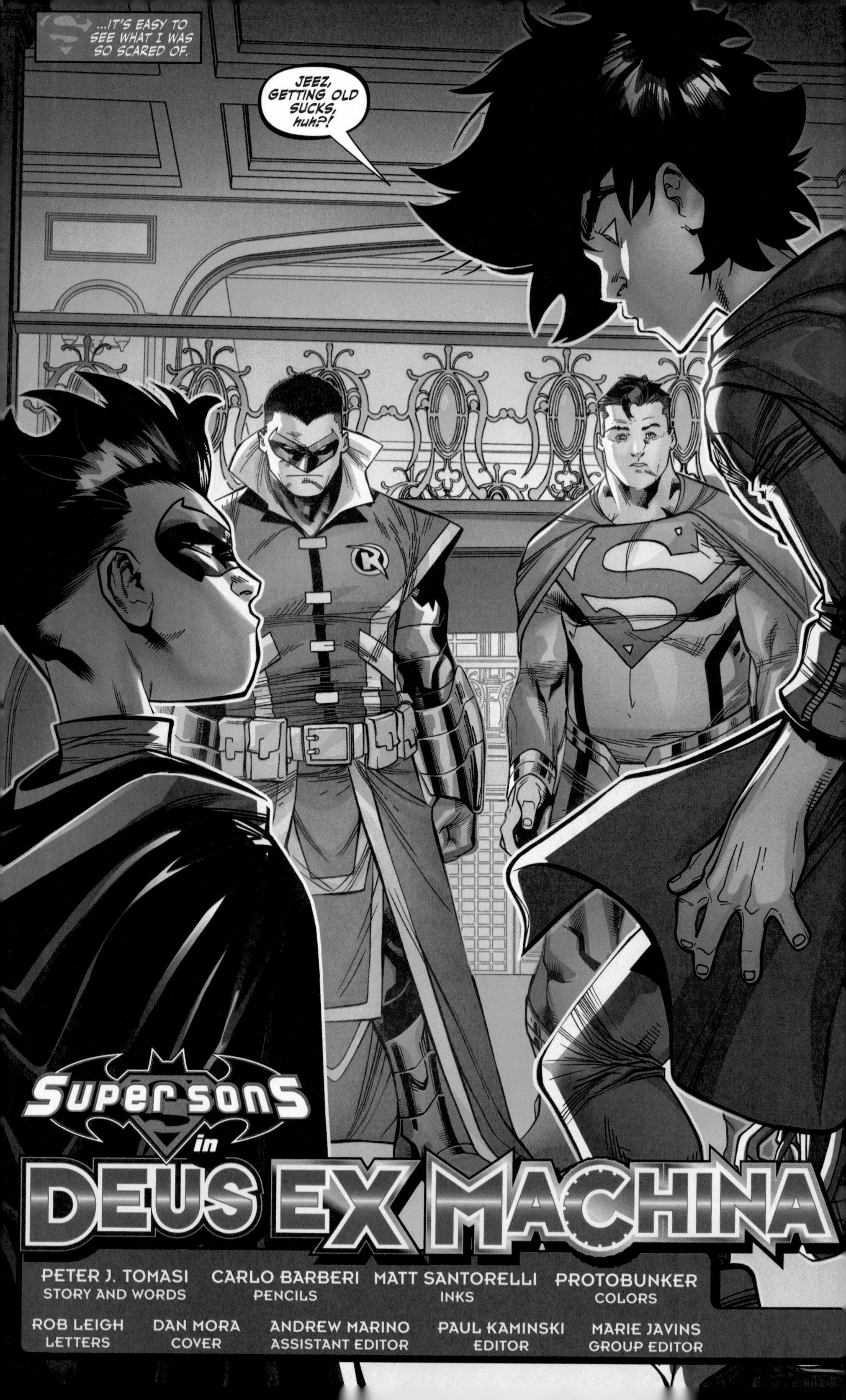
...IT'S EASY TO SEE WHAT I WAS SO SCARED OF.
JEEZ, GETTING OLD SUCKS, huh?!
Super sons in
DEUS EX MACHINA
PETER J. TOMASI STORY AND WORDS
CARLO BARBERI PENCILS
MATT SANTORELLI INKS
PROTOBUNKER COLORS
ROB LEIGH LETTERS
DAN MORA COVER
ANDREW MARINO ASSISTANT EDITOR
PAUL KAMINSKI EDITOR
MARIE JAVINS GROUP EDITOR

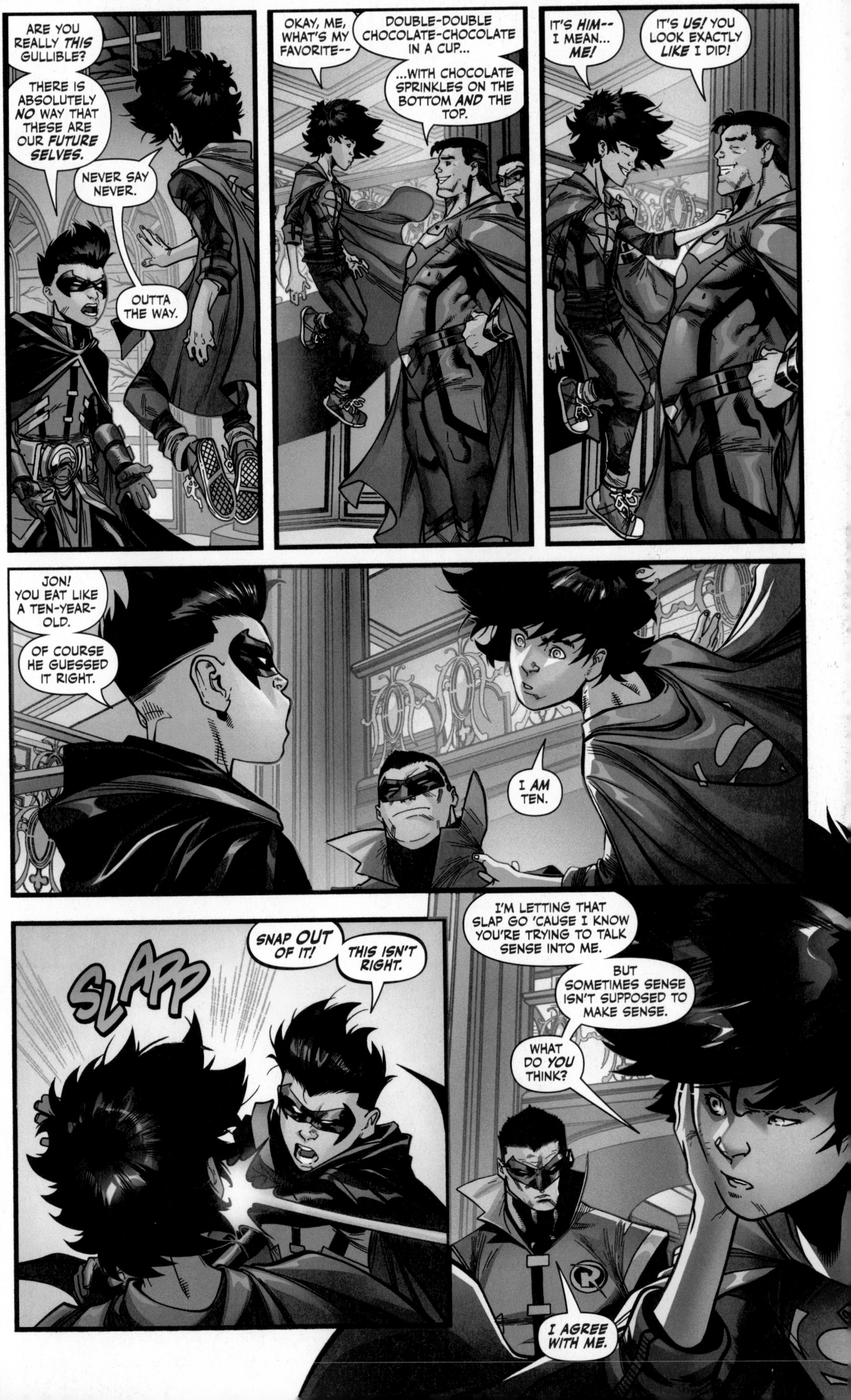
ARE YOU REALLY THIS GULLIBLE?
THERE IS ABSOLUTELY NO WAY THAT THESE ARE OUR FUTURE SELVES.
NEVER SAY NEVER.
OUTTA THE WAY.
OKAY, ME, WHAT'S MY FAVORITE--
DOUBLE-DOUBLE CHOCOLATE-CHOCOLATE IN A CUP...
...WITH CHOCOLATE SPRINKLES ON THE BOTTOM AND THE TOP.
IT'S HIM-- I MEAN... ME!
IT'S US! YOU LOOK EXACTLY LIKE I DID!
JON! YOU EAT LIKE A TEN-YEAR-OLD.
OF COURSE HE GUESSED IT RIGHT.
I AM TEN.
SLAPP
SNAP OUT OF IT!
THIS ISN'T RIGHT.
I'M LETTING THAT SLAP GO 'CAUSE I KNOW YOU'RE TRYING TO TALK SENSE INTO ME.
BUT SOMETIMES SENSE ISN'T SUPPOSED TO MAKE SENSE.
WHAT DO YOU THINK?
I AGREE WITH ME.

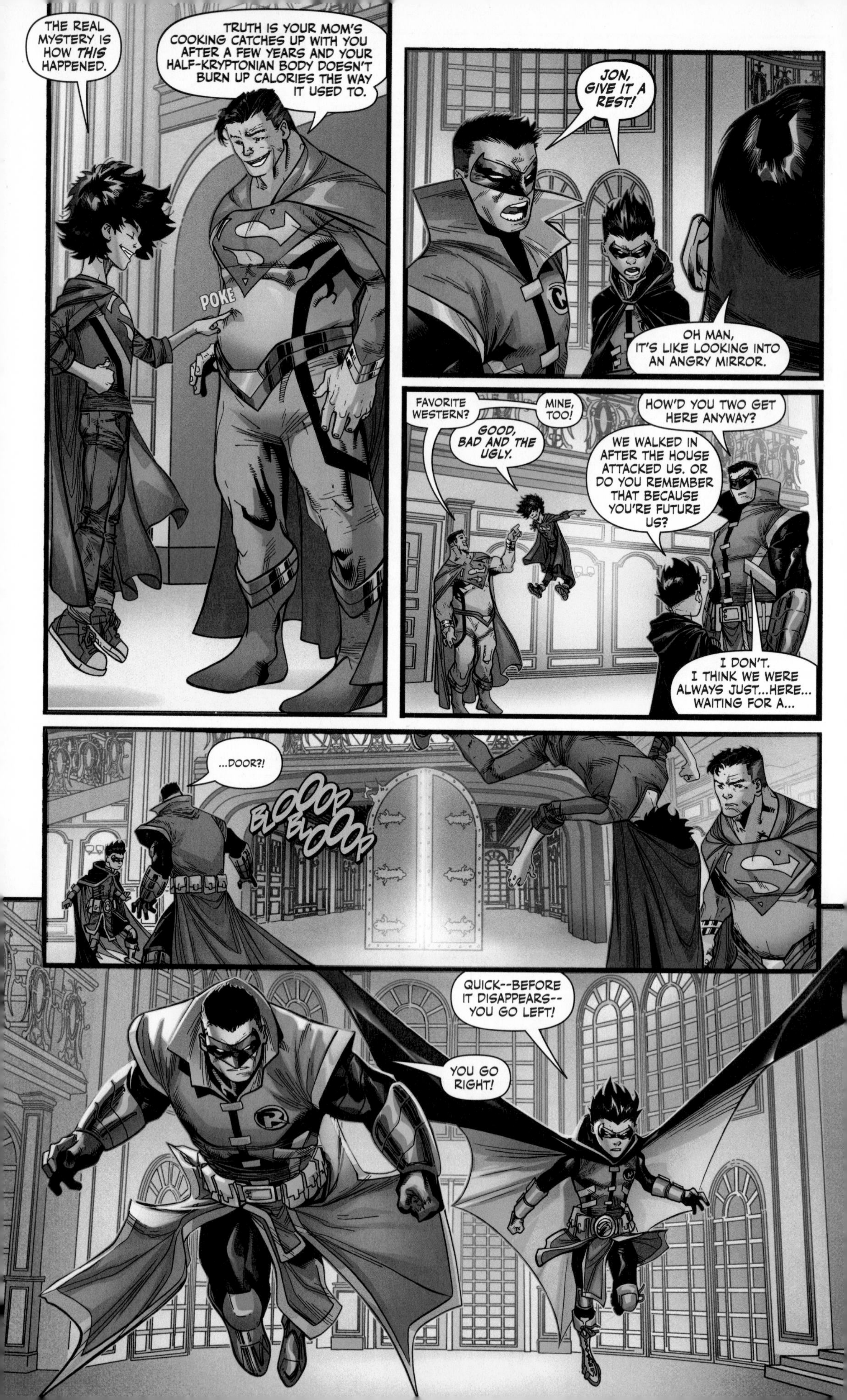
THE REAL MYSTERY IS HOW *THIS* HAPPENED.
TRUTH IS YOUR MOM'S COOKING CATCHES UP WITH YOU AFTER A FEW YEARS AND YOUR HALF-KRYPTONIAN BODY DOESN'T BURN UP CALORIES THE WAY IT USED TO.
POKE
JON, GIVE IT A REST!
OH MAN, IT'S LIKE LOOKING INTO AN ANGRY MIRROR.
FAVORITE WESTERN?
GOOD, BAD AND THE UGLY.
MINE, TOO!
HOW'D YOU TWO GET HERE ANYWAY?
WE WALKED IN AFTER THE HOUSE ATTACKED US. OR DO YOU REMEMBER THAT BECAUSE YOU'RE FUTURE US?
I DON'T. I THINK WE WERE ALWAYS JUST...HERE... WAITING FOR A...
...DOOR?!
BLOOOP BLOOOOP
QUICK--BEFORE IT DISAPPEARS-- YOU GO LEFT!
YOU GO RIGHT!

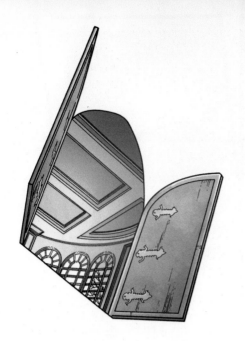

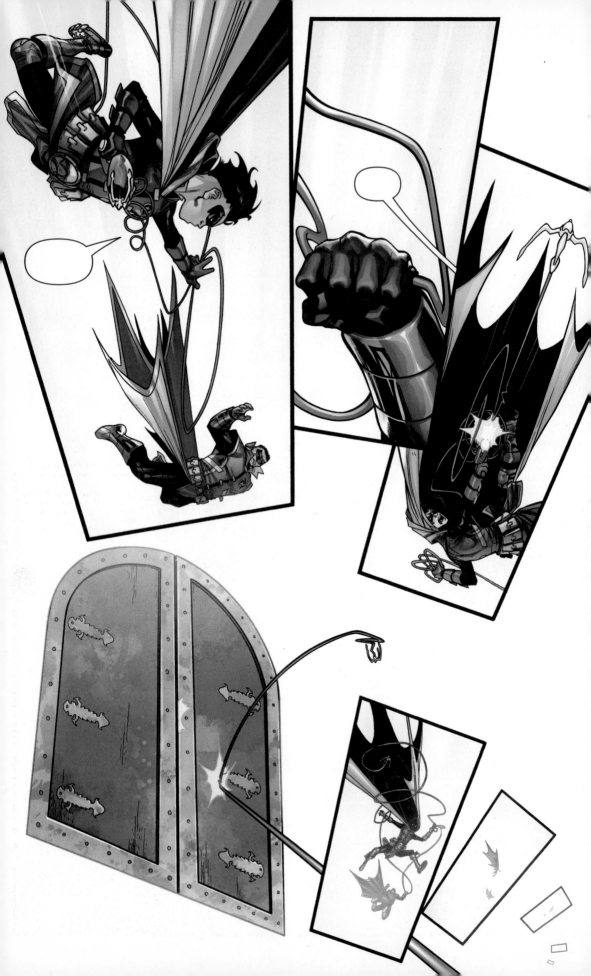

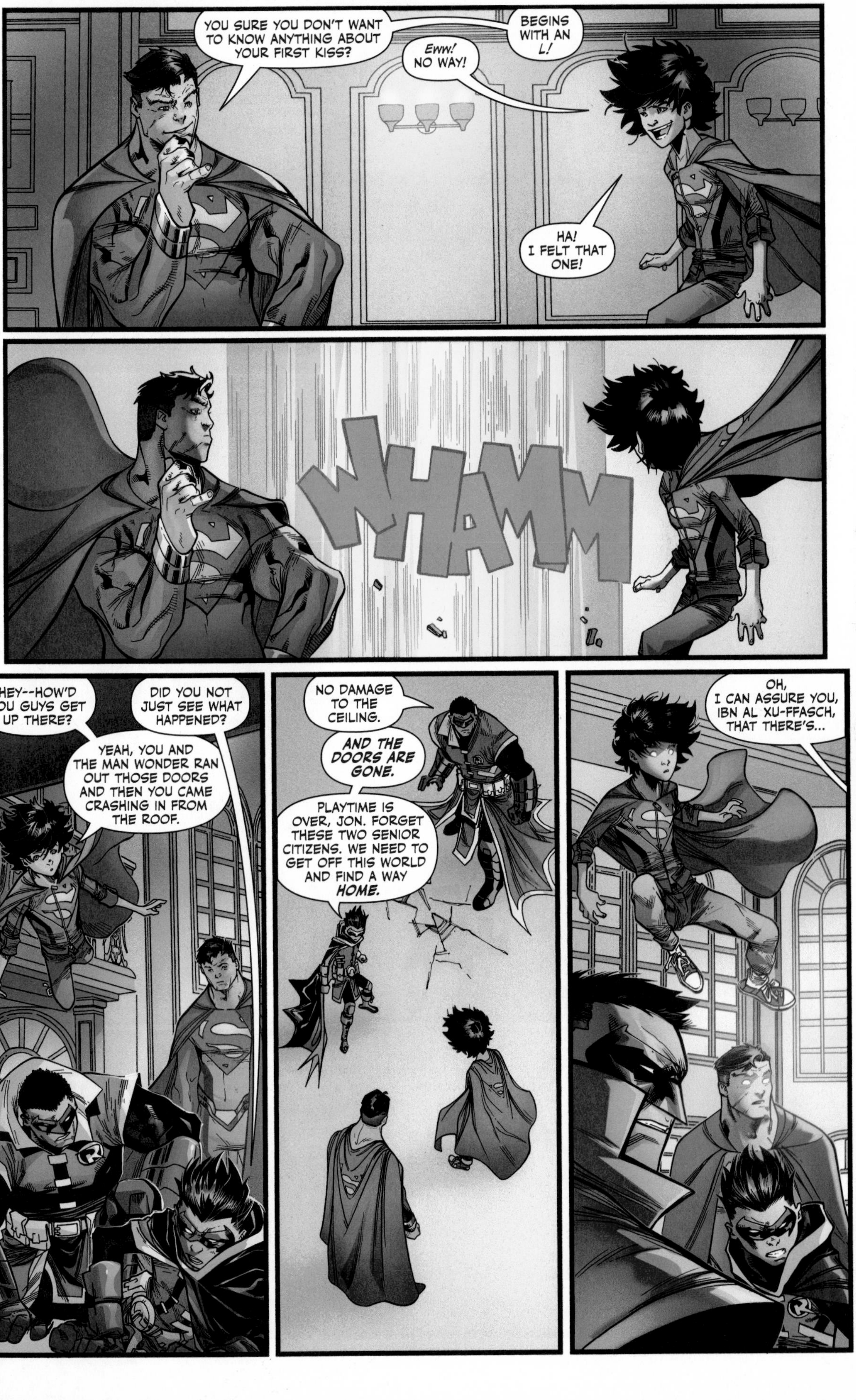
YOU SURE YOU DON'T WANT TO KNOW ANYTHING ABOUT YOUR FIRST KISS?
BEGINS WITH AN *L!*
Eww! NO WAY!
HA! I FELT THAT ONE!
WHAMM
HEY--HOW'D YOU GUYS GET UP THERE?
DID YOU NOT JUST SEE WHAT HAPPENED?
YEAH, YOU AND THE MAN WONDER RAN OUT THOSE DOORS AND THEN YOU CAME CRASHING IN FROM THE ROOF.
NO DAMAGE TO THE CEILING.
AND THE DOORS ARE GONE.
PLAYTIME IS OVER, JON. FORGET THESE TWO SENIOR CITIZENS. WE NEED TO GET OFF THIS WORLD AND FIND A WAY ***HOME.***
OH, I CAN ASSURE YOU, IBN AL XU-FFASCH, THAT THERE'S...

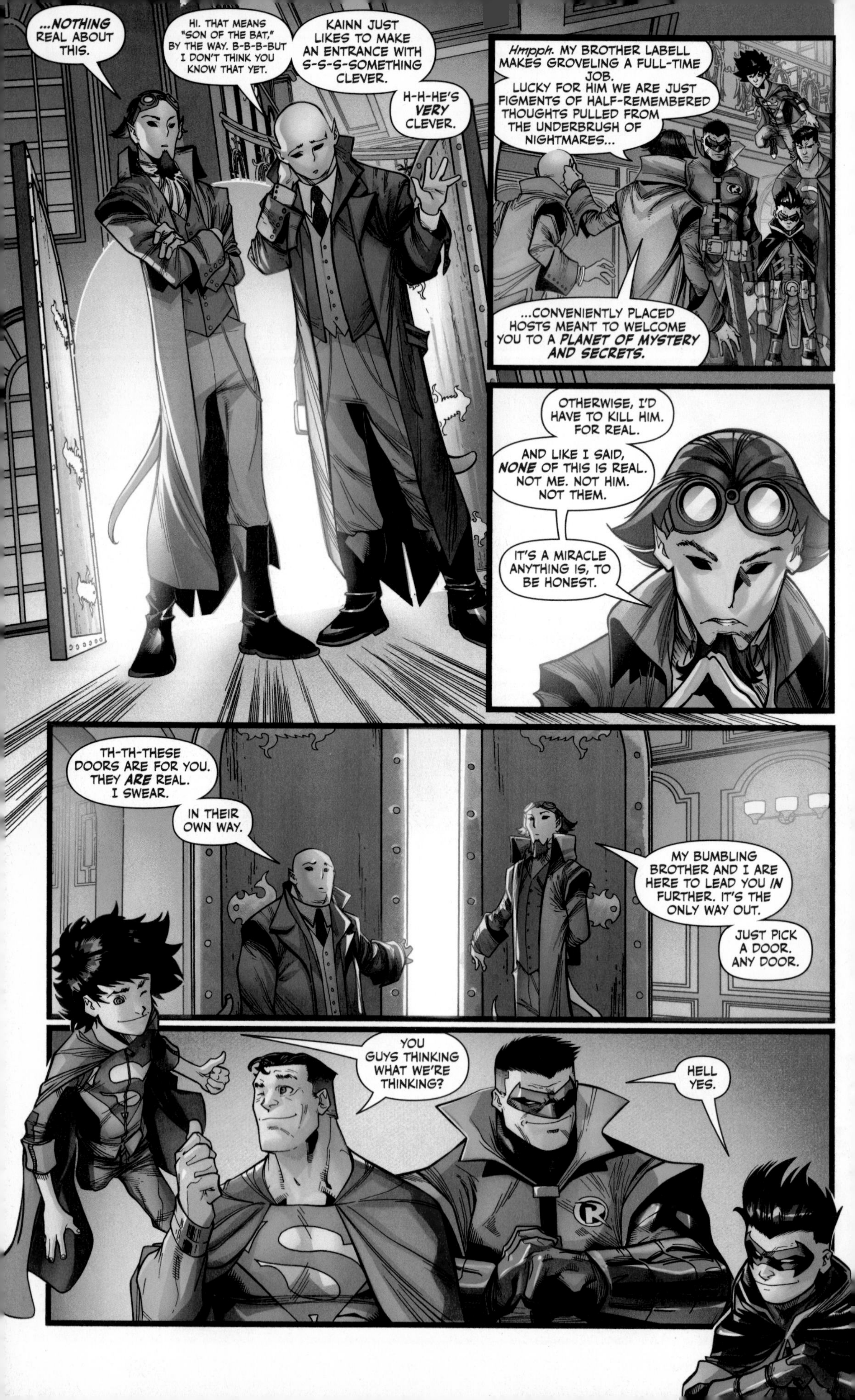
...*NOTHING* REAL ABOUT THIS.
HI. THAT MEANS "SON OF THE BAT," BY THE WAY. B-B-B-BUT I DON'T THINK YOU KNOW THAT YET.
KAINN JUST LIKES TO MAKE AN ENTRANCE WITH S-S-S-SOMETHING CLEVER.
H-H-HE'S *VERY* CLEVER.
Hmpph. MY BROTHER LABELL MAKES GROVELING A FULL-TIME JOB. LUCKY FOR HIM WE ARE JUST FIGMENTS OF HALF-REMEMBERED THOUGHTS PULLED FROM THE UNDERBRUSH OF NIGHTMARES...
...CONVENIENTLY PLACED HOSTS MEANT TO WELCOME YOU TO A *PLANET OF MYSTERY AND SECRETS.*
OTHERWISE, I'D HAVE TO KILL HIM. FOR REAL.
AND LIKE I SAID, *NONE* OF THIS IS REAL. NOT ME. NOT HIM. NOT THEM.
IT'S A MIRACLE ANYTHING IS, TO BE HONEST.
TH-TH-THESE DOORS ARE FOR YOU. THEY *ARE* REAL. I SWEAR.
IN THEIR OWN WAY.
MY BUMBLING BROTHER AND I ARE HERE TO LEAD YOU *IN* FURTHER. IT'S THE ONLY WAY OUT.
JUST PICK A DOOR. ANY DOOR.
YOU GUYS THINKING WHAT WE'RE THINKING?
HELL YES.

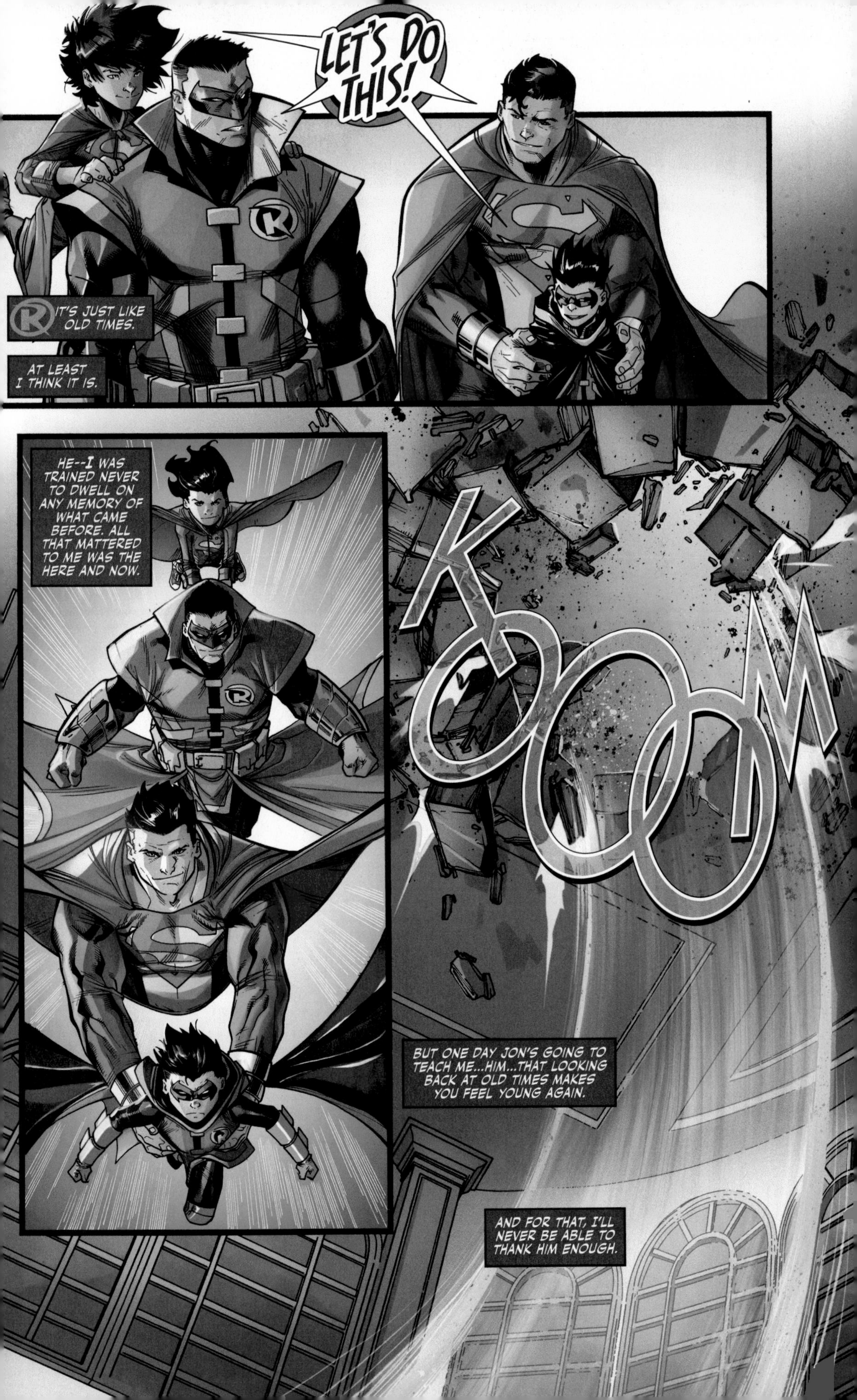
LET'S DO THIS!
IT'S JUST LIKE OLD TIMES.
AT LEAST I THINK IT IS.
HE--I WAS TRAINED NEVER TO DWELL ON ANY MEMORY OF WHAT CAME BEFORE. ALL THAT MATTERED TO ME WAS THE HERE AND NOW.
KOOOM
BUT ONE DAY JON'S GOING TO TEACH ME...HIM...THAT LOOKING BACK AT OLD TIMES MAKES YOU FEEL YOUNG AGAIN.
AND FOR THAT, I'LL NEVER BE ABLE TO THANK HIM ENOUGH.

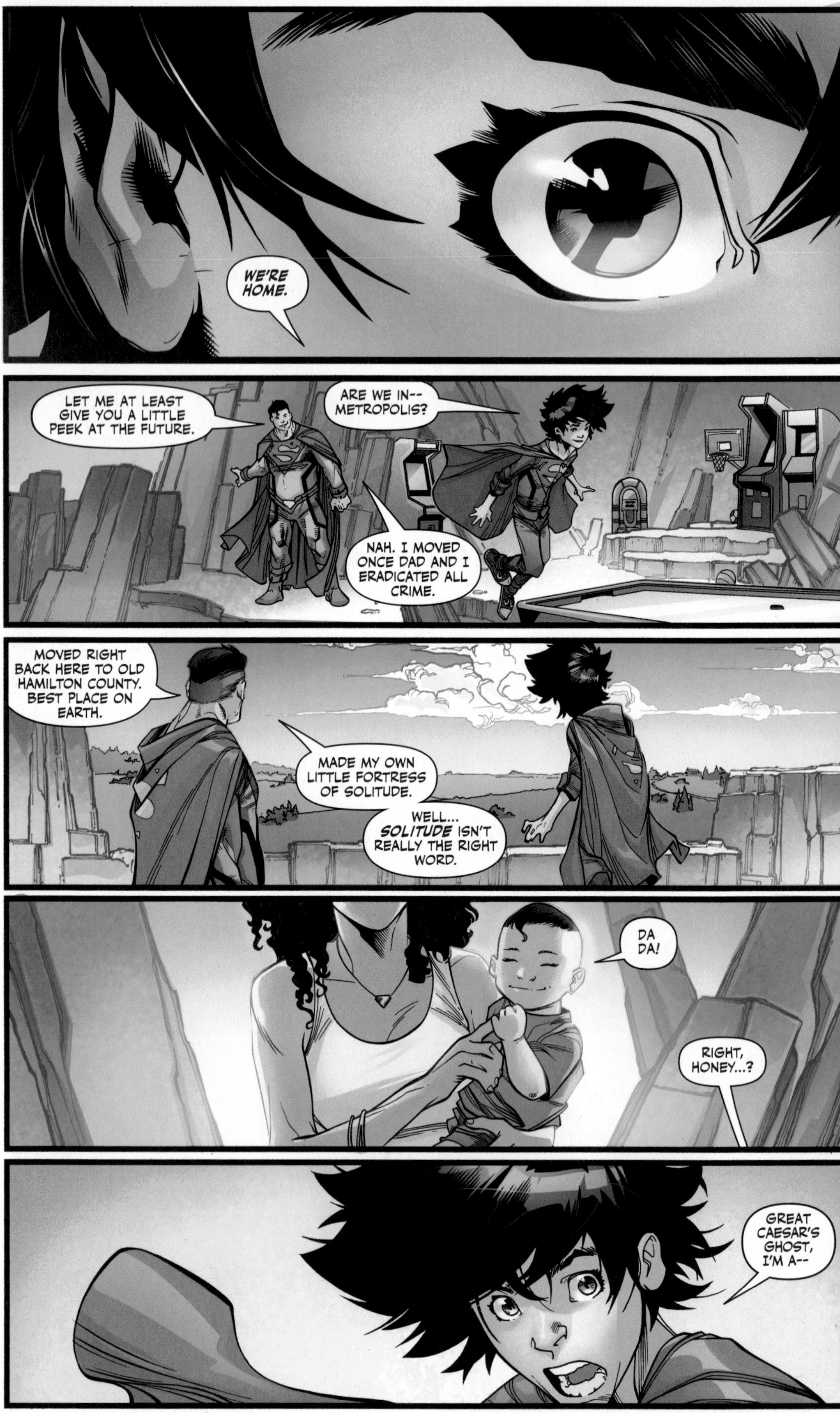
WE'RE HOME.
LET ME AT LEAST GIVE YOU A LITTLE PEEK AT THE FUTURE.
ARE WE IN-- METROPOLIS?
NAH. I MOVED ONCE DAD AND I ERADICATED ALL CRIME.
MOVED RIGHT BACK HERE TO OLD HAMILTON COUNTY. BEST PLACE ON EARTH.
MADE MY OWN LITTLE FORTRESS OF SOLITUDE.
WELL... SOLITUDE ISN'T REALLY THE RIGHT WORD.
DA DA!
RIGHT, HONEY...?
GREAT CAESAR'S GHOST, I'M A--

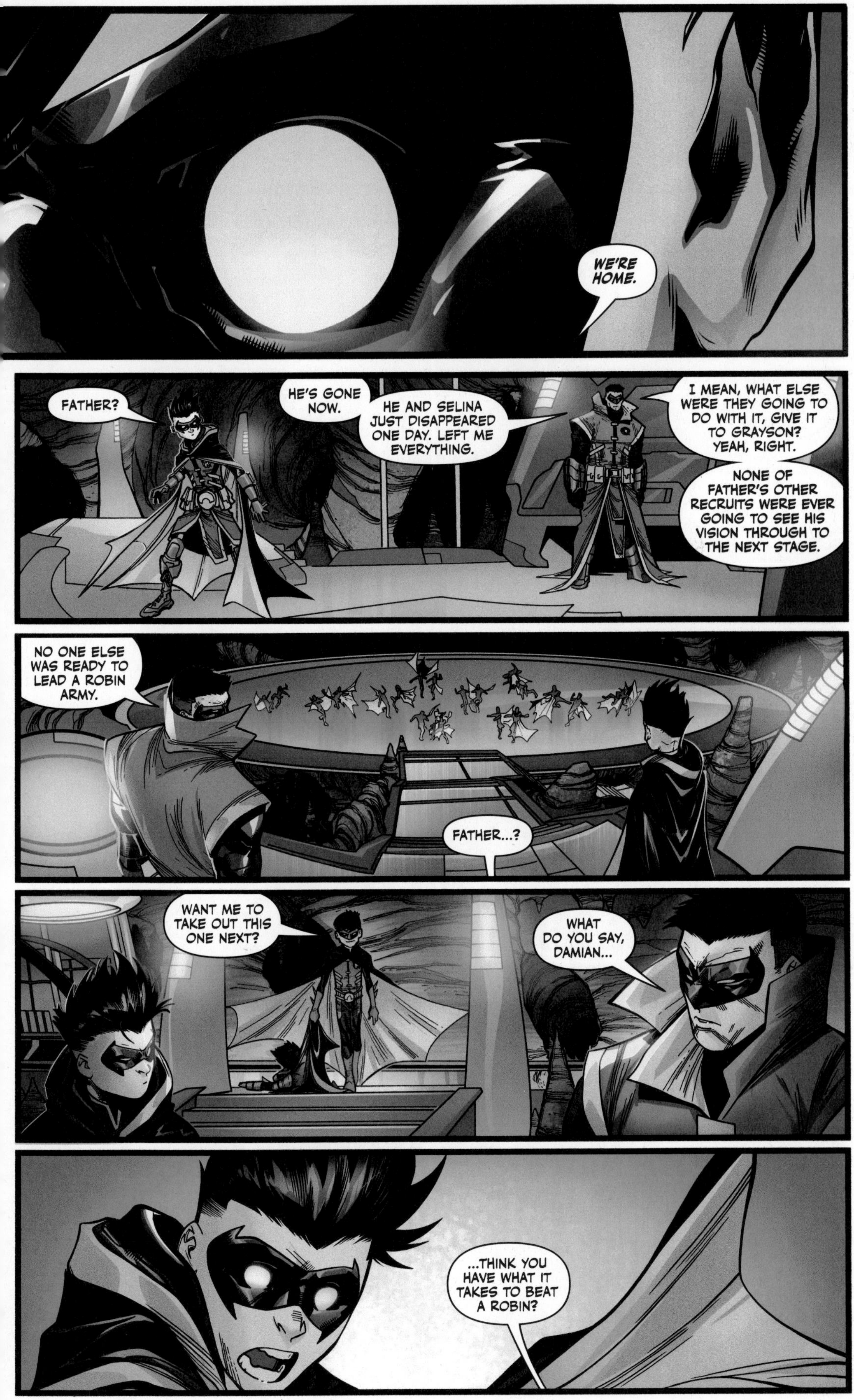
WE'RE HOME.
FATHER?
HE'S GONE NOW.
HE AND SELINA JUST DISAPPEARED ONE DAY. LEFT ME EVERYTHING.
I MEAN, WHAT ELSE WERE THEY GOING TO DO WITH IT, GIVE IT TO GRAYSON? YEAH, RIGHT.
NONE OF FATHER'S OTHER RECRUITS WERE EVER GOING TO SEE HIS VISION THROUGH TO THE NEXT STAGE.
NO ONE ELSE WAS READY TO LEAD A ROBIN ARMY.
FATHER...?
WANT ME TO TAKE OUT THIS ONE NEXT?
WHAT DO YOU SAY, DAMIAN...
...THINK YOU HAVE WHAT IT TAKES TO BEAT A ROBIN?

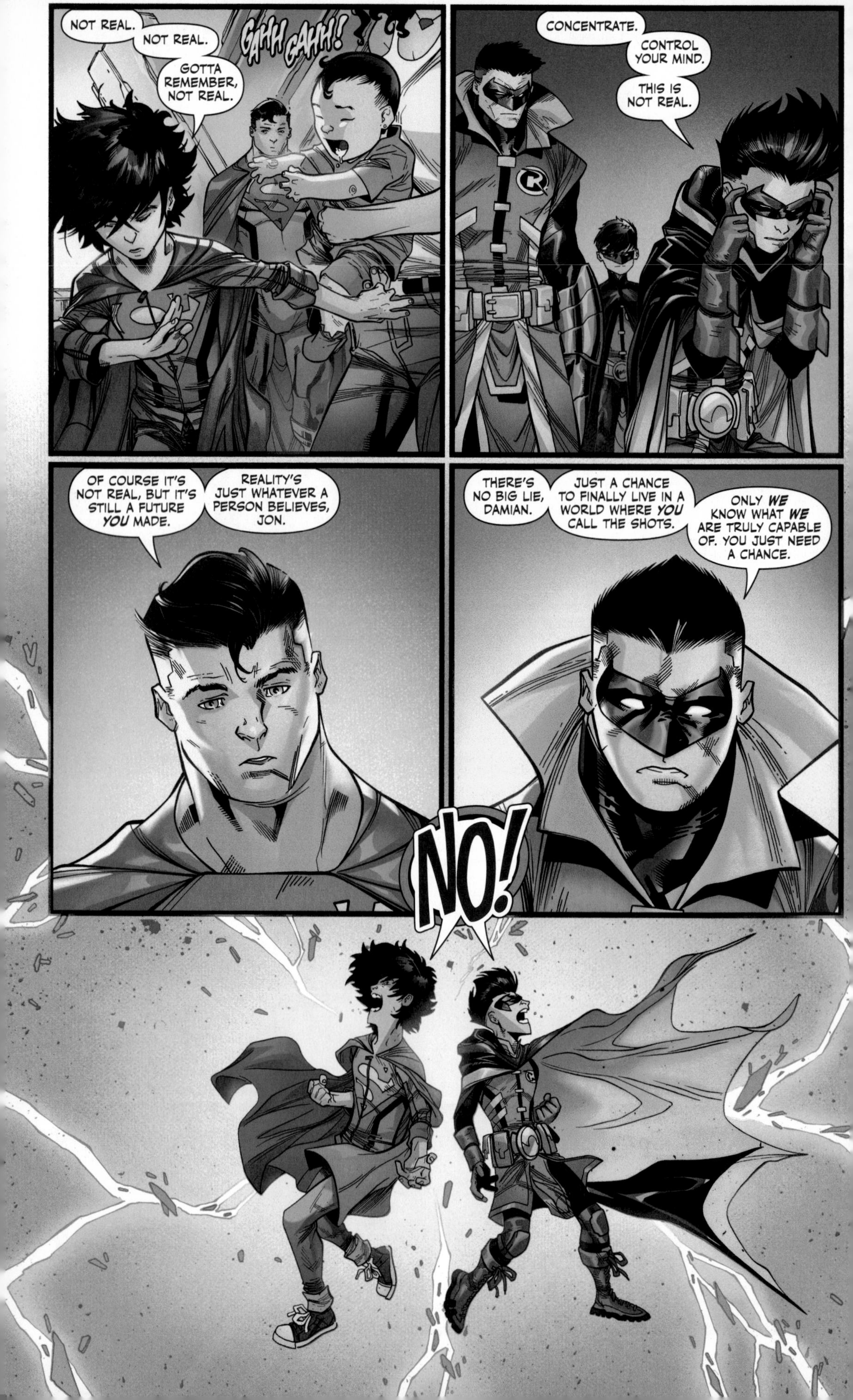

NOT REAL.
NOT REAL.
GOTTA REMEMBER, NOT REAL.
GAHH GAHH!
CONCENTRATE.
CONTROL YOUR MIND.
THIS IS NOT REAL.
OF COURSE IT'S NOT REAL, BUT IT'S STILL A FUTURE *YOU* MADE.
REALITY'S JUST WHATEVER A PERSON BELIEVES, JON.
THERE'S NO BIG LIE, DAMIAN.
JUST A CHANCE TO FINALLY LIVE IN A WORLD WHERE *YOU* CALL THE SHOTS.
ONLY *WE* KNOW WHAT *WE* ARE TRULY CAPABLE OF. YOU JUST NEED A CHANCE.
NO!

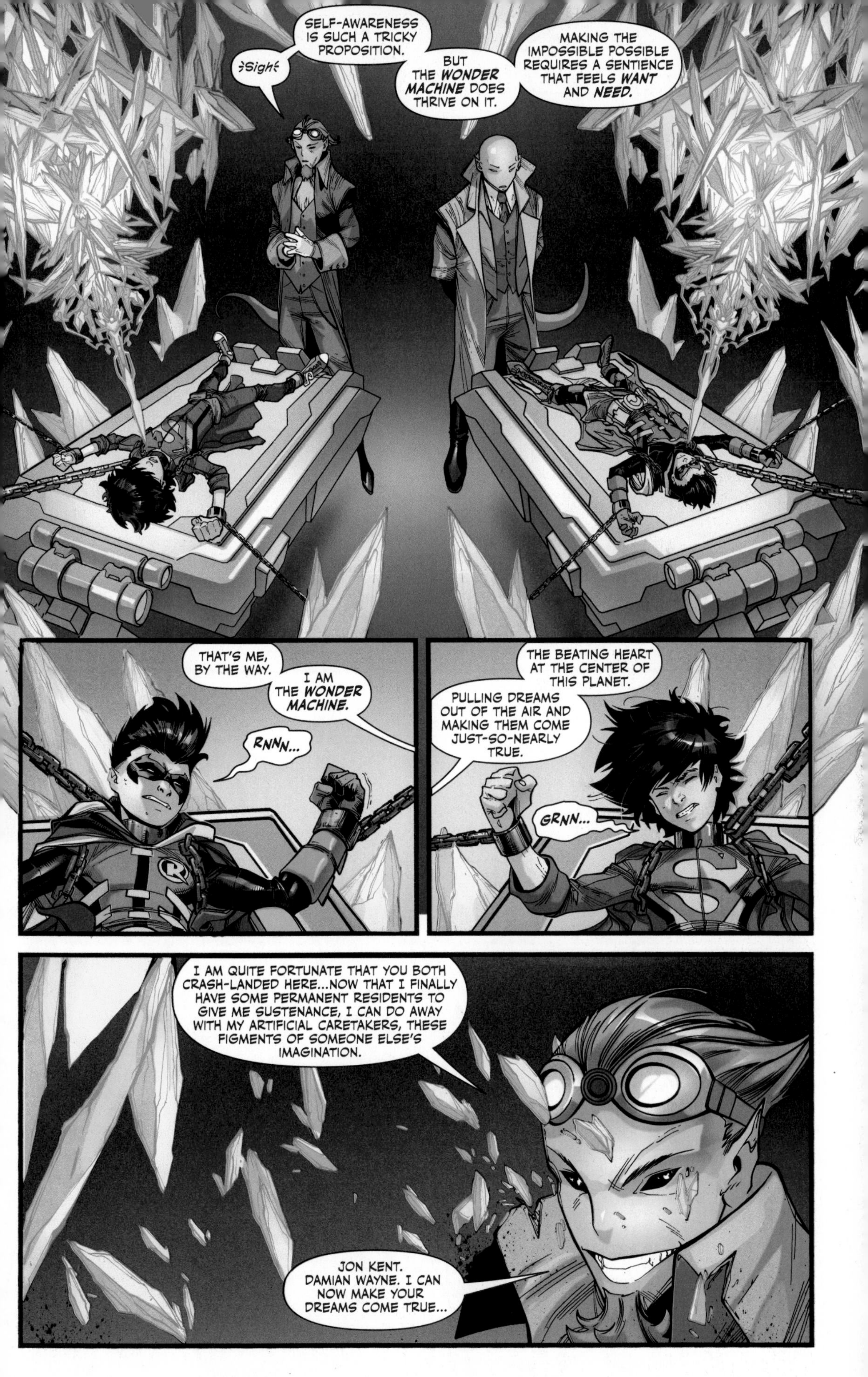
SELF-AWARENESS IS SUCH A TRICKY PROPOSITION.
Sigh
BUT THE WONDER MACHINE DOES THRIVE ON IT.
MAKING THE IMPOSSIBLE POSSIBLE REQUIRES A SENTIENCE THAT FEELS WANT AND NEED.
THAT'S ME, BY THE WAY.
I AM THE WONDER MACHINE.
RNNN...
THE BEATING HEART AT THE CENTER OF THIS PLANET.
PULLING DREAMS OUT OF THE AIR AND MAKING THEM COME JUST-SO-NEARLY TRUE.
GRNN...
I AM QUITE FORTUNATE THAT YOU BOTH CRASH-LANDED HERE...NOW THAT I FINALLY HAVE SOME PERMANENT RESIDENTS TO GIVE ME SUSTENANCE, I CAN DO AWAY WITH MY ARTIFICIAL CARETAKERS, THESE FIGMENTS OF SOMEONE ELSE'S IMAGINATION.
JON KENT. DAMIAN WAYNE. I CAN NOW MAKE YOUR DREAMS COME TRUE...

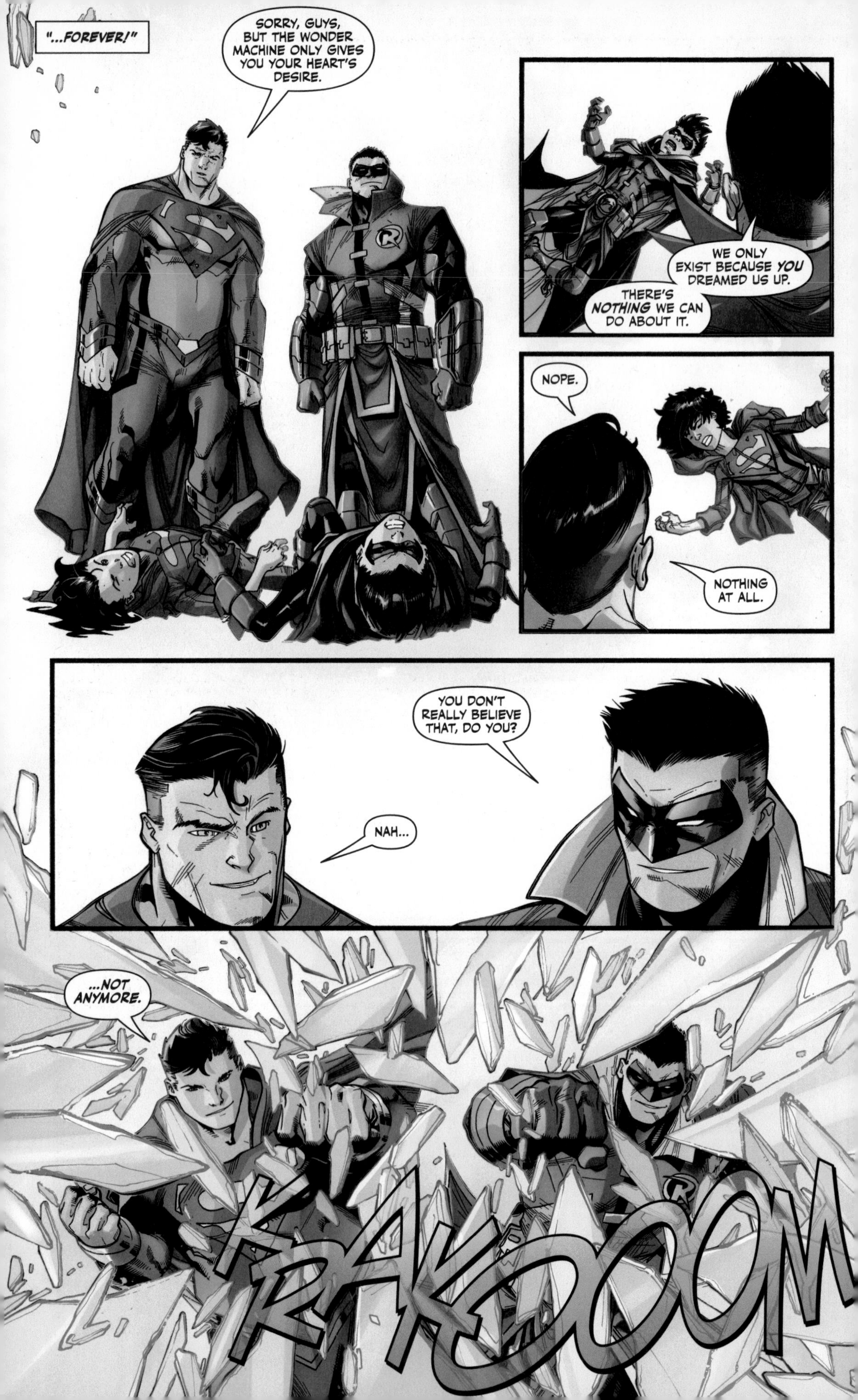
"...FOREVER!"
SORRY, GUYS, BUT THE WONDER MACHINE ONLY GIVES YOU YOUR HEART'S DESIRE.
WE ONLY EXIST BECAUSE YOU DREAMED US UP.
THERE'S NOTHING WE CAN DO ABOUT IT.
NOPE.
NOTHING AT ALL.
YOU DON'T REALLY BELIEVE THAT, DO YOU?
NAH...
...NOT ANYMORE.
KRAKOOOM

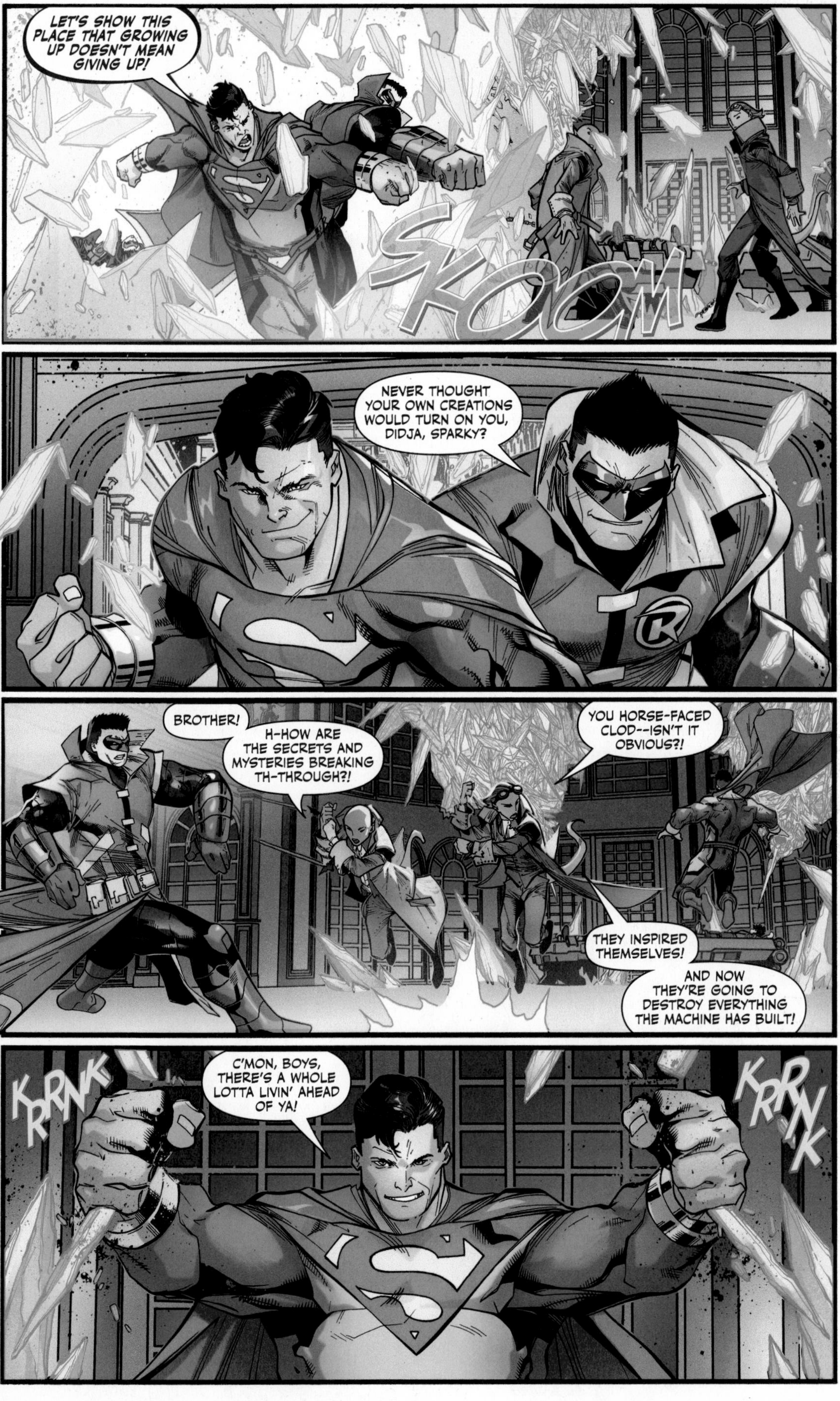
LET'S SHOW THIS PLACE THAT GROWING UP DOESN'T MEAN GIVING UP!
SKOOM
NEVER THOUGHT YOUR OWN CREATIONS WOULD TURN ON YOU, DIDJA, SPARKY?
BROTHER!
H-HOW ARE THE SECRETS AND MYSTERIES BREAKING TH-THROUGH?!
YOU HORSE-FACED CLOD--ISN'T IT OBVIOUS?!
THEY INSPIRED THEMSELVES!
AND NOW THEY'RE GOING TO DESTROY EVERYTHING THE MACHINE HAS BUILT!
KRRNK
C'MON, BOYS, THERE'S A WHOLE LOTTA LIVIN' AHEAD OF YA!
KRRNK

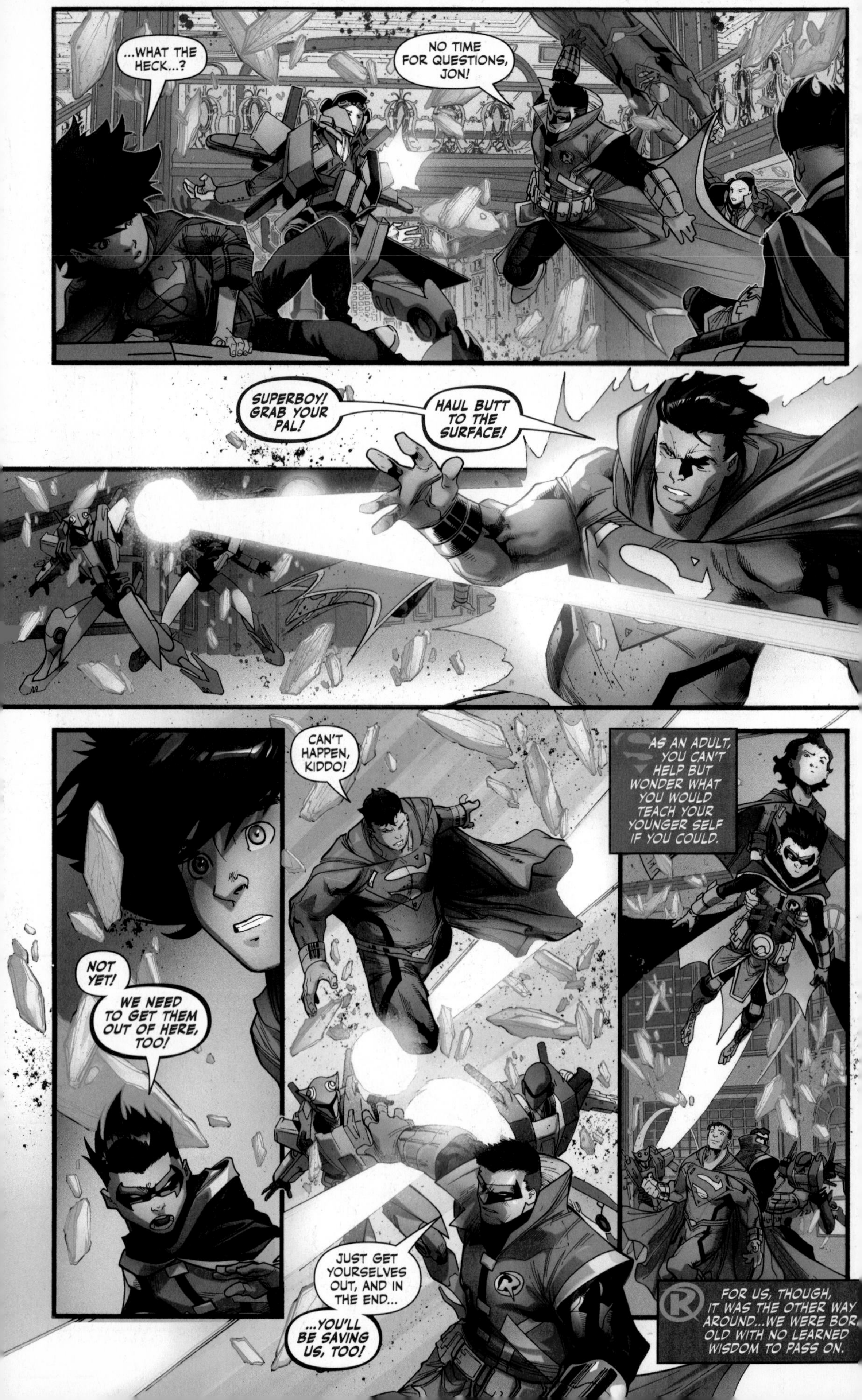
...WHAT THE HECK...?
NO TIME FOR QUESTIONS, JON!
SUPERBOY! GRAB YOUR PAL!
HAUL BUTT TO THE SURFACE!
NOT YET! WE NEED TO GET THEM OUT OF HERE, TOO!
CAN'T HAPPEN, KIDDO!
JUST GET YOURSELVES OUT, AND IN THE END...
...YOU'LL BE SAVING US, TOO!
AS AN ADULT, YOU CAN'T HELP BUT WONDER WHAT YOU WOULD TEACH YOUR YOUNGER SELF IF YOU COULD.
FOR US, THOUGH, IT WAS THE OTHER WAY AROUND...WE WERE BORN OLD WITH NO LEARNED WISDOM TO PASS ON.

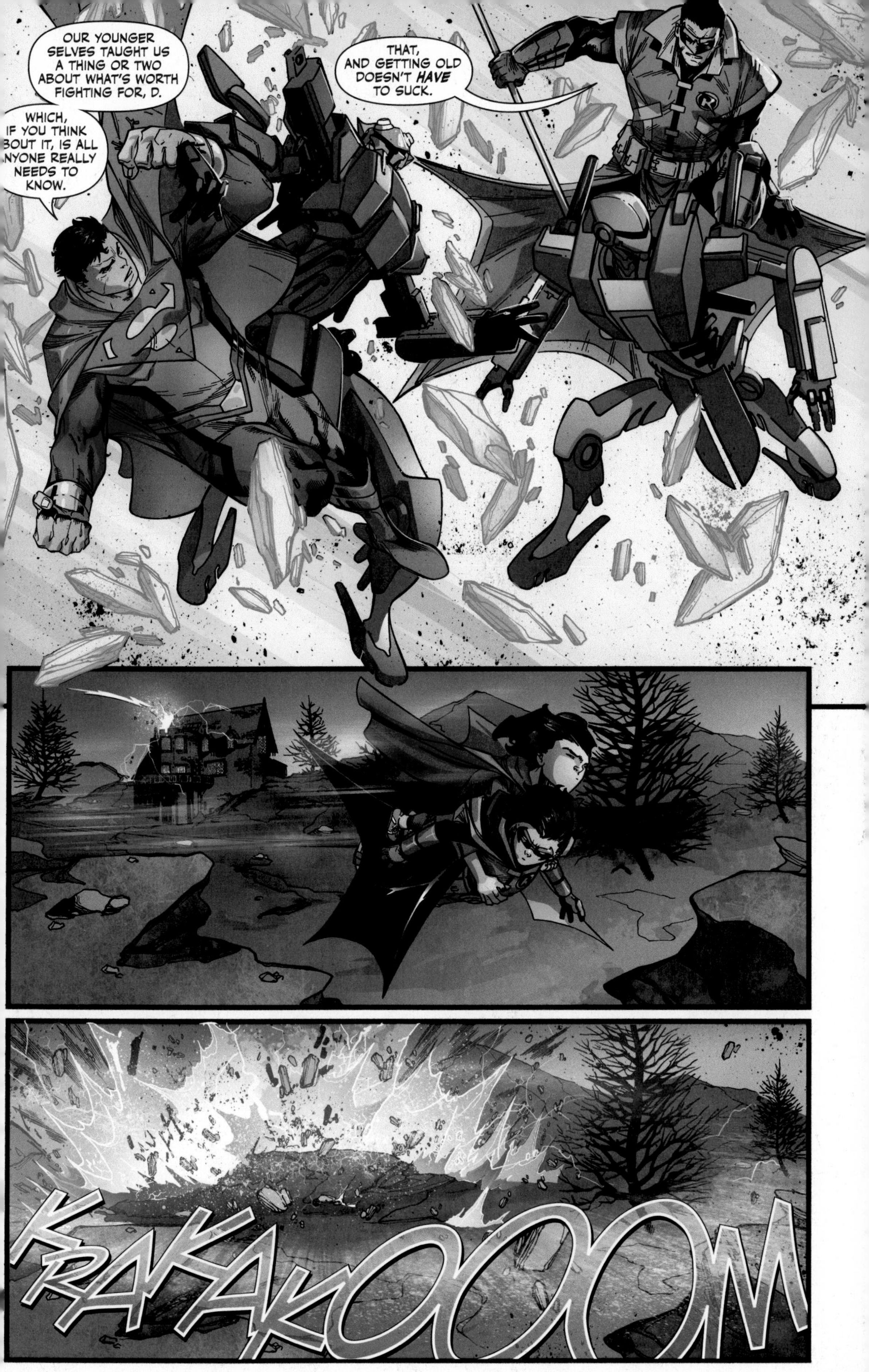
OUR YOUNGER SELVES TAUGHT US A THING OR TWO ABOUT WHAT'S WORTH FIGHTING FOR, D.
THAT, AND GETTING OLD DOESN'T *HAVE* TO SUCK.
WHICH, IF YOU THINK BOUT IT, IS ALL NYONE REALLY NEEDS TO KNOW.
KRAKAKOOOM

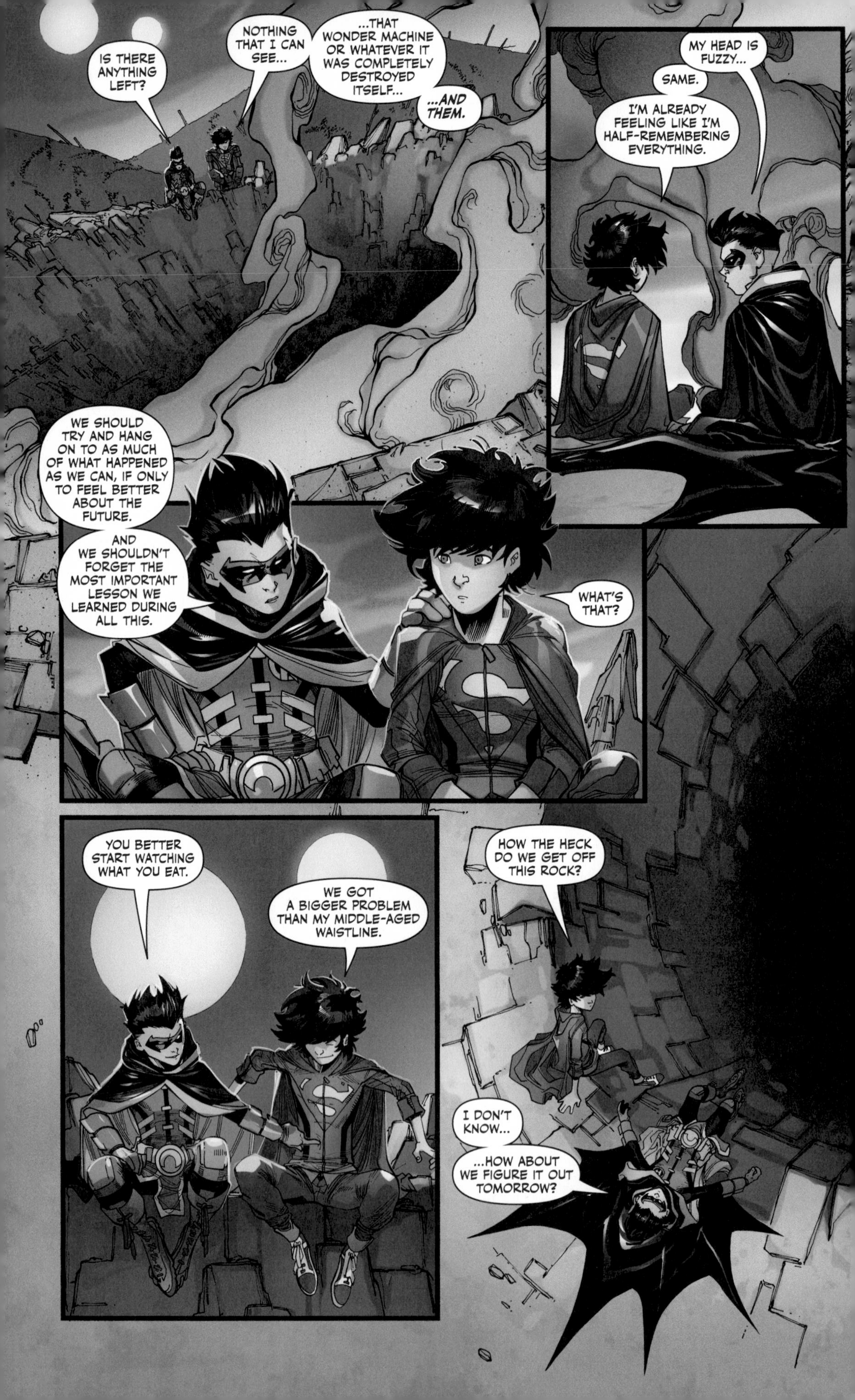
IS THERE ANYTHING LEFT?
NOTHING THAT I CAN SEE...
...THAT WONDER MACHINE OR WHATEVER IT WAS COMPLETELY DESTROYED ITSELF...
...AND THEM.
MY HEAD IS FUZZY...
SAME.
I'M ALREADY FEELING LIKE I'M HALF-REMEMBERING EVERYTHING.
WE SHOULD TRY AND HANG ON TO AS MUCH OF WHAT HAPPENED AS WE CAN, IF ONLY TO FEEL BETTER ABOUT THE FUTURE.
AND WE SHOULDN'T FORGET THE MOST IMPORTANT LESSON WE LEARNED DURING ALL THIS.
WHAT'S THAT?
YOU BETTER START WATCHING WHAT YOU EAT.
WE GOT A BIGGER PROBLEM THAN MY MIDDLE-AGED WAISTLINE.
HOW THE HECK DO WE GET OFF THIS ROCK?
I DON'T KNOW...
...HOW ABOUT WE FIGURE IT OUT TOMORROW?

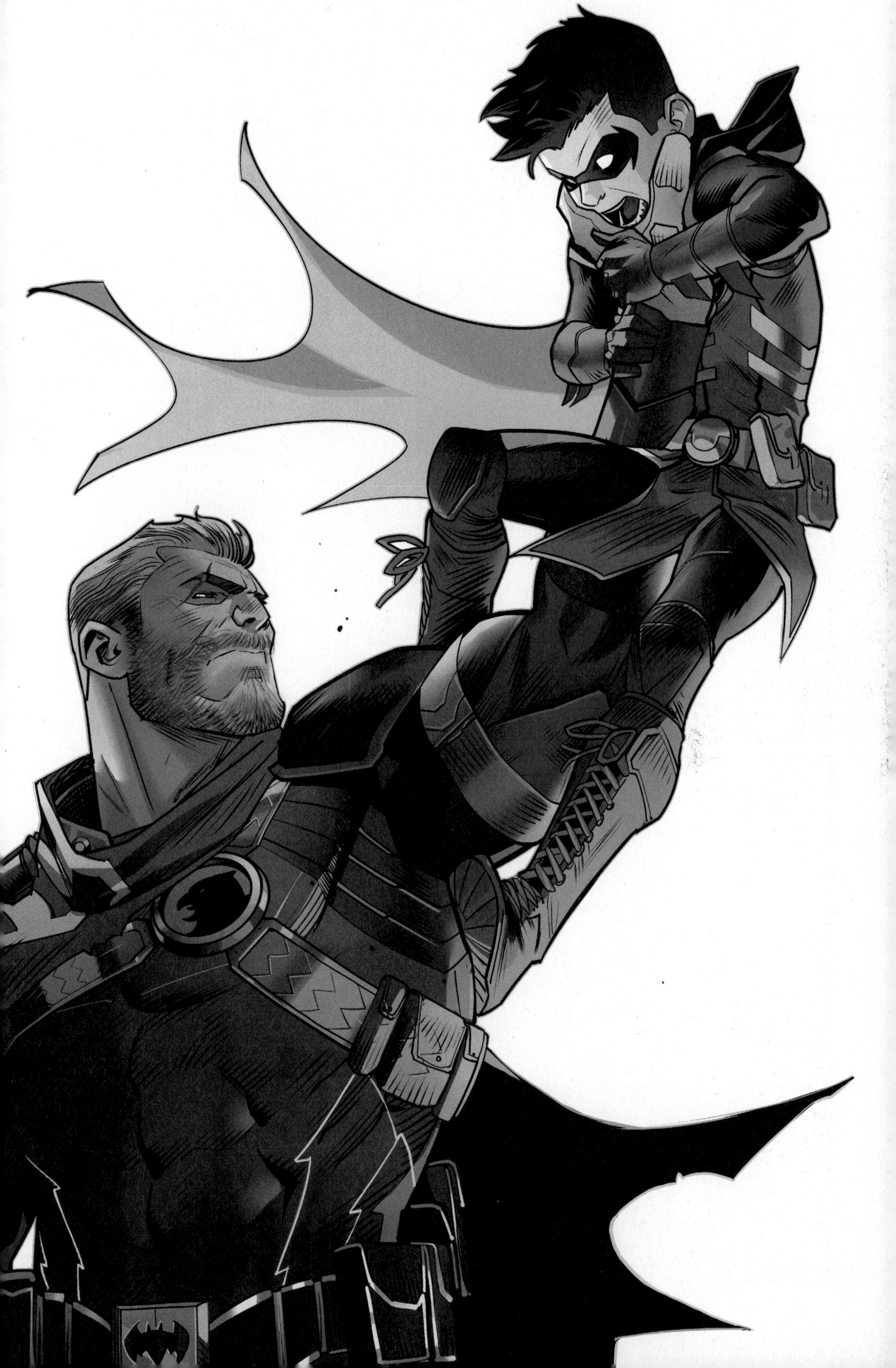

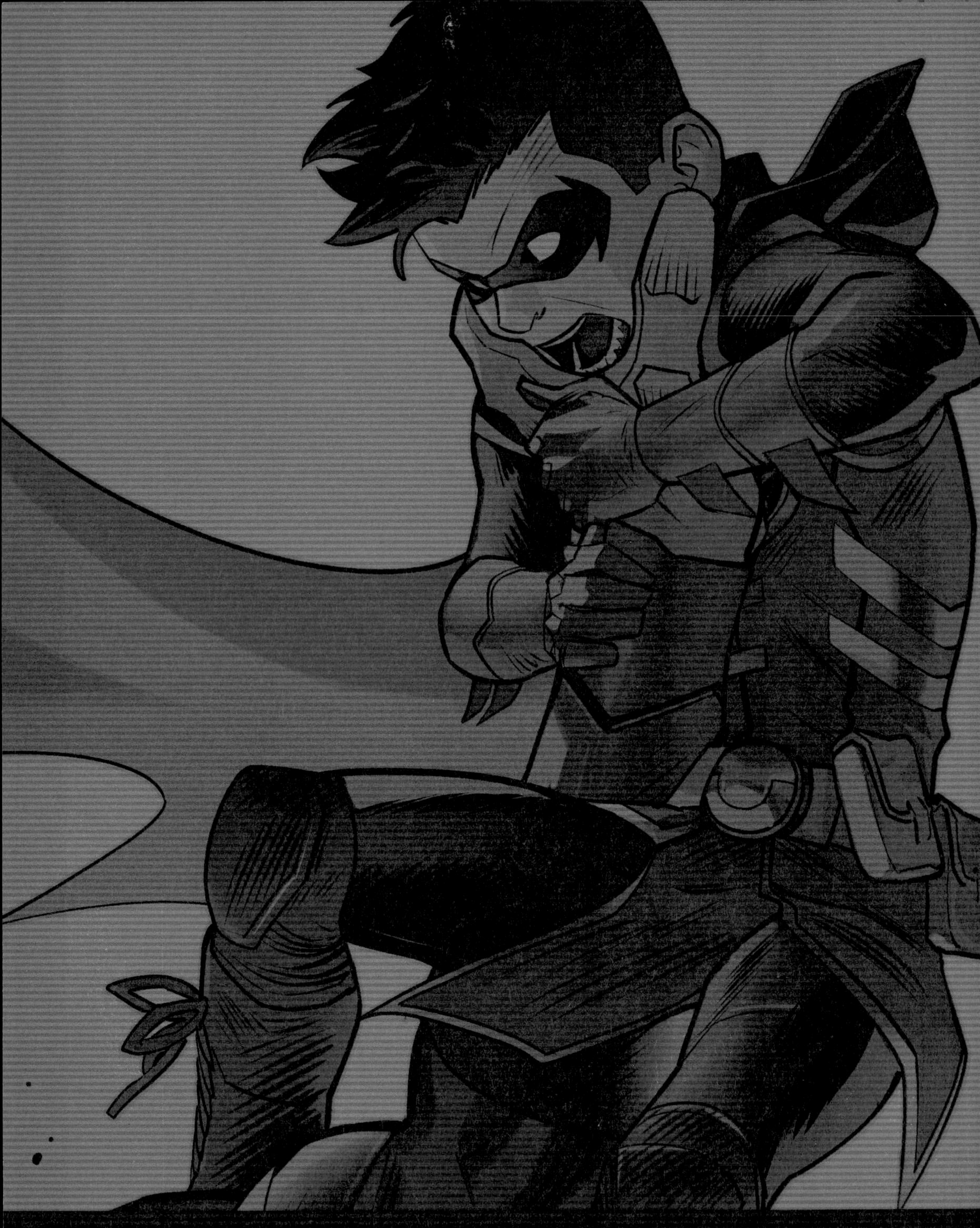

ADVENTURES OF THE SUPER SONS

#6

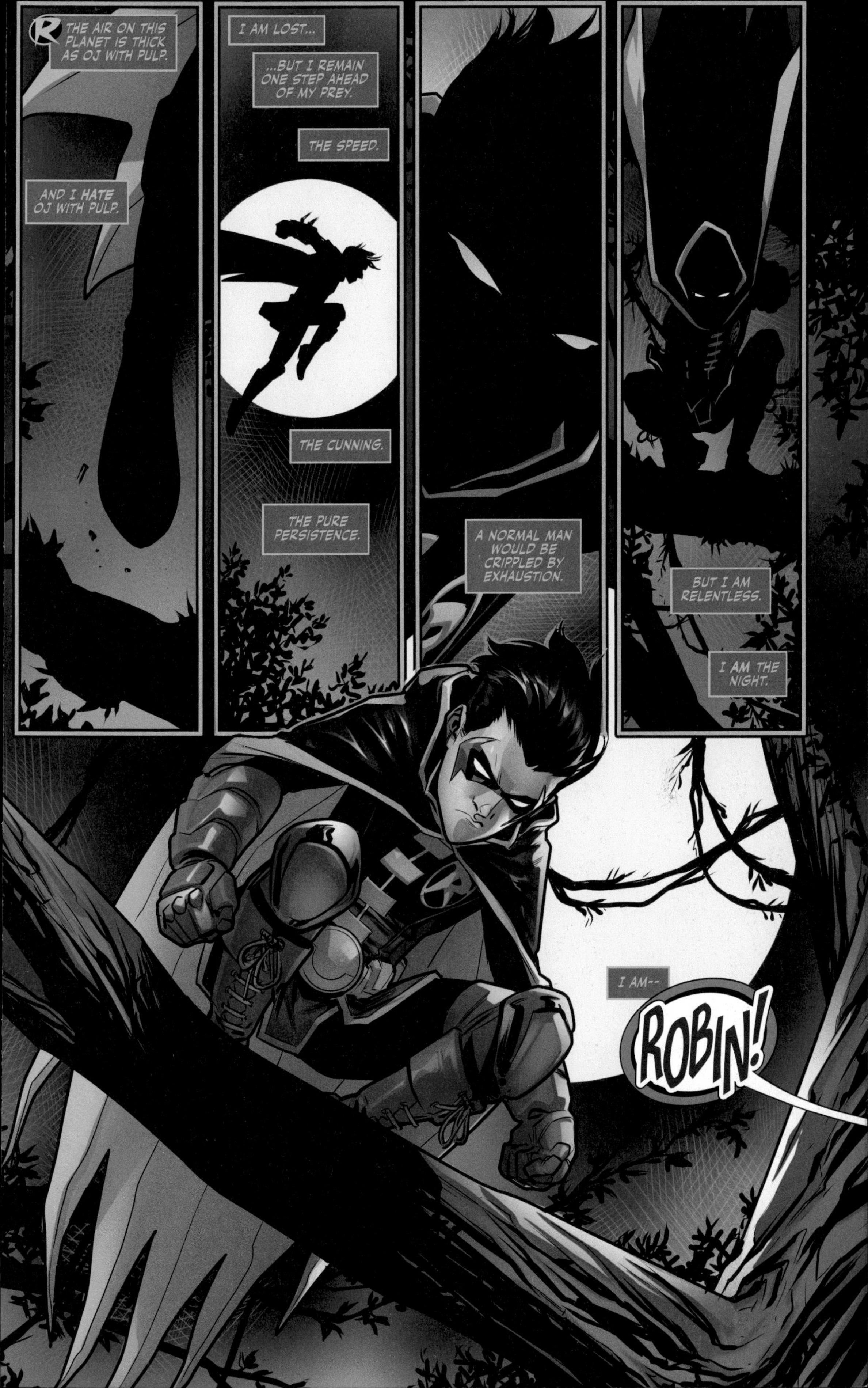
THE AIR ON THIS PLANET IS THICK AS OJ WITH PULP.
AND I HATE OJ WITH PULP.
I AM LOST...
...BUT I REMAIN ONE STEP AHEAD OF MY PREY.
THE SPEED.
THE CUNNING.
THE PURE PERSISTENCE.
A NORMAL MAN WOULD BE CRIPPLED BY EXHAUSTION.
BUT I AM RELENTLESS.
I AM THE NIGHT.
I AM--
ROBIN!

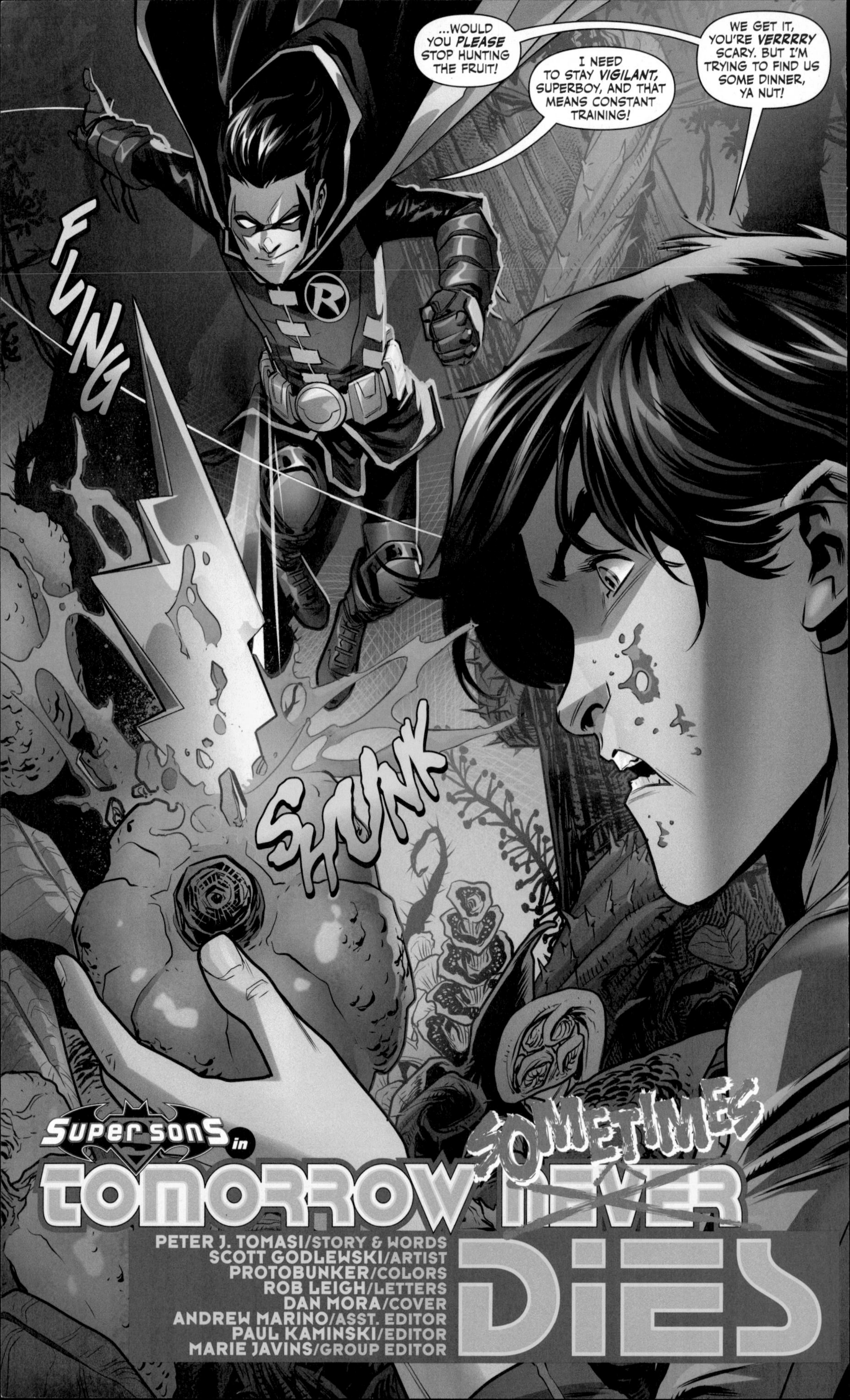
...WOULD YOU *PLEASE* STOP HUNTING THE FRUIT!
I NEED TO STAY *VIGILANT,* SUPERBOY, AND THAT MEANS CONSTANT TRAINING!
WE GET IT, YOU'RE *VERRRRY* SCARY. BUT I'M TRYING TO FIND US SOME DINNER, YA NUT!
FLING
SHUNK
SUPER SONS in
TOMORROW ~~NEVER~~ SOMETIMES DIES
PETER J. TOMASI/STORY & WORDS
SCOTT GODLEWSKI/ARTIST
PROTOBUNKER/COLORS
ROB LEIGH/LETTERS
DAN MORA/COVER
ANDREW MARINO/ASST. EDITOR
PAUL KAMINSKI/EDITOR
MARIE JAVINS/GROUP EDITOR

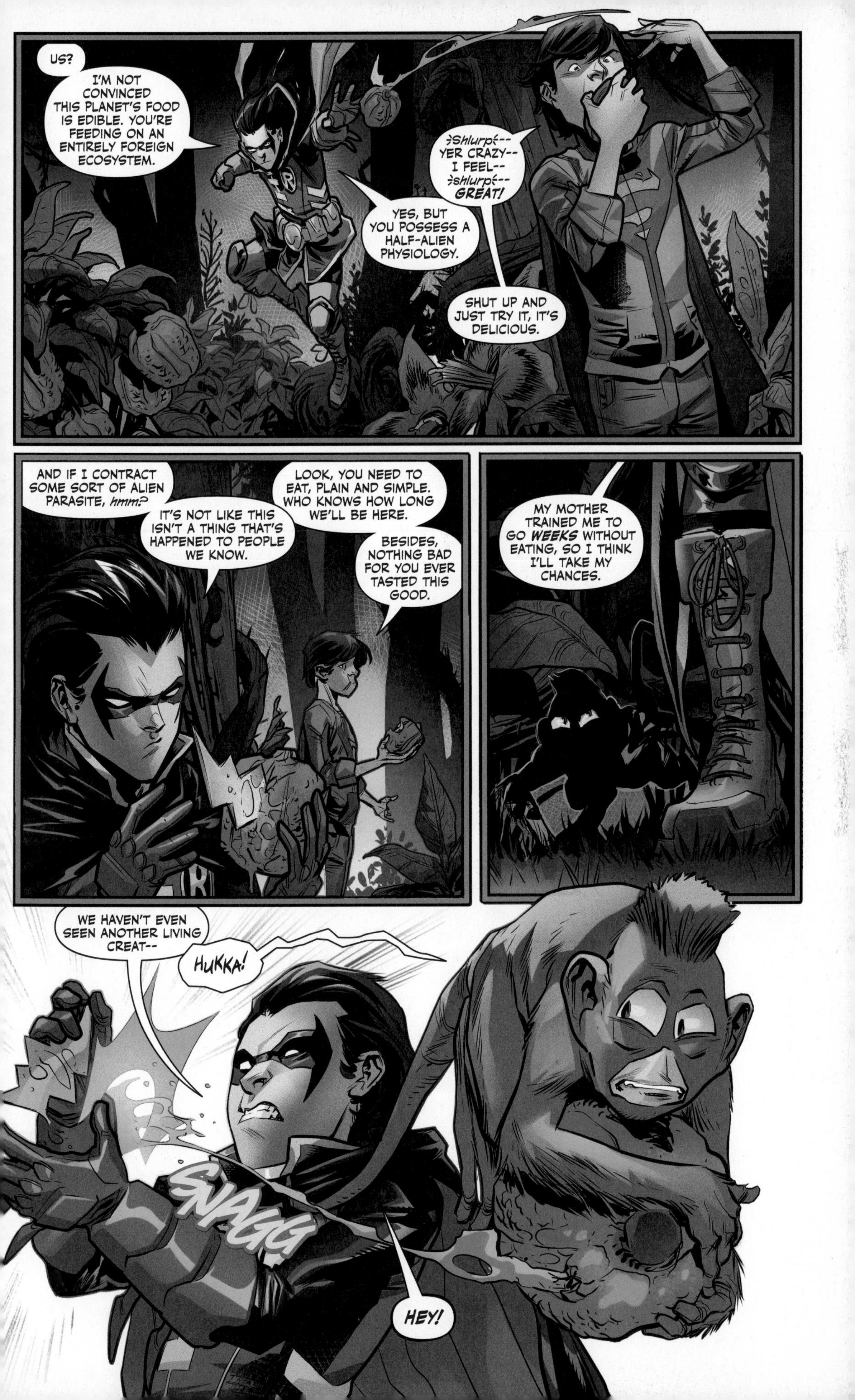
US?
I'M NOT CONVINCED THIS PLANET'S FOOD IS EDIBLE. YOU'RE FEEDING ON AN ENTIRELY FOREIGN ECOSYSTEM.
shlurp-- YER CRAZY-- I FEEL-- *shlurp*-- **GREAT!**
YES, BUT YOU POSSESS A HALF-ALIEN PHYSIOLOGY.
SHUT UP AND JUST TRY IT, IT'S DELICIOUS.
AND IF I CONTRACT SOME SORT OF ALIEN PARASITE, *hmm?*
IT'S NOT LIKE THIS ISN'T A THING THAT'S HAPPENED TO PEOPLE WE KNOW.
LOOK, YOU NEED TO EAT, PLAIN AND SIMPLE. WHO KNOWS HOW LONG WE'LL BE HERE.
BESIDES, NOTHING BAD FOR YOU EVER TASTED THIS GOOD.
MY MOTHER TRAINED ME TO GO ***WEEKS*** WITHOUT EATING, SO I THINK I'LL TAKE MY CHANCES.
WE HAVEN'T EVEN SEEN ANOTHER LIVING CREAT--
HUKKA!
SNAGG
HEY!

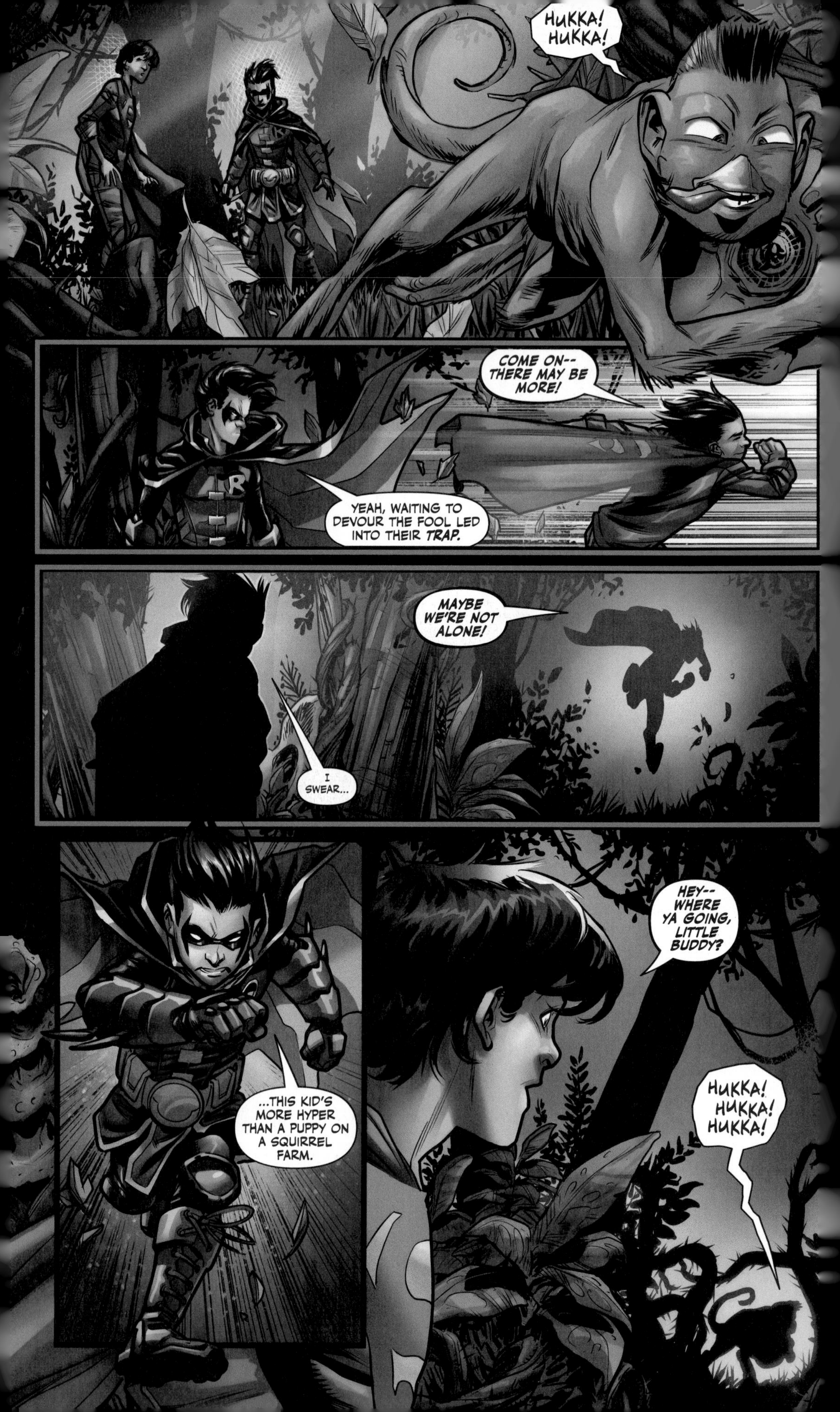
HUKKA! HUKKA!
COME ON-- THERE MAY BE MORE!
YEAH, WAITING TO DEVOUR THE FOOL LED INTO THEIR TRAP.
MAYBE WE'RE NOT ALONE!
I SWEAR...
...THIS KID'S MORE HYPER THAN A PUPPY ON A SQUIRREL FARM.
HEY-- WHERE YA GOING, LITTLE BUDDY?
HUKKA! HUKKA! HUKKA!

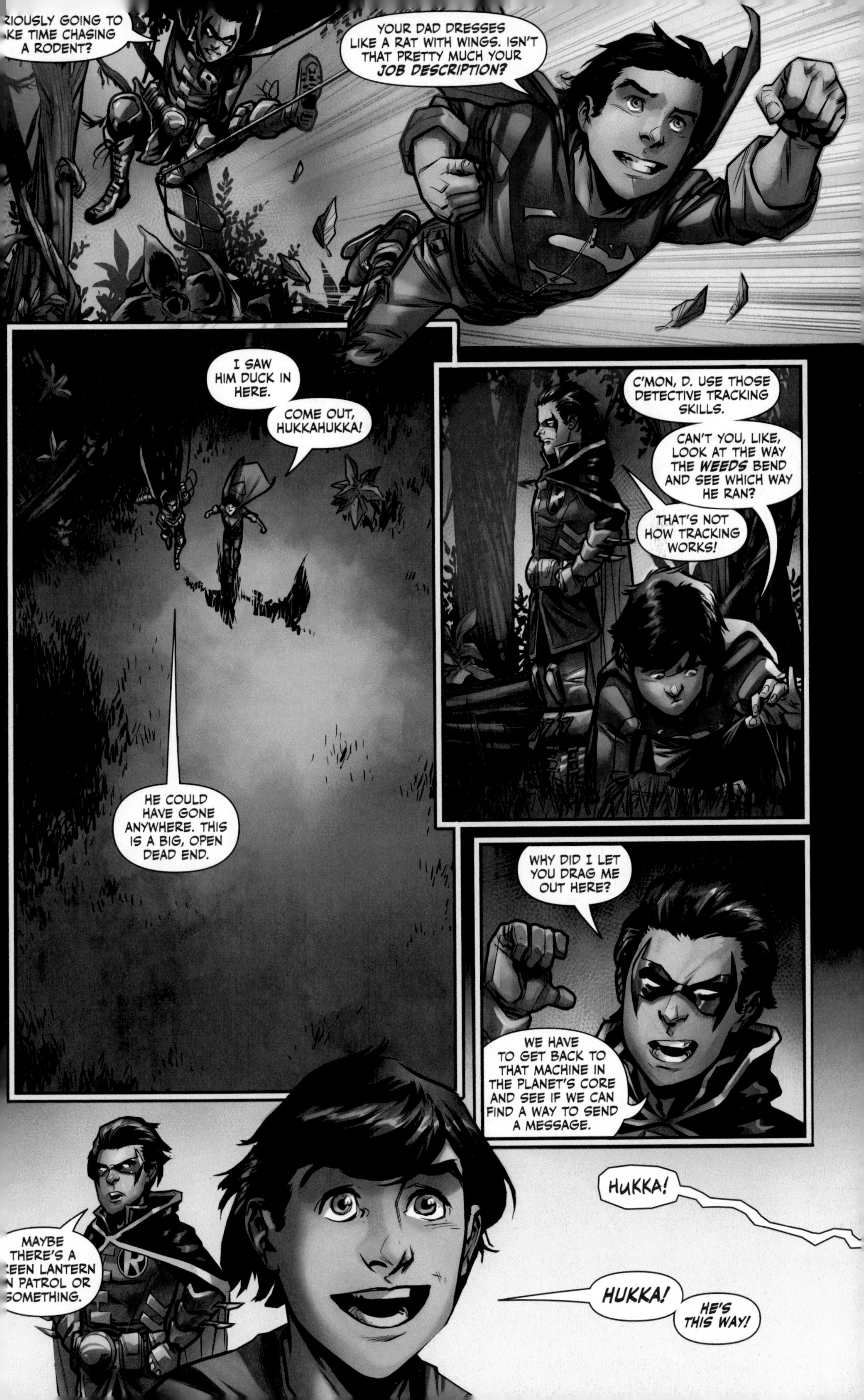

RIOUSLY GOING TO
AKE TIME CHASING
A RODENT?
YOUR DAD DRESSES LIKE A RAT WITH WINGS. ISN'T THAT PRETTY MUCH YOUR *JOB DESCRIPTION?*
I SAW HIM DUCK IN HERE.
COME OUT, HUKKAHUKKA!
HE COULD HAVE GONE ANYWHERE. THIS IS A BIG, OPEN DEAD END.
C'MON, D. USE THOSE DETECTIVE TRACKING SKILLS.
CAN'T YOU, LIKE, LOOK AT THE WAY THE *WEEDS* BEND AND SEE WHICH WAY HE RAN?
THAT'S NOT HOW TRACKING WORKS!
WHY DID I LET YOU DRAG ME OUT HERE?
WE HAVE TO GET BACK TO THAT MACHINE IN THE PLANET'S CORE AND SEE IF WE CAN FIND A WAY TO SEND A MESSAGE.
MAYBE THERE'S A
EEN LANTERN
N PATROL OR
SOMETHING.
HUKKA!
HUKKA!
HE'S THIS WAY!

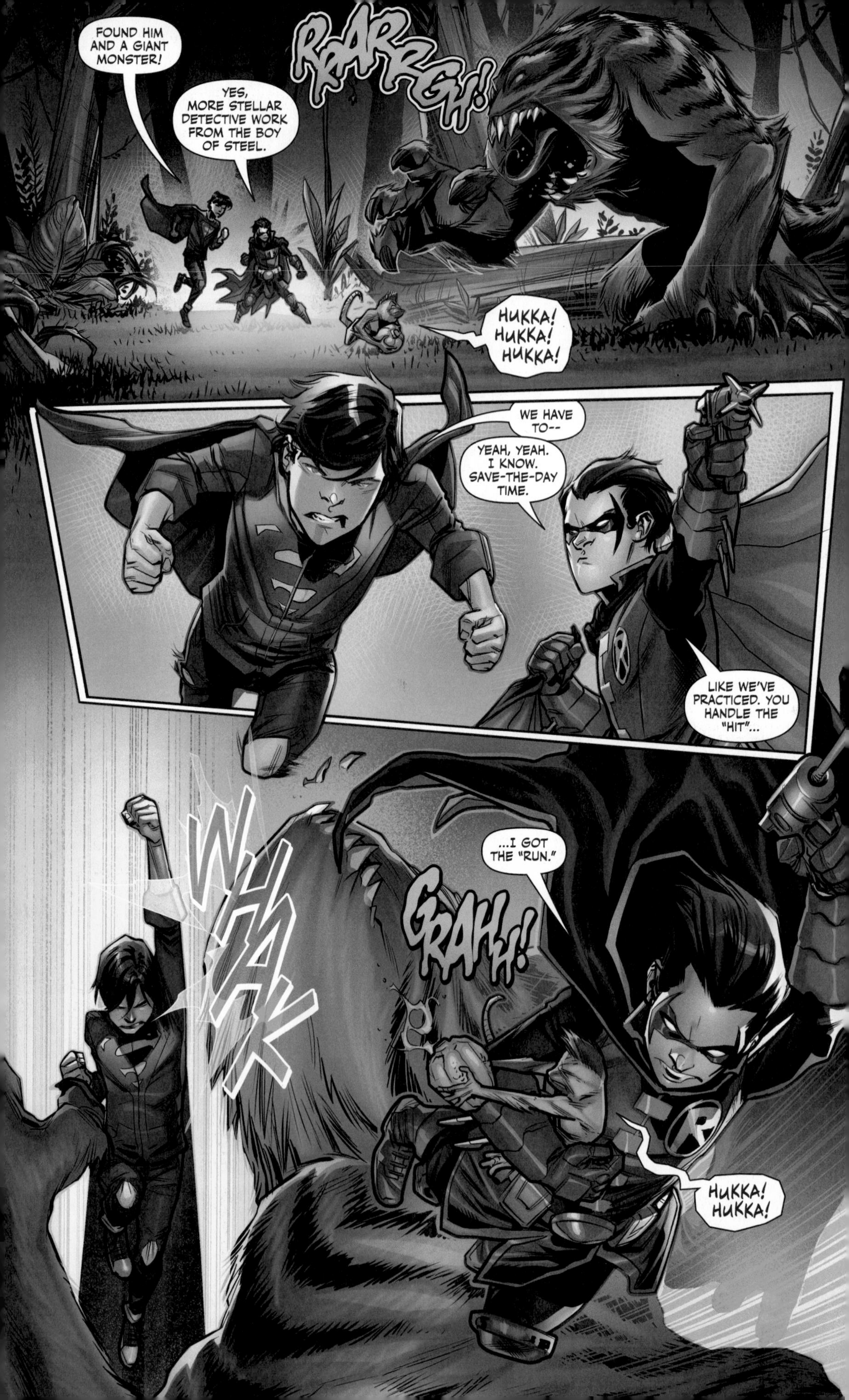
FOUND HIM AND A GIANT MONSTER!
RRARRGH!
YES, MORE STELLAR DETECTIVE WORK FROM THE BOY OF STEEL.
HUKKA! HUKKA! HUKKA!
WE HAVE TO--
YEAH, YEAH. I KNOW. SAVE-THE-DAY TIME.
LIKE WE'VE PRACTICED. YOU HANDLE THE "HIT"...
WHAK
...I GOT THE "RUN."
GRAHH!
HUKKA! HUKKA!

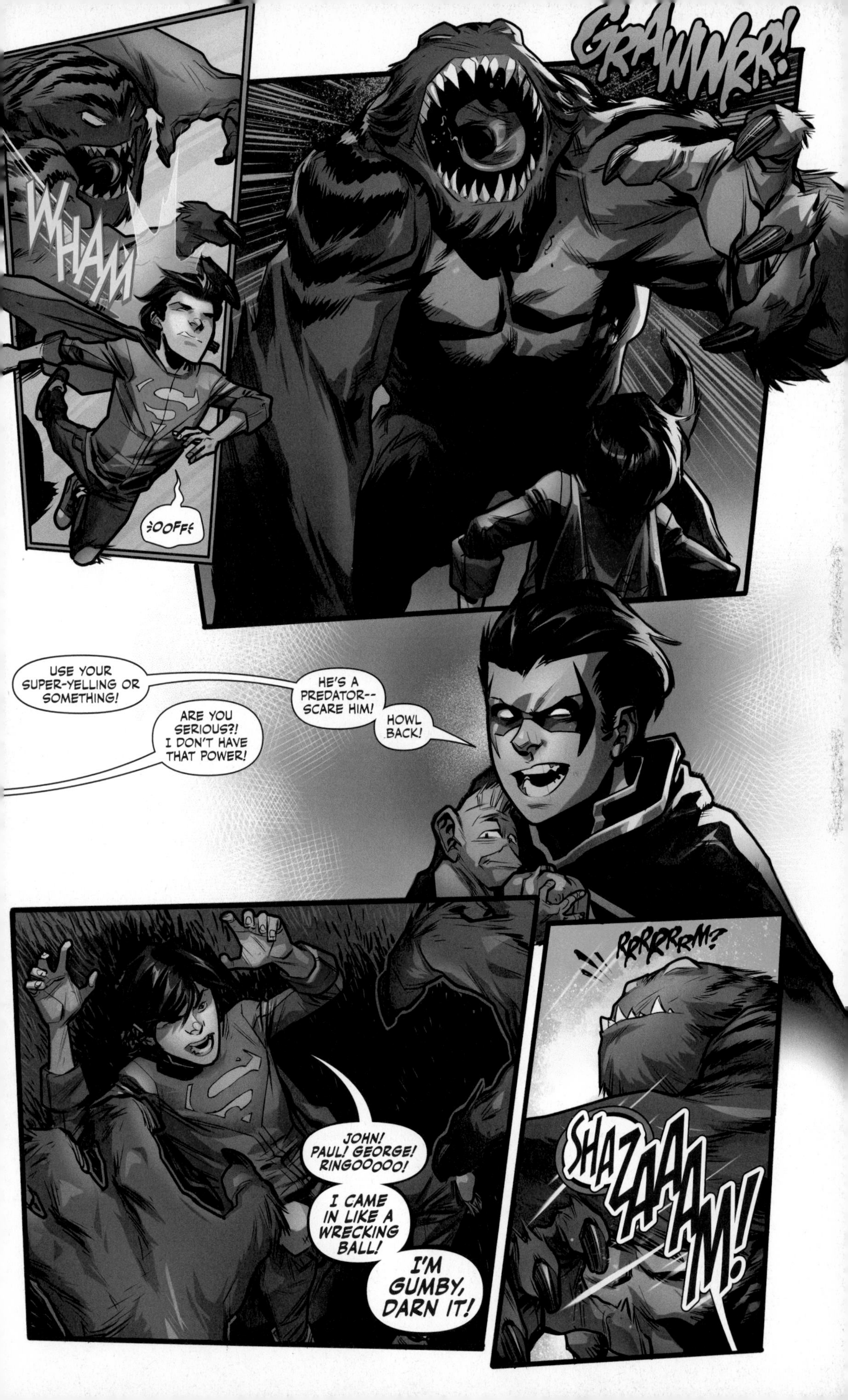
WHAM
GRAWWR!
OOFF
USE YOUR SUPER-YELLING OR SOMETHING!
HE'S A PREDATOR-- SCARE HIM!
HOWL BACK!
ARE YOU SERIOUS?! I DON'T HAVE THAT POWER!
JOHN! PAUL! GEORGE! RINGOOOOO!
I CAME IN LIKE A WRECKING BALL!
I'M GUMBY, DARN IT!
RRRRRRM?
SHAZAAAAM!

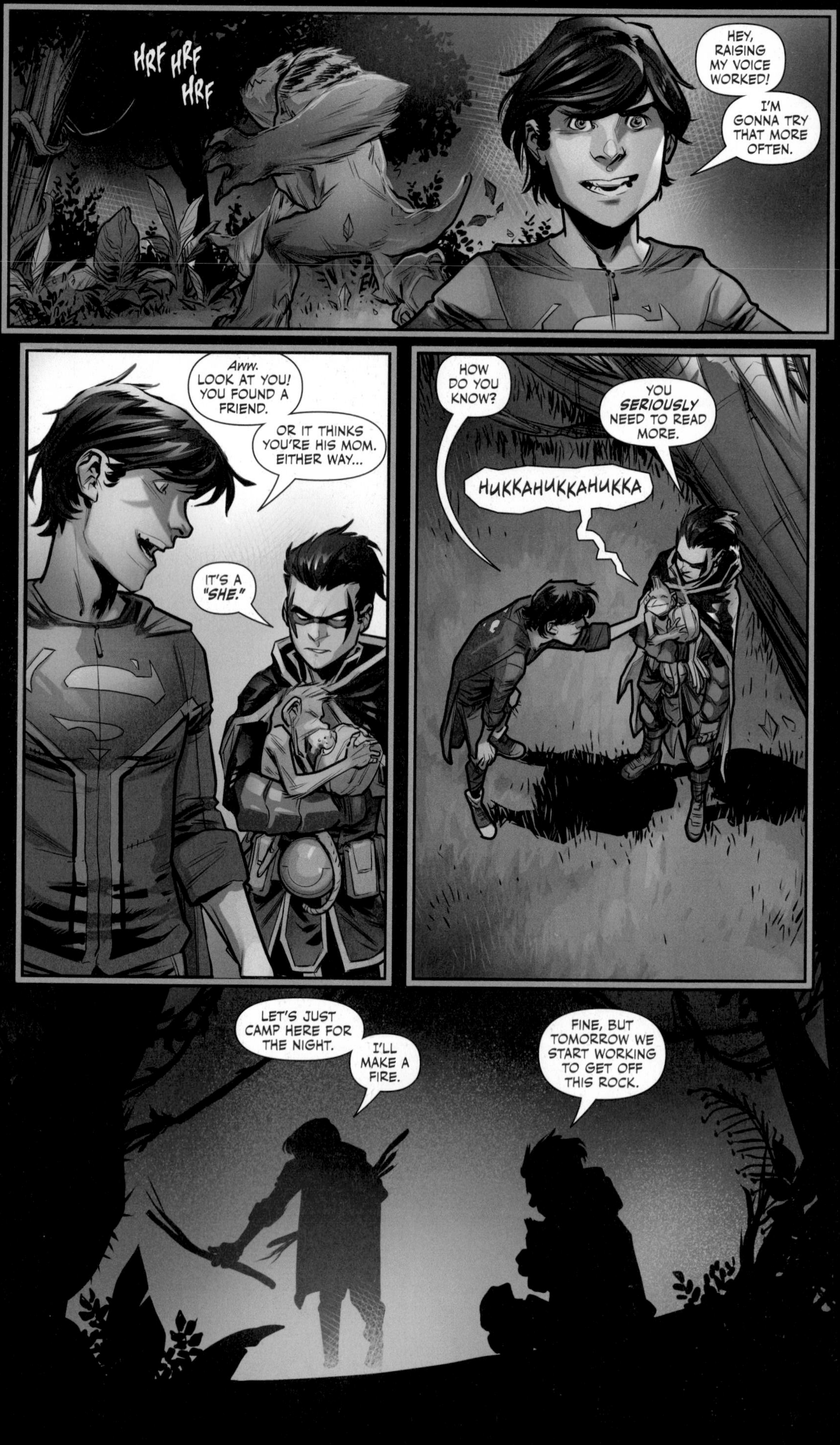
HRF HRF HRF
HEY, RAISING MY VOICE WORKED!
I'M GONNA TRY THAT MORE OFTEN.
AWW. LOOK AT YOU! YOU FOUND A FRIEND.
OR IT THINKS YOU'RE HIS MOM. EITHER WAY...
IT'S A "SHE."
HOW DO YOU KNOW?
YOU SERIOUSLY NEED TO READ MORE.
HUKKAHUKKAHUKKA
LET'S JUST CAMP HERE FOR THE NIGHT.
I'LL MAKE A FIRE.
FINE, BUT TOMORROW WE START WORKING TO GET OFF THIS ROCK.

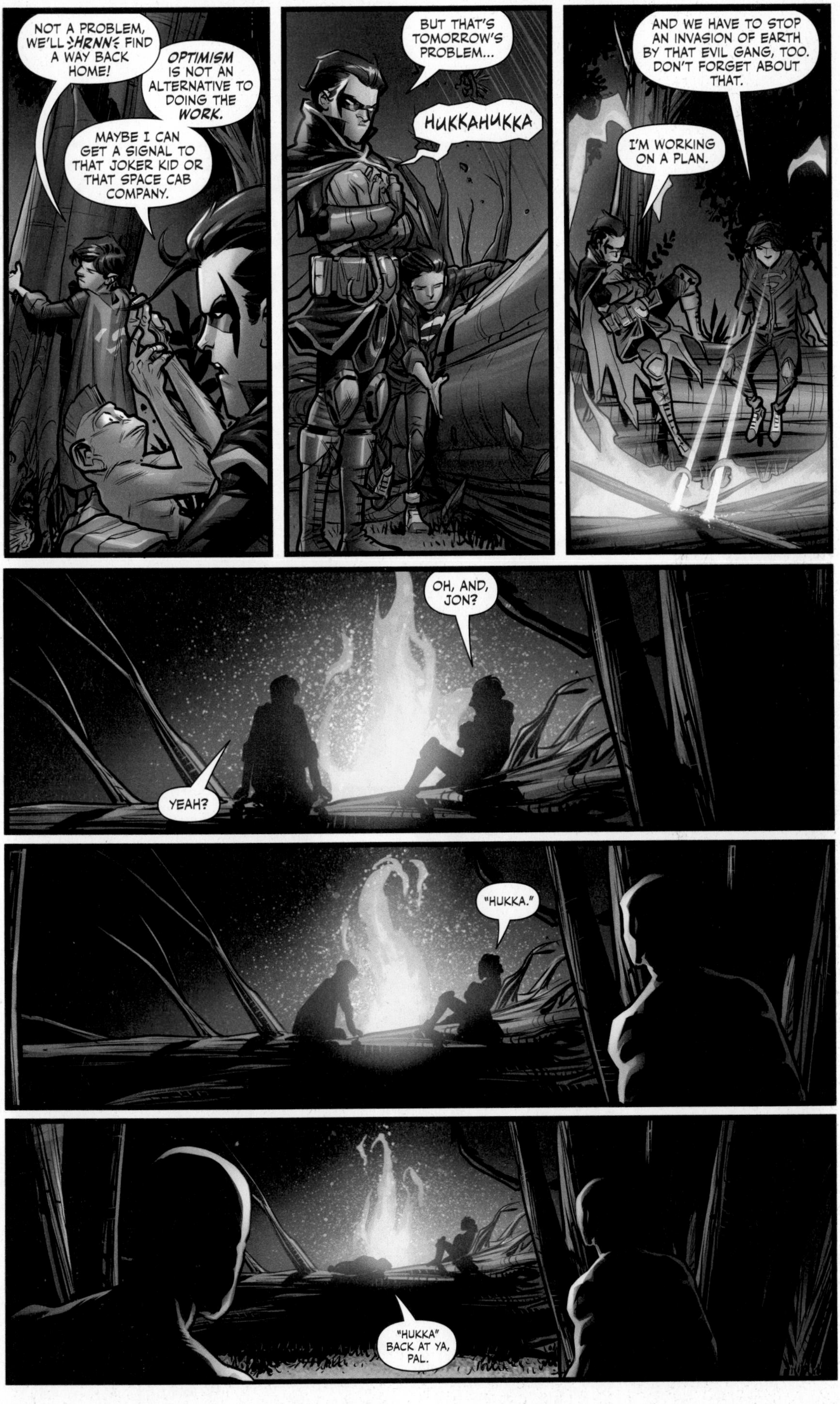
NOT A PROBLEM, WE'LL HRNN FIND A WAY BACK HOME!
OPTIMISM IS NOT AN ALTERNATIVE TO DOING THE WORK.
MAYBE I CAN GET A SIGNAL TO THAT JOKER KID OR THAT SPACE CAB COMPANY.
BUT THAT'S TOMORROW'S PROBLEM...
HUKKAHUKKA
AND WE HAVE TO STOP AN INVASION OF EARTH BY THAT EVIL GANG, TOO. DON'T FORGET ABOUT THAT.
I'M WORKING ON A PLAN.
OH, AND, JON?
YEAH?
"HUKKA."
"HUKKA" BACK AT YA, PAL.

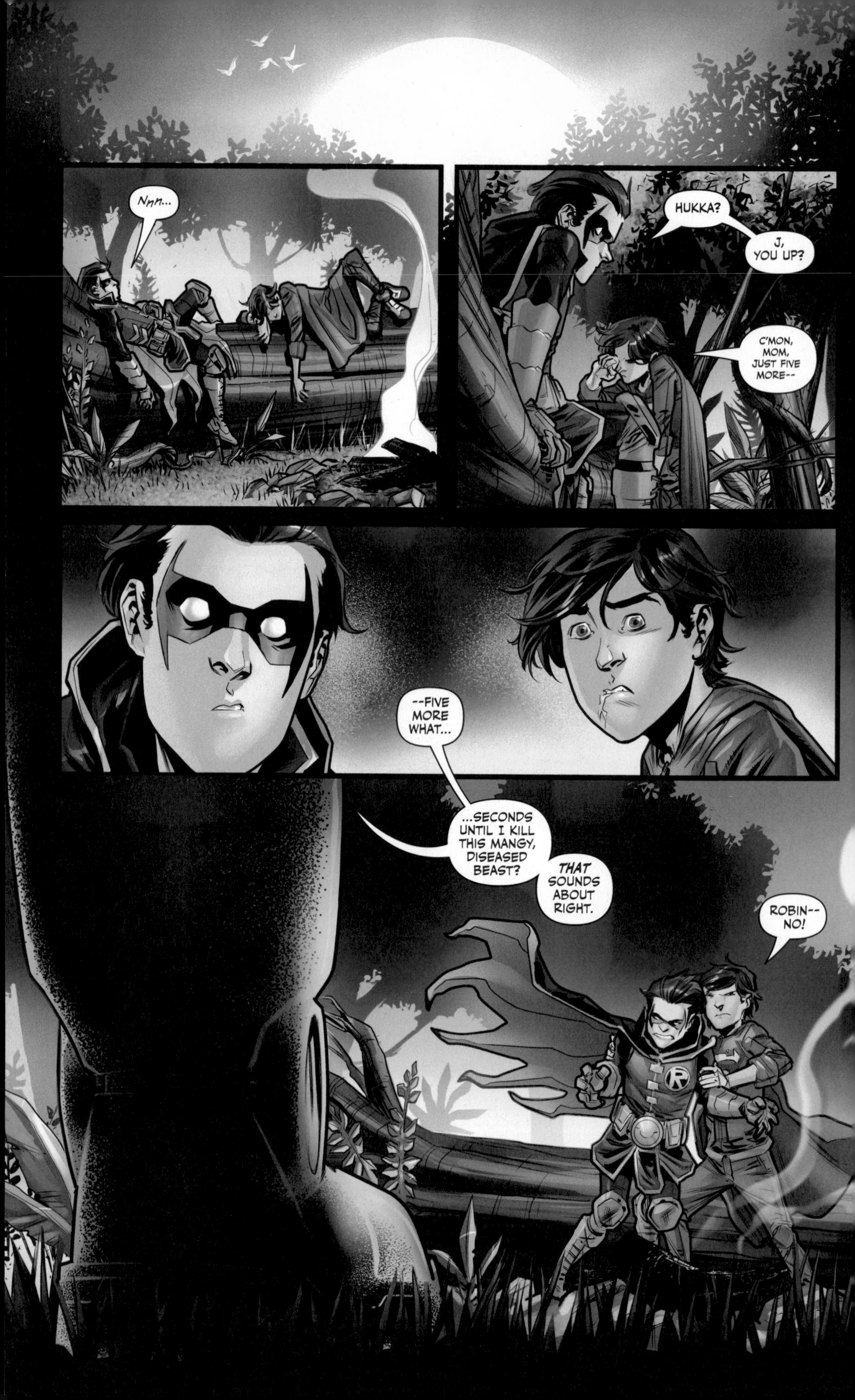
Nnn...
HUKKA?
J, YOU UP?
C'MON, MOM, JUST FIVE MORE--
--FIVE MORE WHAT...
...SECONDS UNTIL I KILL THIS MANGY, DISEASED BEAST?
THAT SOUNDS ABOUT RIGHT.
ROBIN-- NO!

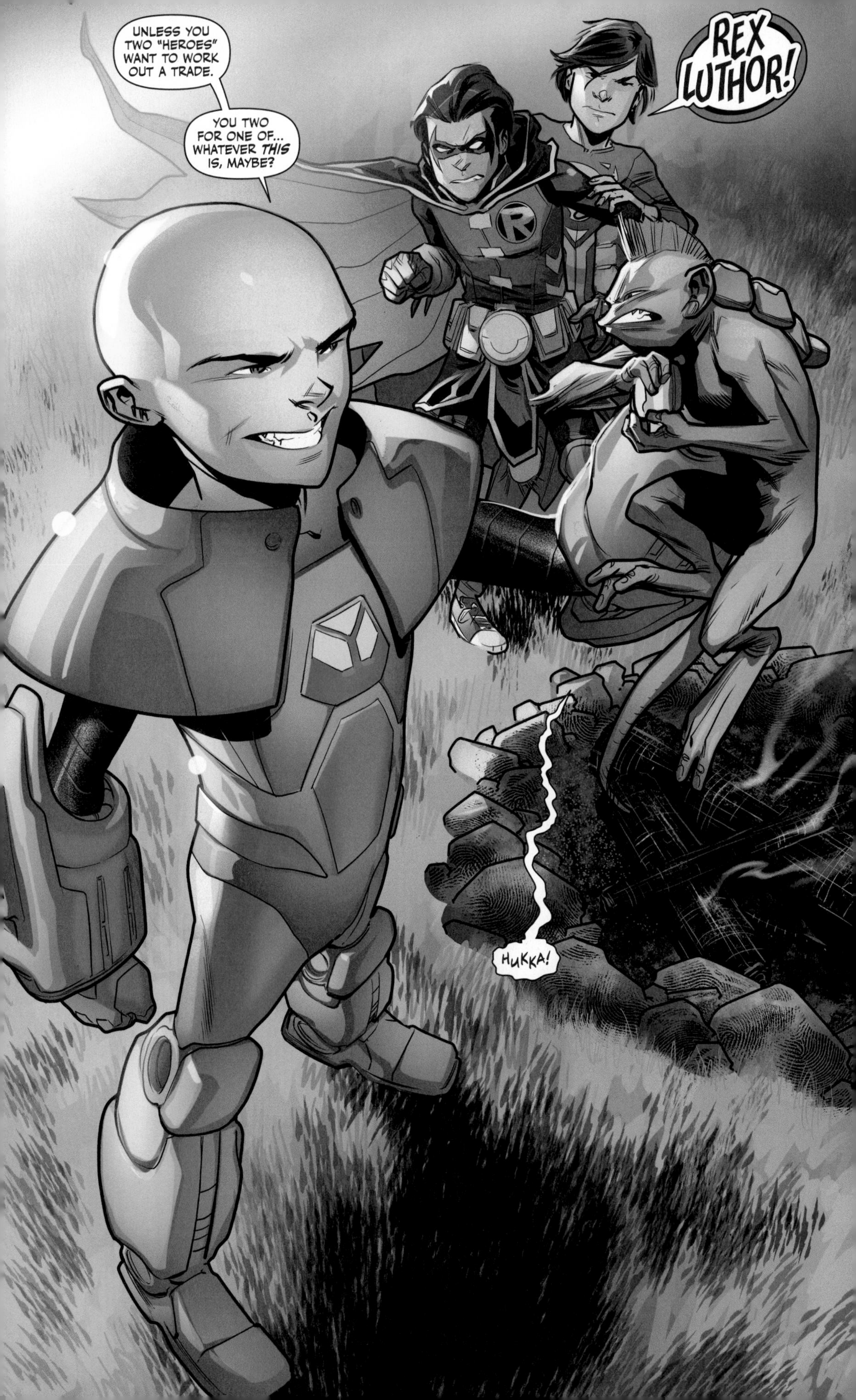
UNLESS YOU TWO "HEROES" WANT TO WORK OUT A TRADE.
YOU TWO FOR ONE OF... WHATEVER *THIS* IS, MAYBE?
REX LUTHOR!
HUKKA!

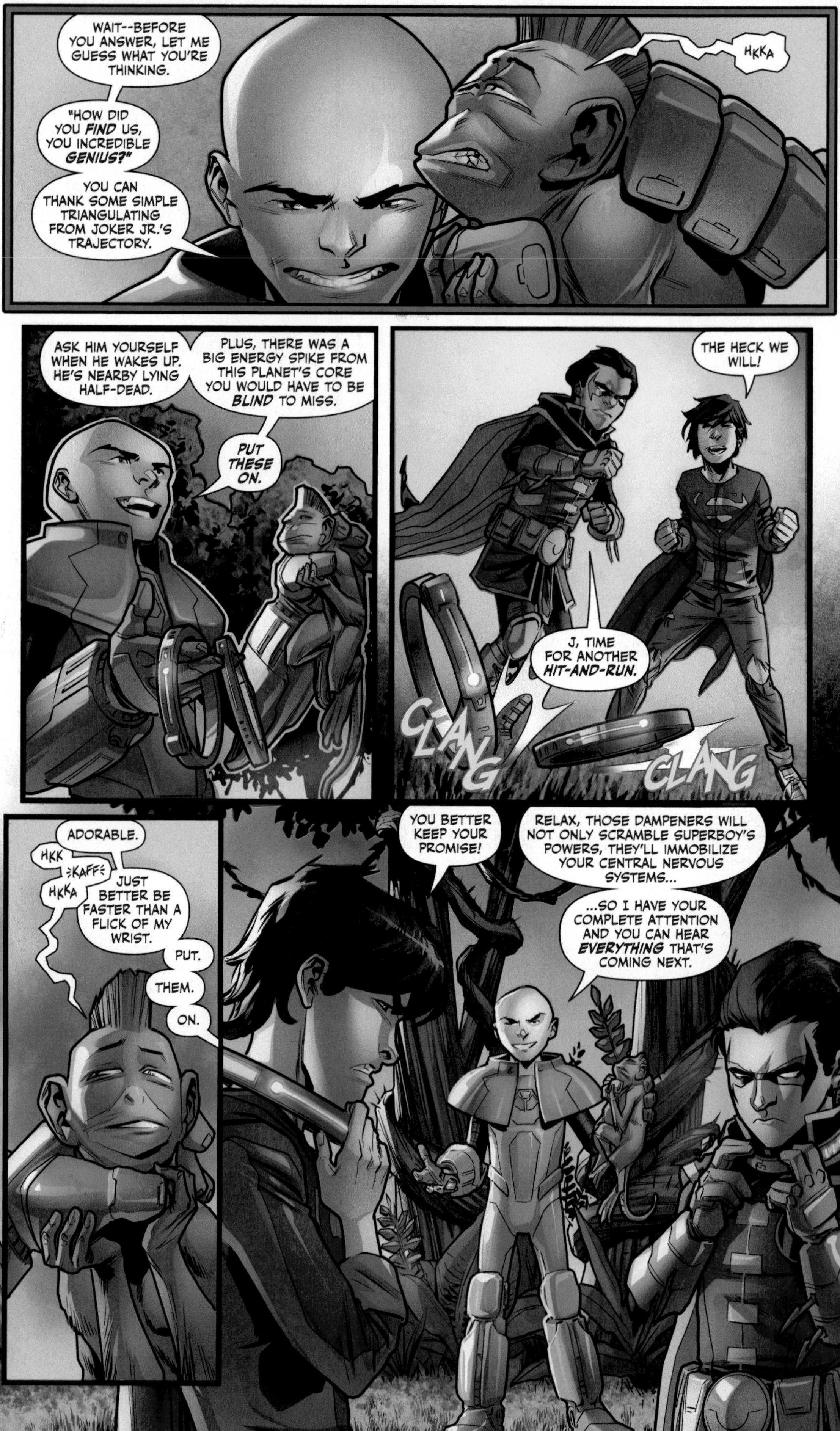
WAIT--BEFORE YOU ANSWER, LET ME GUESS WHAT YOU'RE THINKING.
"HOW DID YOU FIND US, YOU INCREDIBLE GENIUS?"
YOU CAN THANK SOME SIMPLE TRIANGULATING FROM JOKER JR.'S TRAJECTORY.
HKKA
ASK HIM YOURSELF WHEN HE WAKES UP. HE'S NEARBY LYING HALF-DEAD.
PLUS, THERE WAS A BIG ENERGY SPIKE FROM THIS PLANET'S CORE YOU WOULD HAVE TO BE BLIND TO MISS.
PUT THESE ON.
THE HECK WE WILL!
J, TIME FOR ANOTHER HIT-AND-RUN.
CLANG
CLANG
ADORABLE.
HKK
KAFF
HKKA
JUST BETTER BE FASTER THAN A FLICK OF MY WRIST.
PUT.
THEM.
ON.
YOU BETTER KEEP YOUR PROMISE!
RELAX, THOSE DAMPENERS WILL NOT ONLY SCRAMBLE SUPERBOY'S POWERS, THEY'LL IMMOBILIZE YOUR CENTRAL NERVOUS SYSTEMS...
...SO I HAVE YOUR COMPLETE ATTENTION AND YOU CAN HEAR EVERYTHING THAT'S COMING NEXT.

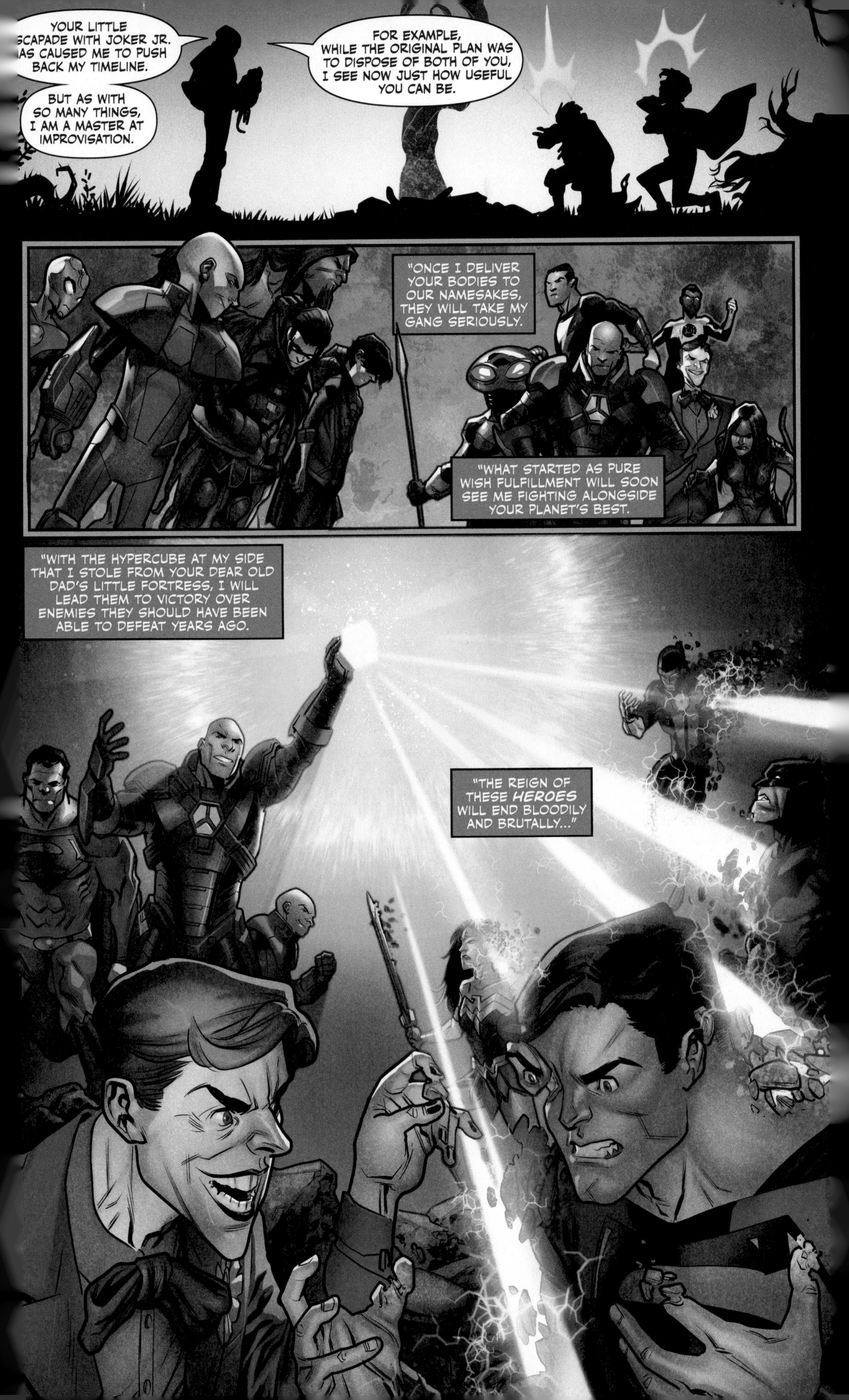
YOUR LITTLE
SCAPADE WITH JOKER JR.
HAS CAUSED ME TO PUSH
BACK MY TIMELINE.
BUT AS WITH
SO MANY THINGS,
I AM A MASTER AT
IMPROVISATION.
FOR EXAMPLE,
WHILE THE ORIGINAL PLAN WAS
TO DISPOSE OF BOTH OF YOU,
I SEE NOW JUST HOW USEFUL
YOU CAN BE.
"ONCE I DELIVER
YOUR BODIES TO
OUR NAMESAKES,
THEY WILL TAKE MY
GANG SERIOUSLY.
"WHAT STARTED AS PURE
WISH FULFILLMENT WILL SOON
SEE ME FIGHTING ALONGSIDE
YOUR PLANET'S BEST.
"WITH THE HYPERCUBE AT MY SIDE
THAT I STOLE FROM YOUR DEAR OLD
DAD'S LITTLE FORTRESS, I WILL
LEAD THEM TO VICTORY OVER
ENEMIES THEY SHOULD HAVE BEEN
ABLE TO DEFEAT YEARS AGO.
"THE REIGN OF
THESE *HEROES*
WILL END BLOODILY
AND BRUTALLY..."

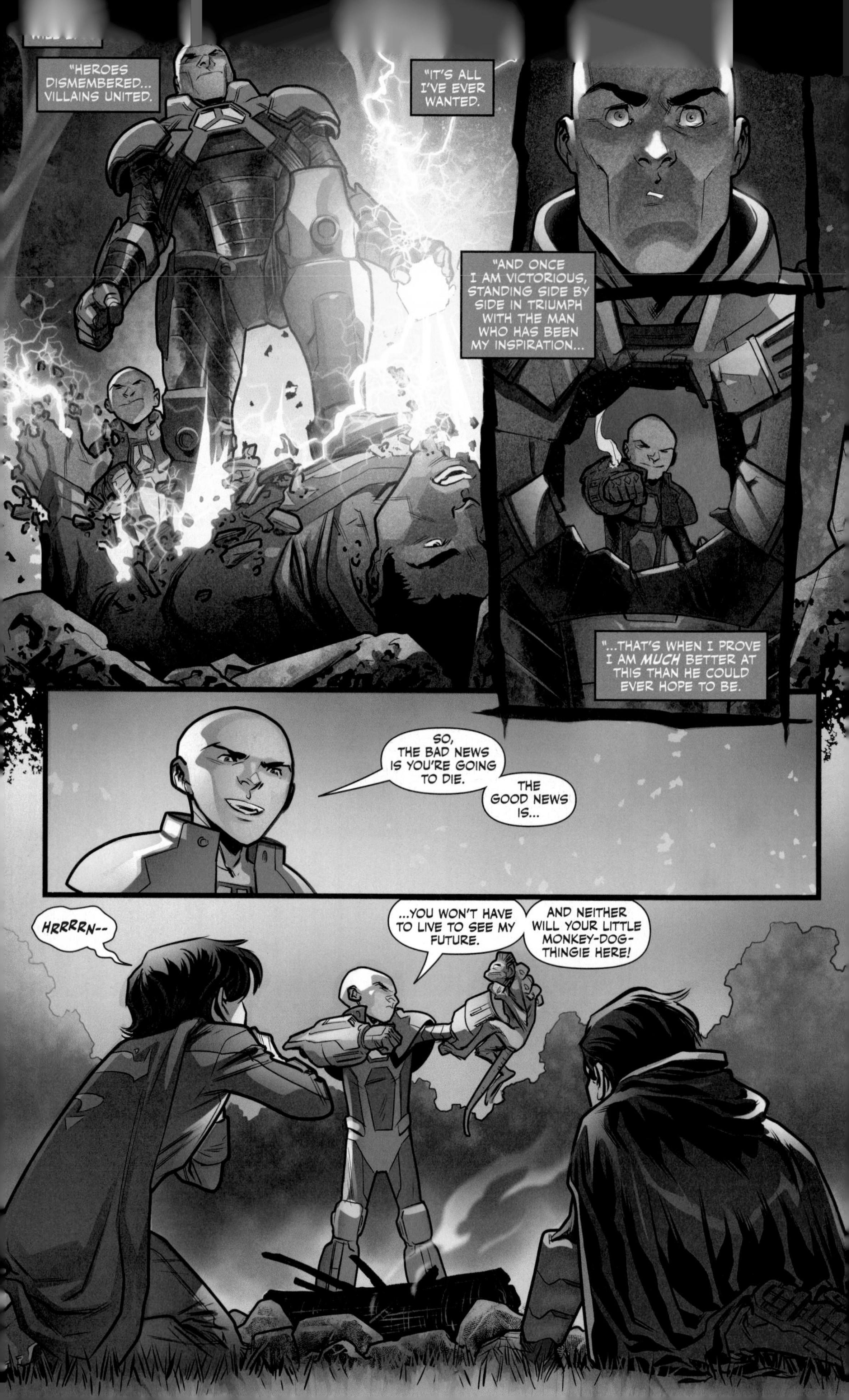
"HEROES DISMEMBERED... VILLAINS UNITED.
"IT'S ALL I'VE EVER WANTED.
"AND ONCE I AM VICTORIOUS, STANDING SIDE BY SIDE IN TRIUMPH WITH THE MAN WHO HAS BEEN MY INSPIRATION...
"...THAT'S WHEN I PROVE I AM *MUCH* BETTER AT THIS THAN HE COULD EVER HOPE TO BE.
SO, THE BAD NEWS IS YOU'RE GOING TO DIE.
THE GOOD NEWS IS...
HRRRRN--
...YOU WON'T HAVE TO LIVE TO SEE MY FUTURE.
AND NEITHER WILL YOUR LITTLE MONKEY-DOG-THINGIE HERE!

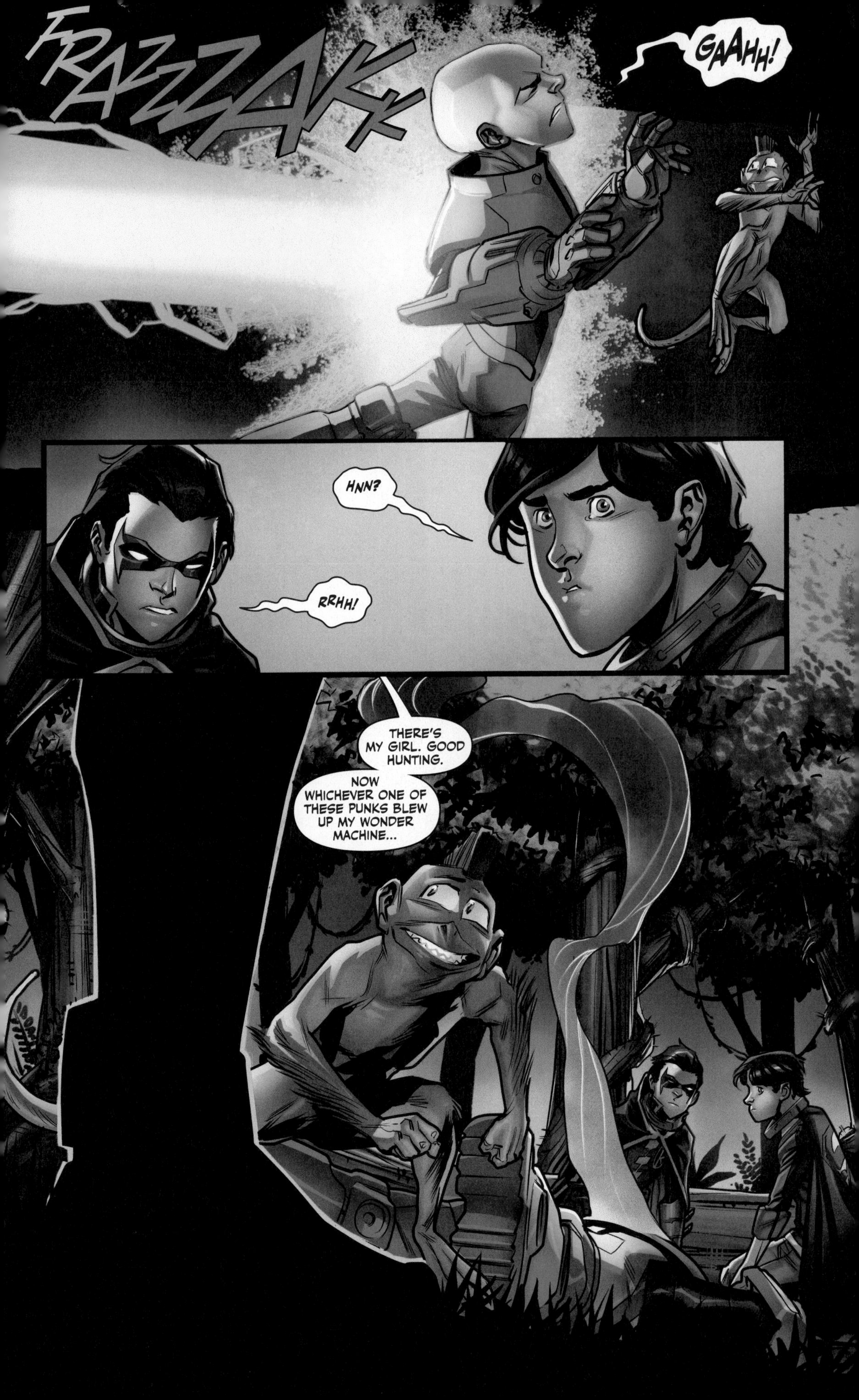
FRAZZZAKK
GAAHH!
HNN?
RRHH!
THERE'S MY GIRL. GOOD HUNTING.
NOW WHICHEVER ONE OF THESE PUNKS BLEW UP MY WONDER MACHINE...

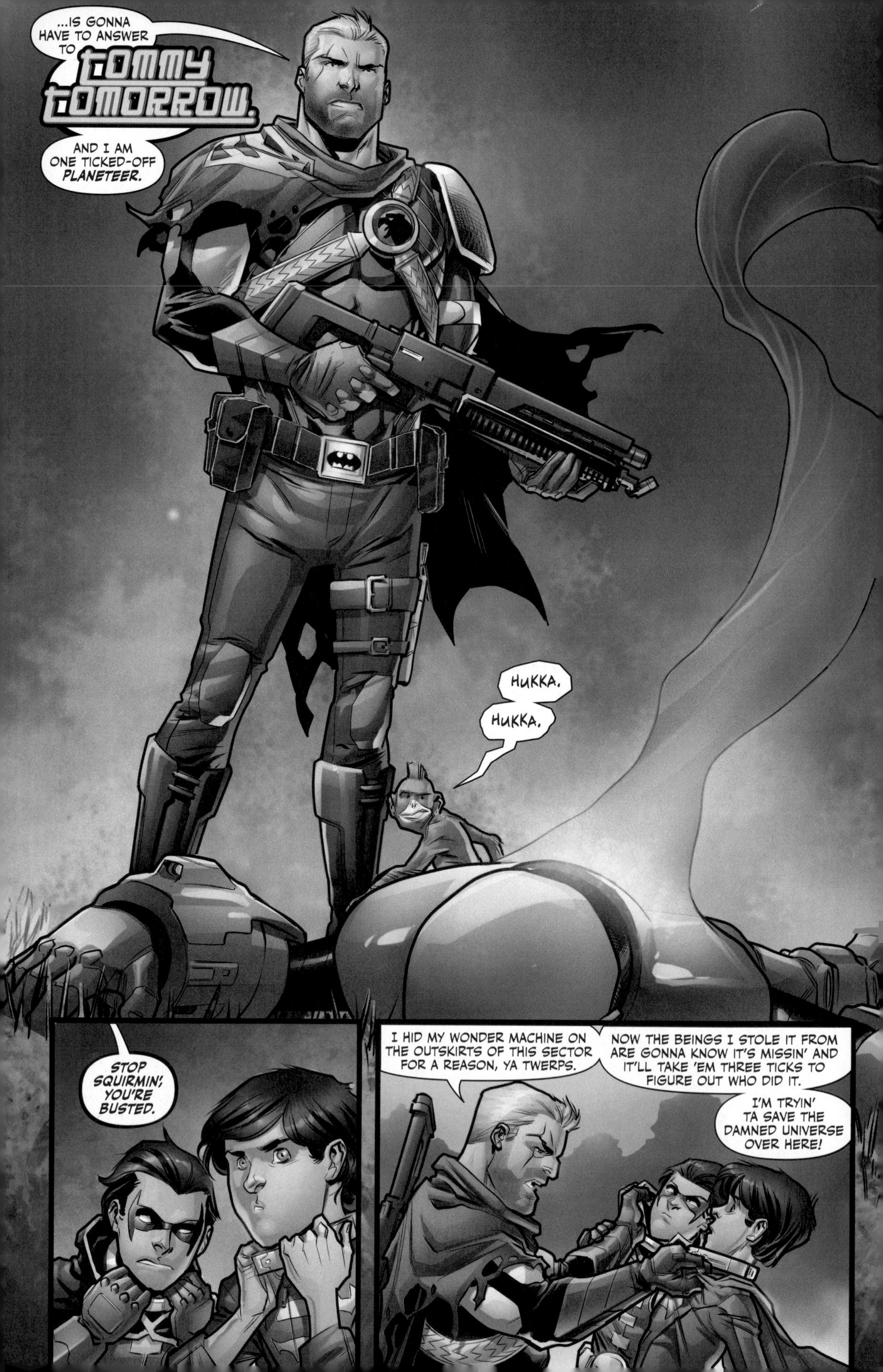
...IS GONNA HAVE TO ANSWER TO
TOMMY TOMORROW.
AND I AM ONE TICKED-OFF PLANETEER.
HUKKA.
HUKKA.
STOP SQUIRMIN'; YOU'RE BUSTED.
I HID MY WONDER MACHINE ON THE OUTSKIRTS OF THIS SECTOR FOR A REASON, YA TWERPS.
NOW THE BEINGS I STOLE IT FROM ARE GONNA KNOW IT'S MISSIN' AND IT'LL TAKE 'EM THREE TICKS TO FIGURE OUT WHO DID IT.
I'M TRYIN' TA SAVE THE DAMNED UNIVERSE OVER HERE!

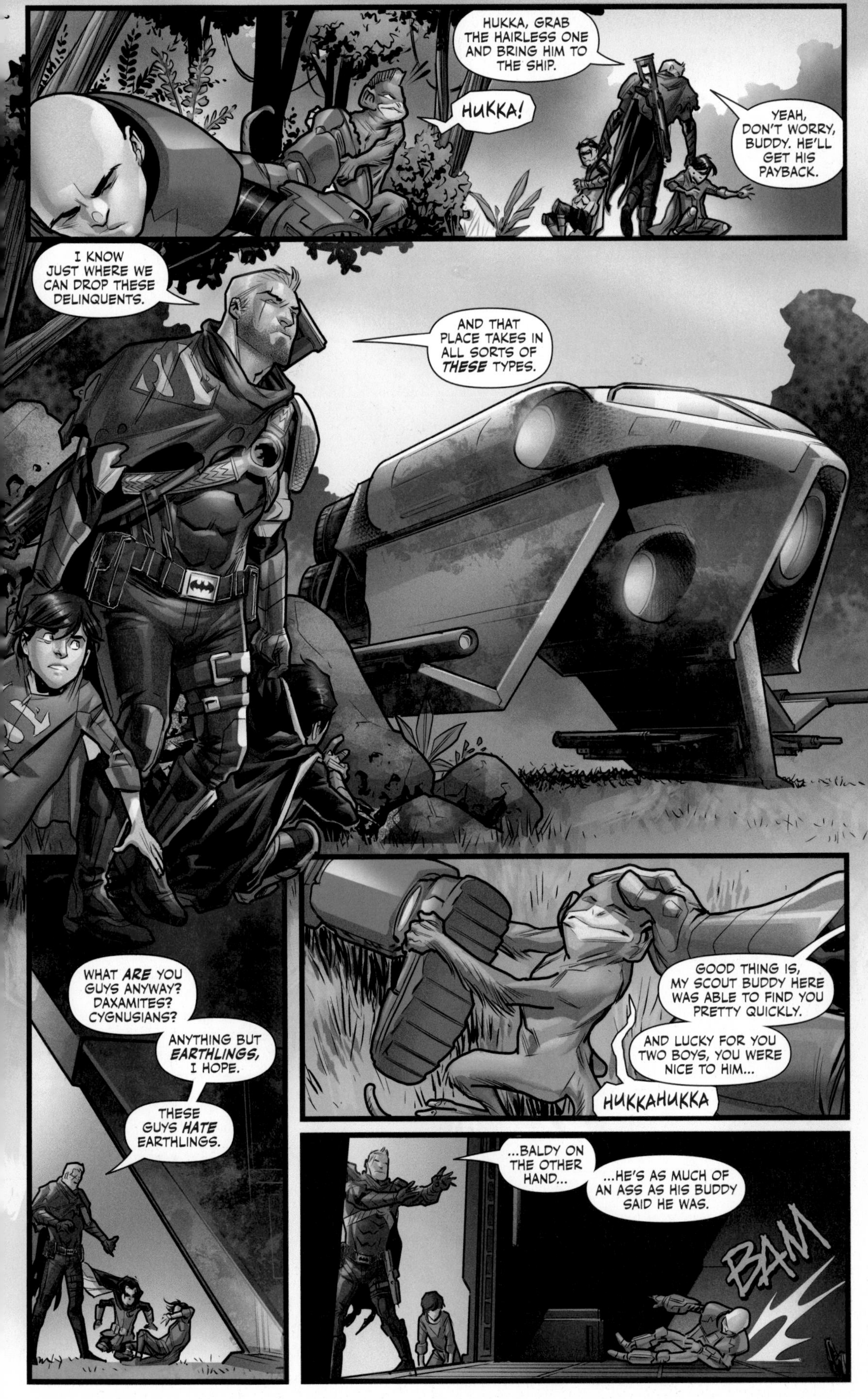
HUKKA, GRAB THE HAIRLESS ONE AND BRING HIM TO THE SHIP.
HUKKA!
YEAH, DON'T WORRY, BUDDY. HE'LL GET HIS PAYBACK.
I KNOW JUST WHERE WE CAN DROP THESE DELINQUENTS.
AND THAT PLACE TAKES IN ALL SORTS OF THESE TYPES.
WHAT ARE YOU GUYS ANYWAY? DAXAMITES? CYGNUSIANS?
ANYTHING BUT EARTHLINGS, I HOPE.
THESE GUYS HATE EARTHLINGS.
GOOD THING IS, MY SCOUT BUDDY HERE WAS ABLE TO FIND YOU PRETTY QUICKLY.
AND LUCKY FOR YOU TWO BOYS, YOU WERE NICE TO HIM...
HUKKAHUKKA
...BALDY ON THE OTHER HAND...
...HE'S AS MUCH OF AN ASS AS HIS BUDDY SAID HE WAS.
BAM

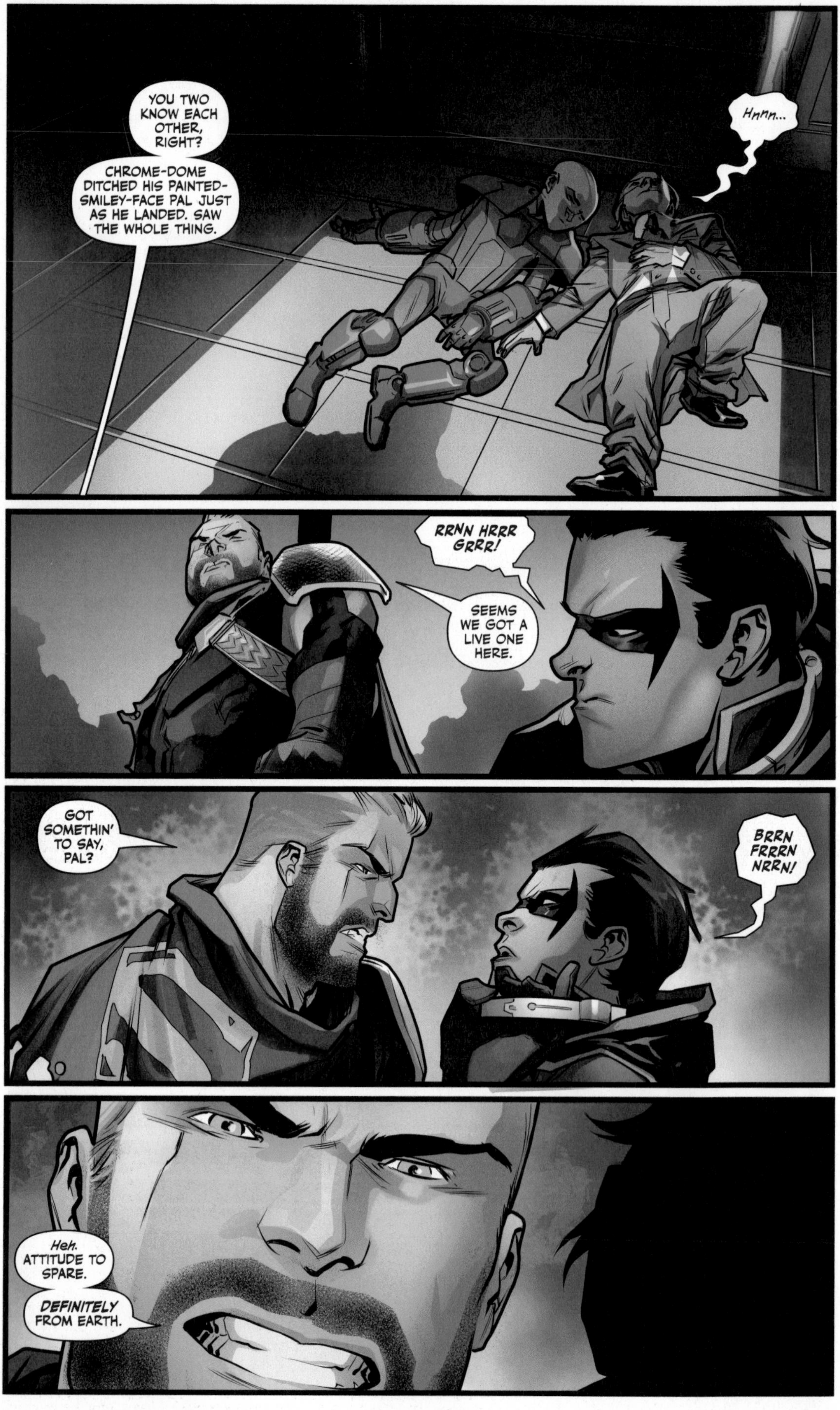
YOU TWO KNOW EACH OTHER, RIGHT?
CHROME-DOME DITCHED HIS PAINTED-SMILEY-FACE PAL JUST AS HE LANDED. SAW THE WHOLE THING.
Hnnn...
RRNN HRRR GRRR!
SEEMS WE GOT A LIVE ONE HERE.
GOT SOMETHIN' TO SAY, PAL?
BRRN FRRRN NRRN!
Heh. ATTITUDE TO SPARE.
DEFINITELY FROM EARTH.

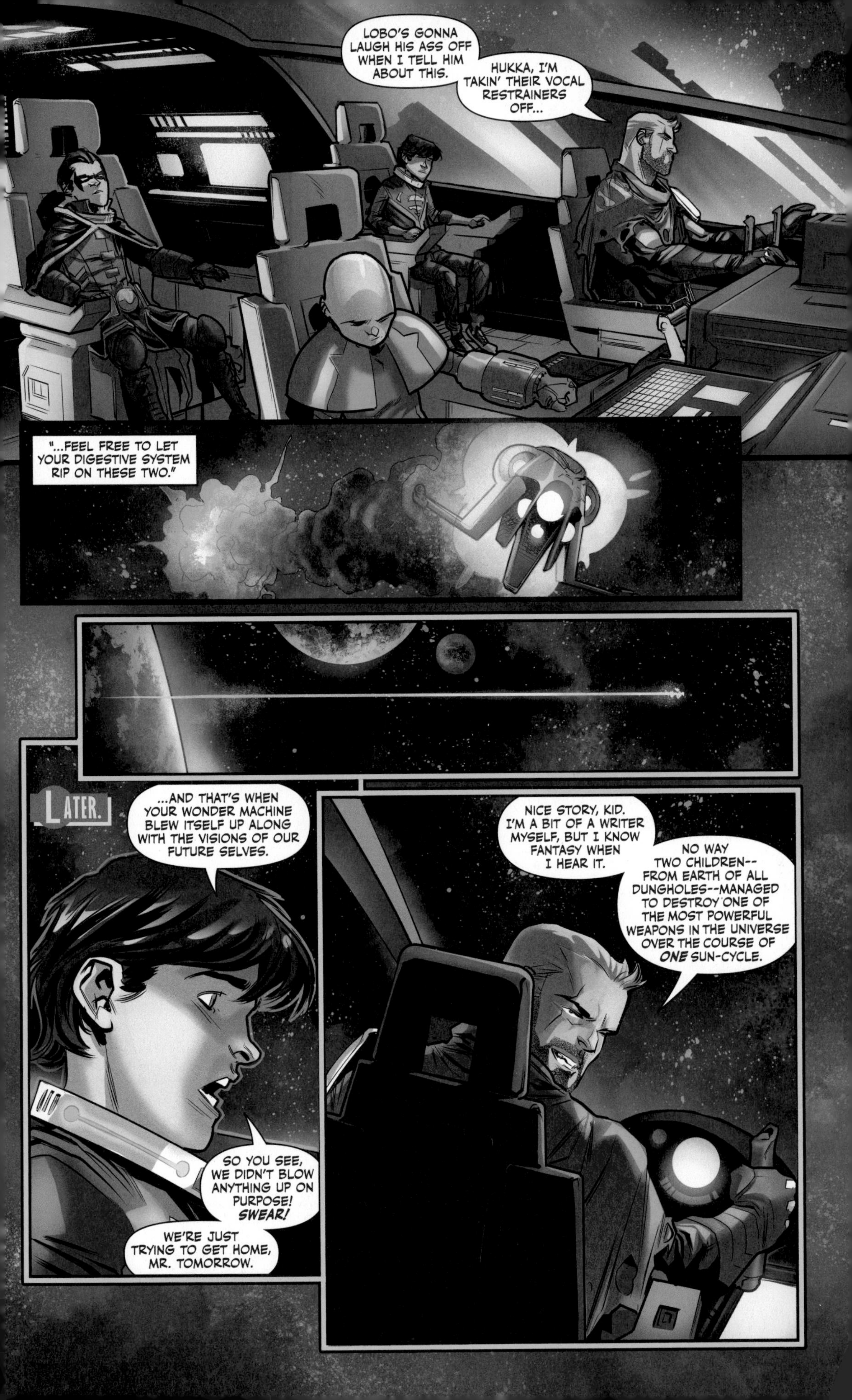
LOBO'S GONNA LAUGH HIS ASS OFF WHEN I TELL HIM ABOUT THIS.
HUKKA, I'M TAKIN' THEIR VOCAL RESTRAINERS OFF...
"...FEEL FREE TO LET YOUR DIGESTIVE SYSTEM RIP ON THESE TWO."
LATER.
...AND THAT'S WHEN YOUR WONDER MACHINE BLEW ITSELF UP ALONG WITH THE VISIONS OF OUR FUTURE SELVES.
SO YOU SEE, WE DIDN'T BLOW ANYTHING UP ON PURPOSE! SWEAR!
WE'RE JUST TRYING TO GET HOME, MR. TOMORROW.
NICE STORY, KID. I'M A BIT OF A WRITER MYSELF, BUT I KNOW FANTASY WHEN I HEAR IT.
NO WAY TWO CHILDREN--FROM EARTH OF ALL DUNGHOLES--MANAGED TO DESTROY ONE OF THE MOST POWERFUL WEAPONS IN THE UNIVERSE OVER THE COURSE OF ONE SUN-CYCLE.

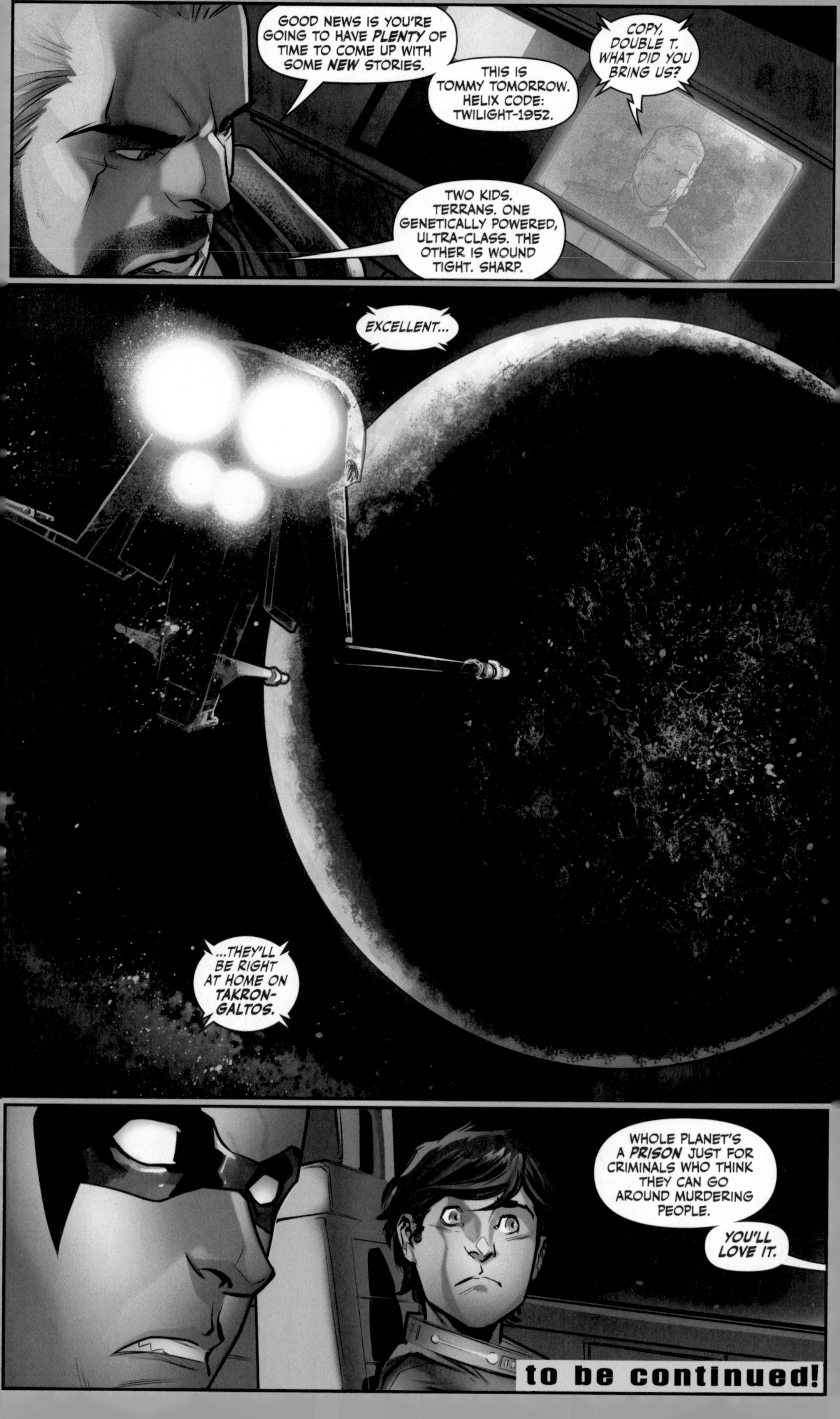
GOOD NEWS IS YOU'RE GOING TO HAVE PLENTY OF TIME TO COME UP WITH SOME NEW STORIES.
THIS IS TOMMY TOMORROW. HELIX CODE: TWILIGHT-1952.
COPY, DOUBLE T. WHAT DID YOU BRING US?
TWO KIDS. TERRANS. ONE GENETICALLY POWERED, ULTRA-CLASS. THE OTHER IS WOUND TIGHT. SHARP.
EXCELLENT...
...THEY'LL BE RIGHT AT HOME ON TAKRON-GALTOS.
WHOLE PLANET'S A PRISON JUST FOR CRIMINALS WHO THINK THEY CAN GO AROUND MURDERING PEOPLE.
YOU'LL LOVE IT.
to be continued!

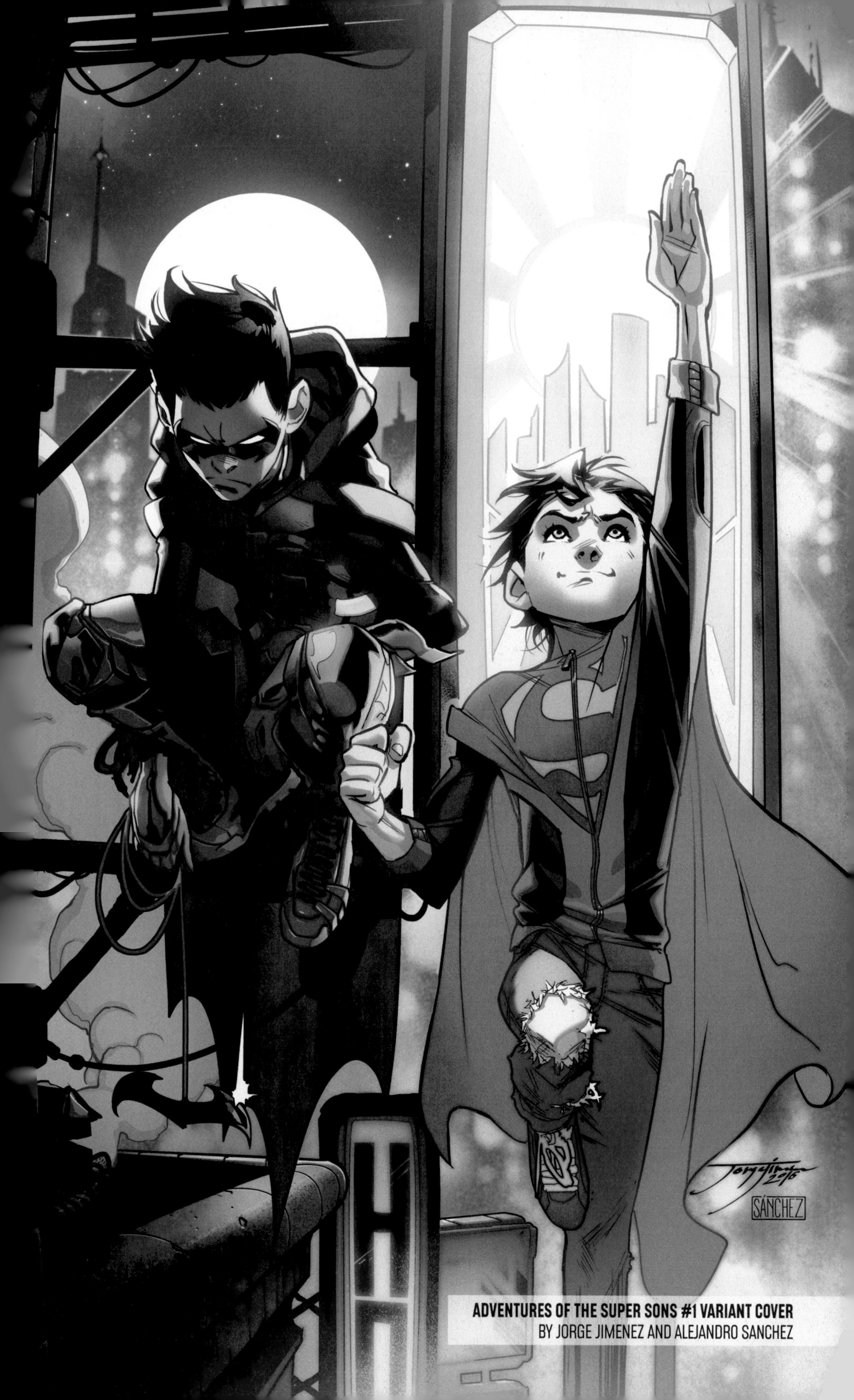
SÁNCHEZ

ADVENTURES OF THE SUPER SONS #1 VARIANT COVER
BY JORGE JIMENEZ AND ALEJANDRO SANCHEZ

FUTURE ROBIN AND SUPERBOY CHARACTER STUDIES BY CARLO BARBERI

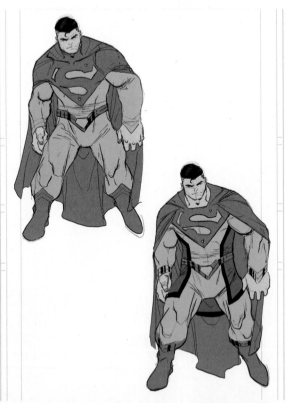

BRAINIAC
ICE PRINCESS

BANG

BRAINIAC, ICE PRINCESS AND JOKER JR. CHARACTER STUDIES BY CARLO BARBERI

KID DEADSHOT

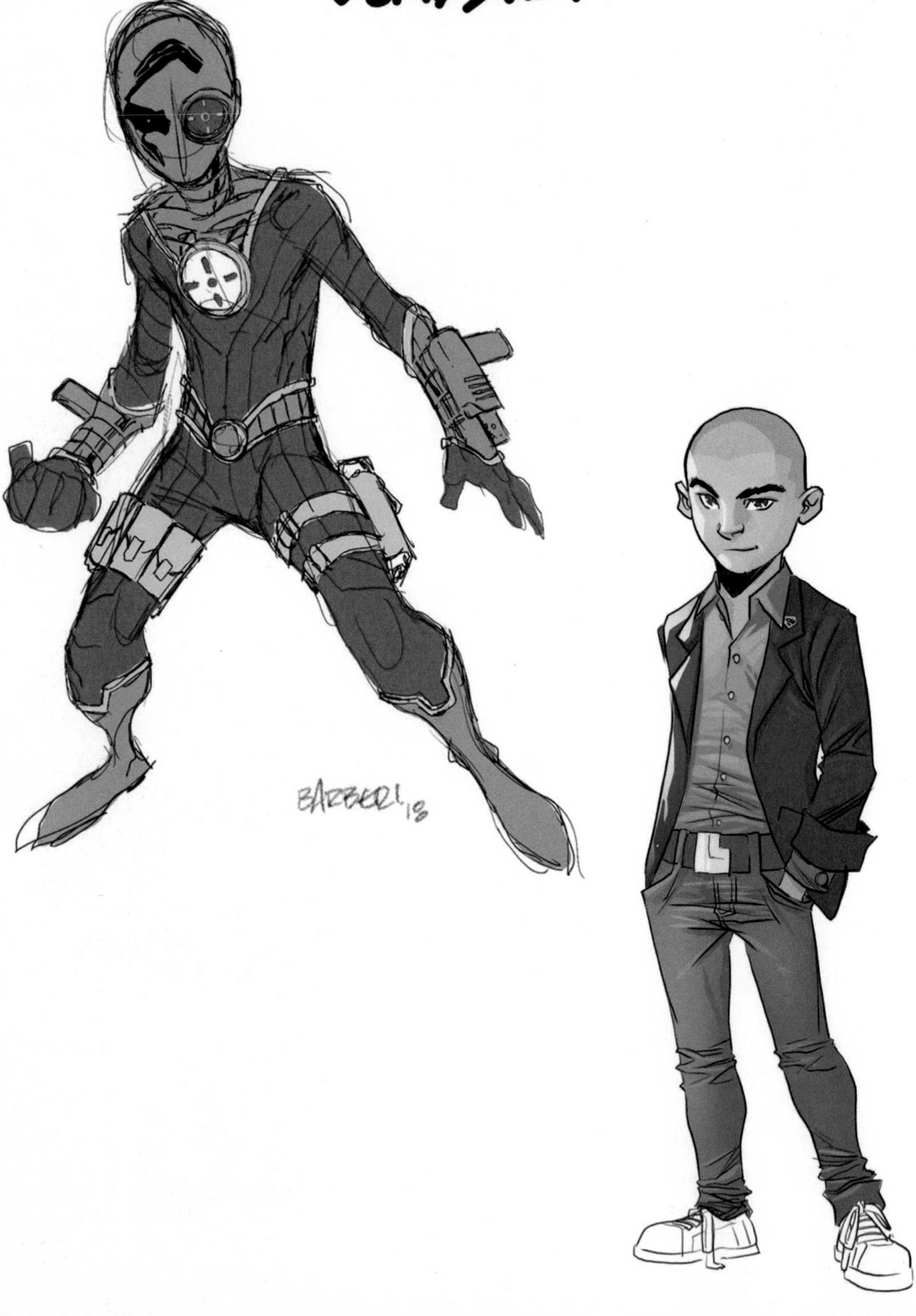
BARBERI '18

KID DEADSHOT AN ARBERI

A

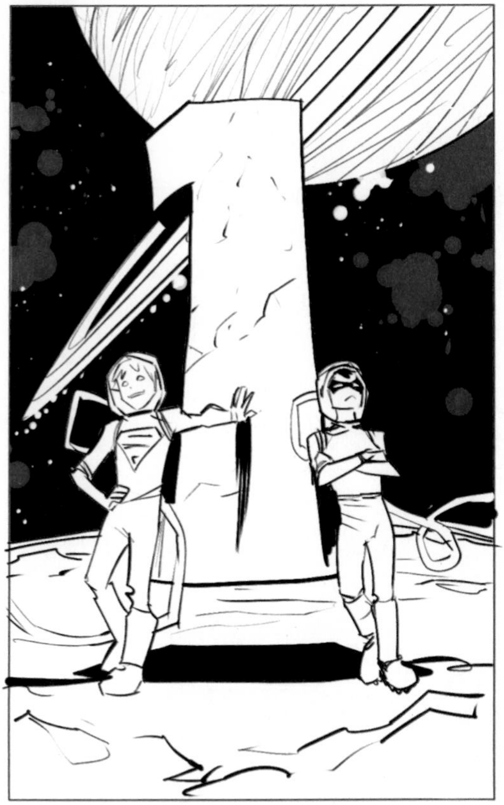

B

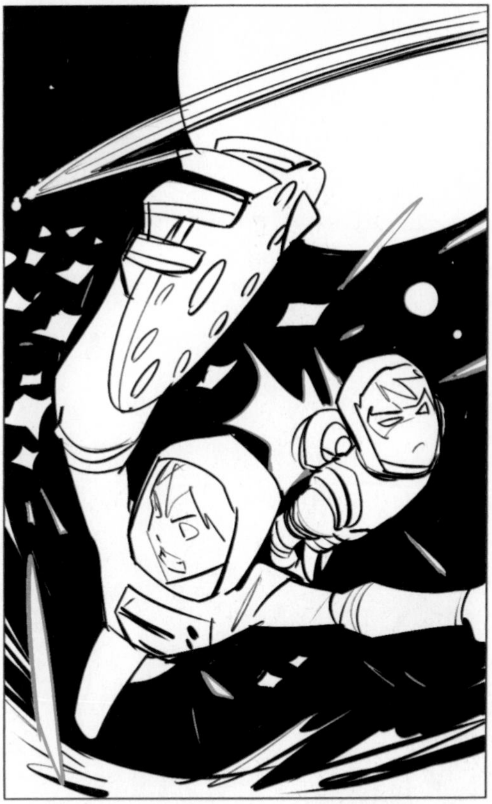

C

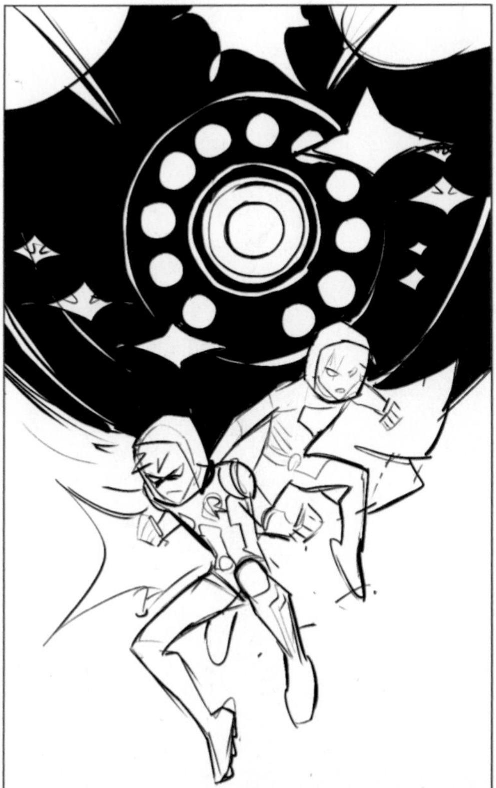

B

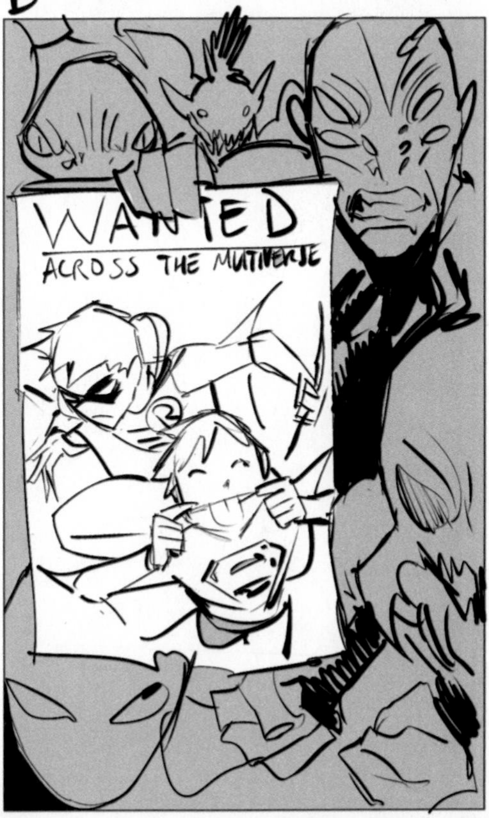
WANTED
ACROSS THE MULTIVERSE

ADVENTURES OF THE SUPER SONS #1 & #2 COVER SKETCHES BY DAN MORA

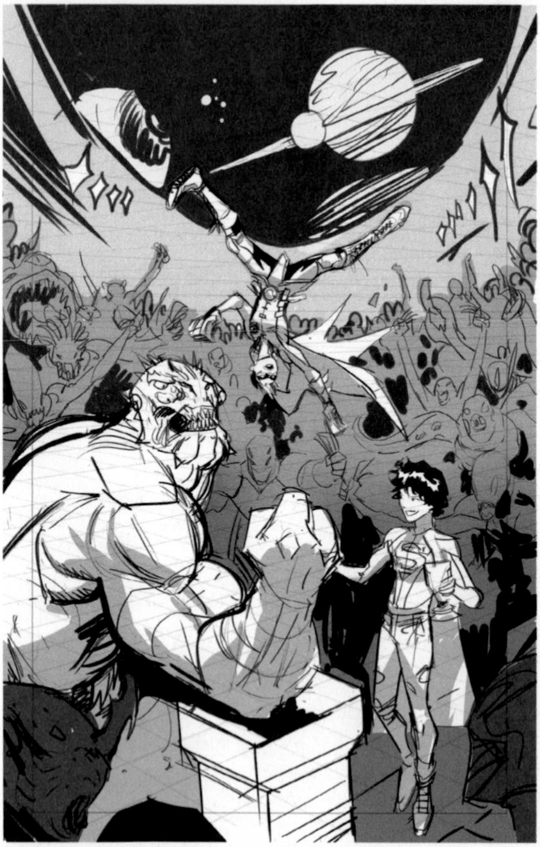

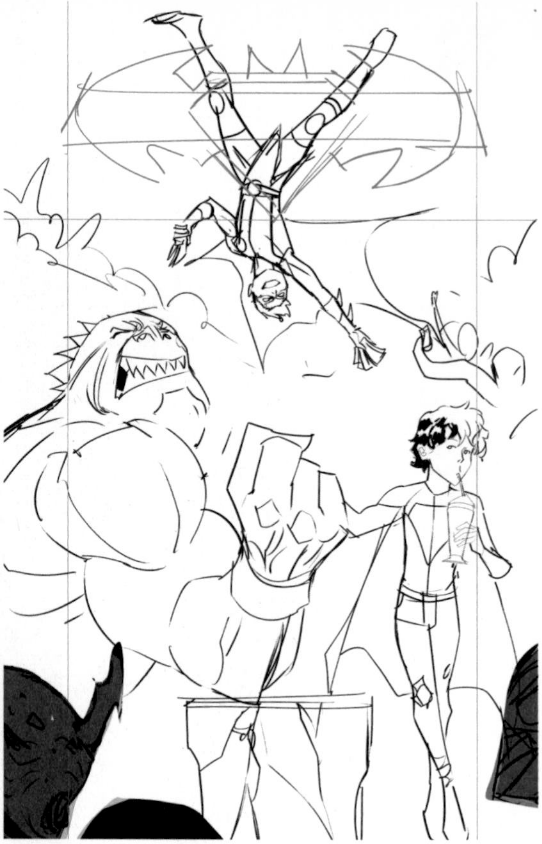

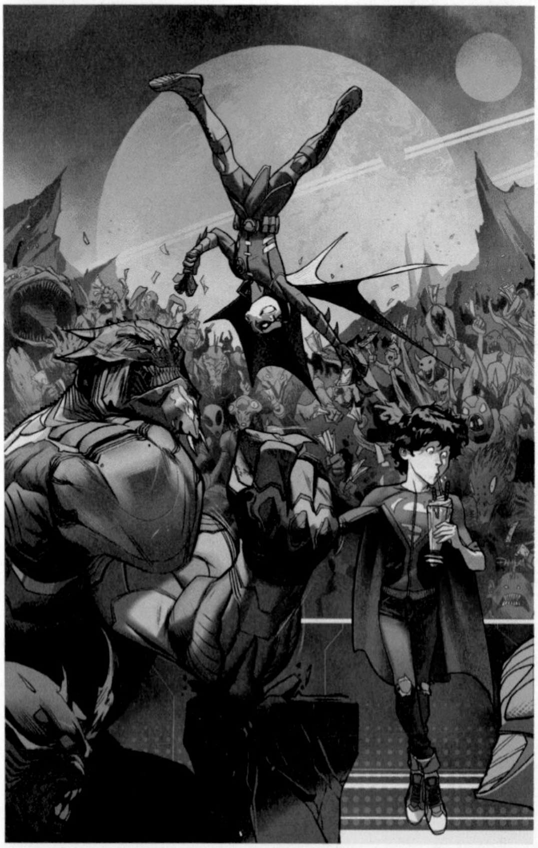

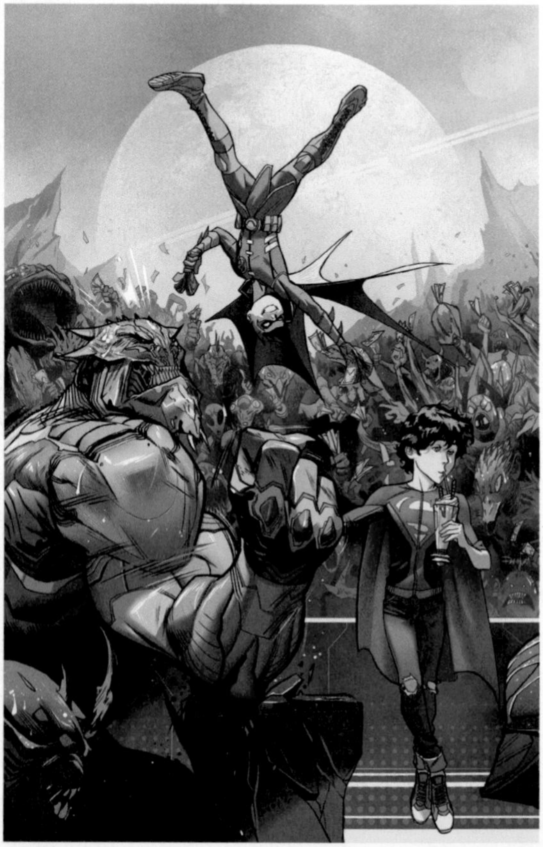

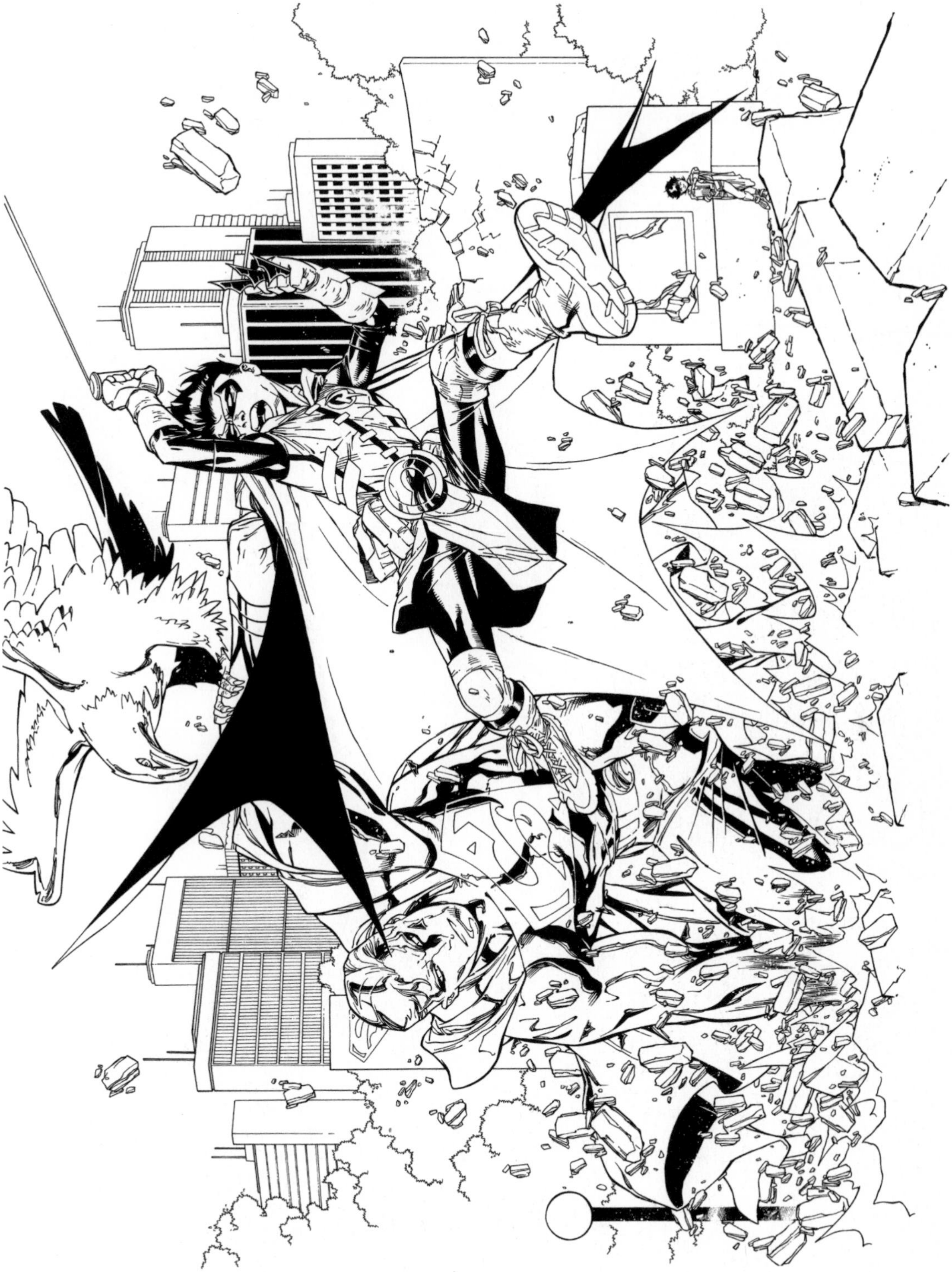

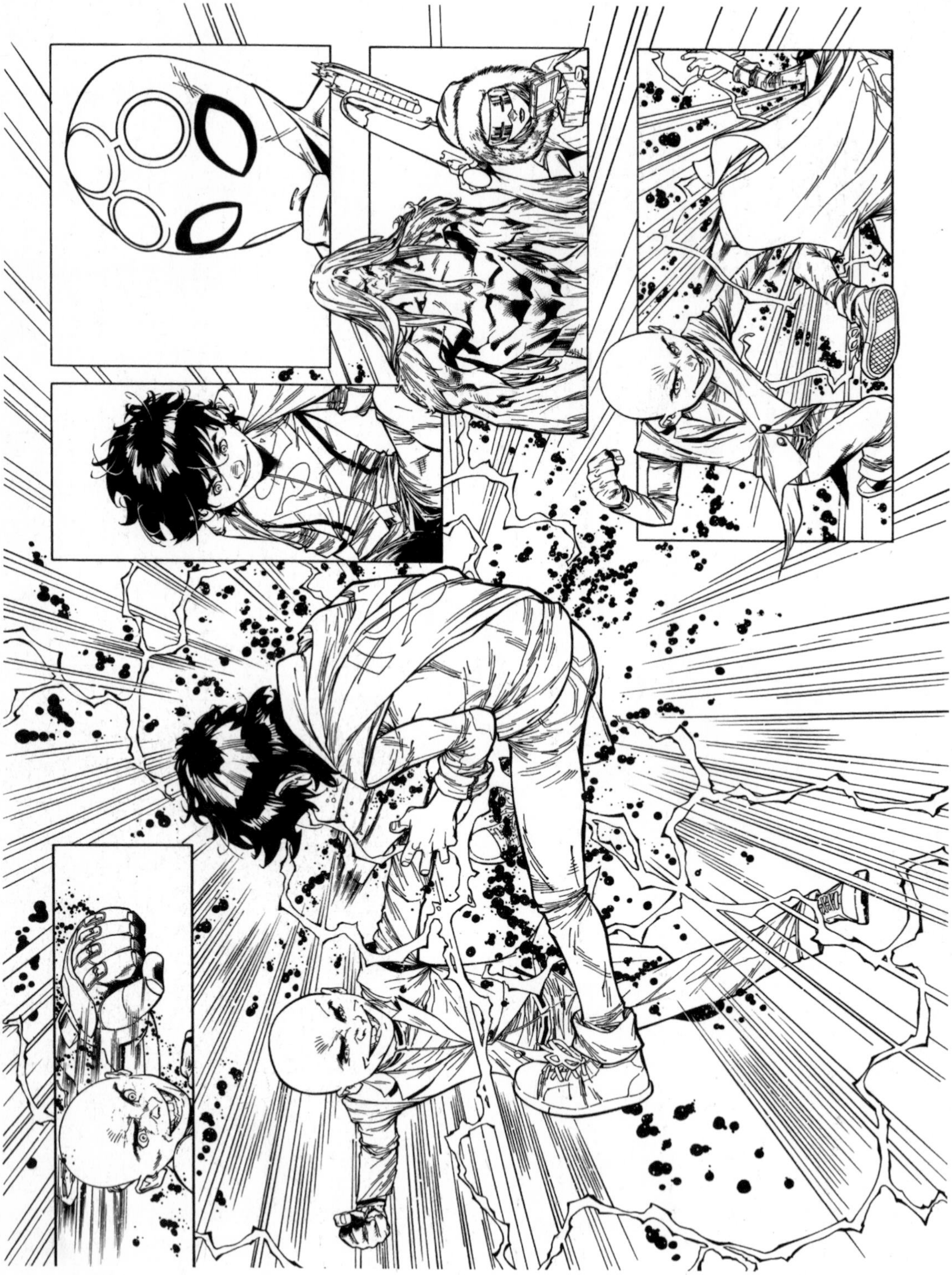